Pierre Teilhard de Chardin
and
Carl Gustav Jung
Side by Side

Pierre Teilhard de Chardin
and
Carl Gustav Jung
Side by Side

Edited with an Introduction
by Fred R. Gustafson, D.Min.

Pierre Teilhard de Chardin and Carl Gustav Jung: Side by Side
[The Fisher King Review Volume 4]

Copyright © 2015 by Fisher King Press
First Edition
ISBN 978-1-77169-014-0 Paperback
ISBN 978-1-77169-015-7 eBook

Published simultaneously in Canada and the United States of America by Fisher King Press. For information on obtaining permission for use of material from this work, submit a written request to:

permissions@fisherkingpress.com

Fisher King Press LLC
109 E 17th St, Ste 80
Cheyenne, WY 82001
www.fisherkingpress.com
fisherking@fisherkingpress.com
+1-831-238-7799

Many thanks to all who have directly or indirectly provided permission to quote their works. Every effort has been made to trace all copyright holders; however, if any have been overlooked, the author will be pleased to make the necessary arrangements at the first opportunity.

CONTENTS

CONTRIBUTORS

Fred R. Gustafson, D. Min. is a Diplomat Jungian Analyst (Zurich) and member of the Chicago Society of Jungian Analysts. He is a senior training analyst with the C.G. Jung Institute of Chicago and a clergy member of the Evangelical Lutheran Church. He has lectured both nationally and internationally on the subjects related to Analytical Psychology and religion. He is the author of *The Black Madonna of Einsiedeln: An Ancient Image for Our Present Time*, *Dancing Between Two Worlds: Jung and the Native American Soul*, *The Moonlit Path: Reflections on the Dark Feminine*, and *Lifting the Veil* (co-authored with Jane Kamerling of the CSJA).

Rich Hanhardt, MS, MBA, has practiced psychotherapy in many venues and with a variety of clients for over 42 years. He has studied extensively in a variety of traditions. He is currently the Executive Director of The Sacred Bond Center in Wisconsin. He is the author of *Sacred Bond: A Model of Spiritual Transformation for Therapists, Clients, and Seekers* and *Living Waters: Healing Through Meditative Prayer*.

John Giannini, Ph.D., received his diploma in Analytical Psychology in 1980 at the same time that the Chicago Society became a teaching institute. He continues to participate in its committees and teaching assignments. He is also a member of the International Association for Psychological Type and the Jung Society for Scholarly Studies. He has an MBA from Stanford, a MA from the University of Chicago and an M.Div. from St. Albert's College, Oakland, California.

Jon Magnuson, M.Div., MSW, has taught with American Indian Studies programs at the University of Washington and Northern Michigan University. He has written numerous articles on psychology and religion for publications including *The Christian Century*, *Sojourners*, *Theology Today*, *Montana Magazine*, and *The Journal of Asian Martial Arts*. A former Peace Corps volunteer in Nepal, he is a licensed psychotherapist and ordained Lutheran (ELCA) pastor and currently lives in rural Northern Michigan, serving as the Director for The Cedar Tree Institute, a nonprofit organization that initiates projects and provides services in the areas of mental health, religion, and the environment.

Stan V. McDaniel, Ph.D., is Professor of Philosophy Emeritus at Sonoma State University in California. During his 25-year tenure, he taught cross-disciplinary and innovative courses including The Philosophy of Jung, Philosophy of Alchemy, Evolutionary Cosmology, and Eastern Philosophy, as well as the general philosophy curriculum. He was also the organizer and speaker at several symposia on the relation between Philosophy and Psychology. He is presently engaged in private research on the concept of development in western and eastern esoteric systems.

Steven Herrmann, Ph.D., MFT, is a Jungian psychotherapist with an office in Oakland, California. Steven is the author of over twenty published essays and articles on analytical psychology and American poetry. He is the author of two books *William Everson: The Shaman's Call,* and *Walt Whitman: Shamanism, Spiritual Democracy, and the World Soul.* He lives and teaches in the San Francisco Bay Area.

Sister Barbara Faris boasts being the daughter of a small town, neighborhood barkeeper. It was there that she learned about community from parents whose "earthy" spirituality focused on care for and about the people they served for 40 years. She began her own life in community 57 years ago, joining the Sisters of St. Francis in Milwaukee, Wisconsin. Her professional career includes that of elementary and high school educator, education of post Vatican II laity, living and working among the inner city and Native American communities, and hospital and hospice chaplaincy. She returned to academic studies at age 60 completing an MA and PhD in Mythological Studies with Emphasis on Depth Psychology from Pacifica Graduate Institute in California. Barbara presently shares life with 60 retired sisters. She volunteers services in teaching and prison ministries in the Milwaukee area.

John Dourley, Ph.D., is a Jungian analyst, Zurich, 1980, practicing in Ottawa, Canada. He is professor emeritus, Department of Religion, Carleton University, Ottawa, Canada. He has published on Jung and religion, Routledge, 2008, 2010 and earlier with Inner City Books, Toronto, Canada. He is a Roman Catholic priest and a member of the religious order, the Oblates of Mary Immaculate.

Laura A. Weber, Ph.D., was an educator and administrator in Jesuit universities for over twenty-five years and now serves as Associate Director of Prairiewoods Eco-Spirituality and Retreat Center in Hiawatha, Iowa. Her academic training in philosophy, theology, biblical hermeneutics, classical studies, and spirituality provided the impetus for her exploration of Teilhard's mystical theology. Her current research interests include quantum theology, eco-feminist spirituality, and feminist biblical hermeneutics.

Jane A. Kelley, LCSW, is a Diplomat Jungian Analyst and member of the C.G. Jung Institute of Chicago. She is the founder and director of the Kelley Clinic. Through her over thirty years of using experiential, body-centered therapies, she has guided clients to listen to the innate wisdom of their body's messages for wholeness.

Robert Henderson, D.Min., is a Clinical Pastoral Educator and Jungian psychotherapist living in Glastonbury, Connecticut. He has interviewed over sixty Jungian Analysts throughout the world many of whom are now deceased. Several of these now archival interviews can be found in three volumes titled *Living with Jung: Enterviews with Jungian Analysts* published by Spring Journal.

Peter T. Dunlap, Ph.D., is a psychologist working in private and political practice. Peter is engaged in research at the interface between Jung's analytical psychology, emotion-centered psychotherapy practices, and the political function of affect. He works with social change organizations in order to activate and support their political development. He is the author of *Awakening Our Faith in the Future: The Advent of Psychological Liberalism*, a book about our past and present psycho-cultural development.

Francisco (Paco) Martorell, MSW, is a migrant, un caminante, in search of the fullness of harmony, communion, and co-creativity. He was born and grew up in Mexico, in the state of Michoacán where the Monarch butterflies migrate seeking the sanctuary of the Fir Mountains. When he was eleven he joined the religious congregation of the Misioneros del Espíritu Santo where he earned a bachelor's degree in Philosophy and Masters in Theology. Paco migrated to the United States in the early seventies where he has raised a family and earned a MSW. He worked in Milwaukee Public Schools for 29 years, doing school social work, family psychotherapy, and administering school-community projects. He is a member of an intentional community called Ramos Ignatian Associates. The name Ramos is after Elba Ramos and her daughter Celina who were assassinated along with six Jesuits in the repressive years of El Salvador struggle for justice. This community follows the same Ignatian spirituality that formed Teilhard de Chardin. Along with members of the Ramos Ignatian Associates, Paco is involved in the "Awakening the Dreamer" symposium, a project of the Pachamama Alliance. He volunteers in an interfaith alliance of about 40 congregations focused on social justice in Milwaukee: Milwaukee Inner-city Congregations Allied for Hope (MICAH). Throughout his life he has lived and worked in very diverse cultural, faith, and socio-economic settings.

Dennis L. Merritt has a Ph.D. in entomology from UC-Berkeley and is a graduate of the Zurich Jung Institute. He practices as a Jungian analyst and ecopsychologist in Madison and Milwaukee, Wisconsin. He authored four volumes of *The Dairy Farmer's Guide to the Universe—Jung, Hermes, and Ecopsychology* (Fisher King Press, 2012-2013).

Dedication

To my dear wife and friend, Karen

INTRODUCTION

Fred R. Gustafson, D.Min.

The idea behind the creation of this book has been founded on both a personal and impersonal level. Personally, I first heard of Teilhard de Chardin in the mid 1960s from a professor of ethics, A.D. Mattson, who taught at the Lutheran School of Theology at Chicago. I was a student at the time and had never heard of Chardin. Few of his books had been published in English at this time and, though I knew nothing of this man, Dr. Mattson spoke with such enthusiasm about him that the name stayed with me. Along the way, I purchased and read some of Chardin's books reading parts of them sporadically. But, whatever seed was planted in me back then would not go away. A deeper part of me, of which I knew little, was not going to let me forget. But I did, at least for a while. Life happens, so to speak, marriage, children are born, schools attended, job requirements, moves are made, deaths and births experienced and so forth. And maybe that is the way it is supposed to work for all of us. Life must be lived sometimes to receive and understand more fully what was once so many years prior a dim glow on the horizon of consciousness.

This pattern had been much the same for my studies of Carl Gustav Jung. I knew little of him until I started my doctoral program at Andover Newton Theological School in Boston. The head of the psychology department was Dr. John Billinsky. It turned out he had had a very close relationship with Dr. Jung, was obviously influenced by him and, accordingly, influenced the entire psychology department. Things began to fall into place psychologically and spiritually for me reading Jung, and, for the first time in my life, I focused on my dreams. But again, life happens, ideas sit in the background of consciousness and time passes but not the germinal influences of both Chardin and Jung. So now, at the time of this publication, I can say I have read Chardin and Jung with great enthusiasm much like I imagine Drs. Mattson and Billinsky had done and realize how much they have shaped my professional and personal life.

Behind this personal experience is the impersonal, a less than perfect word to describe the greater effect these two men have had and continue to have on what is best described in Teilhard's language, an emerging planetary consciousness. Though

Jung and Chardin never met, their influence on the world is still being felt and will continue so in this next 21ˢᵗ century and beyond. This is so for any creative endeavor that exceeds the limits of the familiar worldview, be it in the arts, literature, philosophy, religion, or science. Their intellectual and personal paths of inquiry interfaced with each other. Both were concerned with science and religion; both operated within these paradigms. Both of these men shook the world they lived in offering up views, on one hand, of the profound depths of the human psyche and, on the other, presenting a profound re-consideration of evolution as a process leading toward a social unification of the planet.

Jung used the concept of individuation, whereas, Chardin spoke of evolution. Both of these terms were meant by them to describe unfolding processes that were goal directed whether in the soul of an individual or the world soul itself. Each took these concepts to a creative depth so much so that the world they lived in deeply admired or detested them. Each had conflicts in their chosen fields. Jung was a psychologist who used the field of science to explore the religious depths of the human soul by studying mythology, world religions, folk tales, dreams, and human behavior. Chardin used the ground of religion to work in the field of science via paleontology, geology, and physics as he explored a deeper and more relevant understanding of evolution. Though each began from different intellectual platforms, they crisscrossed into the other's territory of inquiry and related their ideas to include the full scope of humanity. They took those two adversaries of world history, science, and religion, and built a bridge between them in such a manner that one can no longer speak of one without including the other.

There are just three supports to this bridge I wish to make before I yield to the unique contributions of the authors in this book. They, more than I alone could ever have done, have thrown light on the parallel supporting linkages connecting science and religion and why today Jung and Chardin stand side by side as major contributors to the human endeavor.

The first is to mention that both of these men were deeply involved with religion from the beginning of their lives up to the end. Chardin was born and raised in the context of the Roman Catholic Theology of his day, whereas, Jung was born and raised in the context of a Swiss Reformed Church environment within which his father was a parish pastor. Chardin spent his entire life dedicated, against tremendous odds, to his priesthood and to the Society of Jesus. Jung wrote extensively on religious issues and told John Freeman of BBC in 1959 at the end of his life that he did not believe God existed; he knew God existed.

The word "religion" regained integrity for these men because the spiritual force behind this word pushed them deep within themselves, past the collective dogmas of their day and left them alone to define their place in the cosmic order of things. Chardin described this descent into himself this way:

> ...And so, for the first time in my life perhaps ... I took the lamp and, leaving the zone of everyday occupations and relationships where everything seems clear, I went down into my inmost self, to the deep abyss whence I feel dimly that my power of action emanates. But as I moved further and further away from the conventional certainties by which social life is superficially illuminated, I became aware that I was losing contact with myself. At each step of the descent a new person was disclosed within me of whose name I was no longer sure, and who no longer obeyed me. And when I had to stop my exploration because the path faded from beneath my steps, I found a bottomless abyss at my feet, and out of it came-arising I know not from where-the current which I dare to call *my* life.[1]

In the Introduction to *Divine Mileau*, Pierre Leroy, S.J. wrote:

> It was during these decisive years that he was ordained priest….He resolved in future to collaborate with all his energies in the cosmogenesis whose reality became for him daily more resplendent. Salvation was no longer to be sought in 'abandoning the world' but in active 'participation' in building it up. He would approach his scientific work no longer as an amateur but as a qualified specialist: and it would be undertaken not for its own sake…but in order to release the Spirit from the crude ore in which it lay hidden or inactive.[2]

Even though he was raised in a loving Christian home by parents who presented Catholicism in a graceful manner and being deeply effected by the natural beauty of the landscape in which he lived, he still had to move beyond such a beginning and look deeply within himself. As for Jung, his descent can be readily seen in any of the accounts of his life. Most notably was his break with Freud that constellated the images and voices that came up from within his inner world. He took his fear of going

---

1 Pierre Teilhard de Chardin, *The Divine Milieu,* pp, 76-7.
2 Teilhard, *The Divine Milieu.* p. 22.

insane seriously, writing out accounts of what he was experiencing, actively dialoguing with the voices and, in the end, giving birth to his unique psychology.

> After the break with Freud, all my friends and acquaintances dropped away. My book [*The Psychology of the Unconscious*] was declared to be rubbish. I was a mystic, and that settled the matter….But I had foreseen my isolation and harbored no illusion about the reactions of my so-called friends. That was a point I had thoroughly considered beforehand. I had known that everything was at stake, and that I had to take a stand for my convictions. I realized that the chapter, 'The Sacrifice,' meant my own sacrifice.[3]

And again:

> …I lived as if under constant inner pressure. At times this became so strong that I suspected there was some psychic disturbance in myself….But this retrospection led to nothing but a fresh acknowledgment of my own ignorance. Thereupon I said to myself, 'Since I know nothing at all, I shall simply do whatever occurs to me.' Thus I consciously submitted myself to the impulses of the unconscious.[4]

Finally, and because of the courage to stay in the dark uncertain ground of his soul, he could say:

> The years when I was pursuing my inner images were the most important in my life– in them everything essential was decided. It all began then; the later details are only supplements and clarifications of the material that burst forth from the unconscious, and at first swamped me. It was the *prima materia* for a lifetime's work.[5]

Finally, to suggest that Jung had no appreciation and concern for the greater collective and the movement of humanity into the future because he was suspicious of collective thinking or of the religious phenomenon is as erroneous as thinking Chardin never looked deeply into himself. For both the evidence proves otherwise.

The second reflection is contained in the word "paleontology." It is true that Chardin was a trained professional paleontologist who studied the forms of life existing in former geologic times. But, Jung also was a paleontologist of the soul. There is, for

---

3 C.G. Jung, *Memories, Dreams, Reflections*, pp, 167-8. (Note: *MDR* refers throughout this publication to C.G. Jung's *Memories, Dreams, Reflections*.)

4 Jung, *MDR*, p. 173.

5 Jung, *MDR*, p. 199.

example, his famous dream of the two storied house in which he descended from the first floor, to the ground fifteenth or sixteenth medieval floor down through a stone stairway that led to the cellar then further down to a vaulted room of Roman times and, finally, down through a stone slab in the floor to the depths where he discovered scattered bones and broken pottery. This dream revived Jung's interest in archeology but, more so, strengthened the foundation for his understanding of the collective unconscious shared by everyone. It was a reflection of the ancient inheritance each of us carries.

Jung's paleontologically oriented psychology is seen here when he states:

> I can only gaze with wonder and awe at the depths and heights of our psychic nature. Its non-spatial universe conceals an untold abundance of images which have accumulated over millions of years of living development and become fixed in the organism.[6]

And again:

> The deeper 'layers' of the psyche lose their individual uniqueness as they retreat farther and farther into darkness. 'Lower down,' that is to say as they approach the autonomous functional systems, they become increasingly collective until they are universalized and extinguished in the body's materiality, i.e., in chemical substances. The body's carbon is simply carbon. Hence 'at bottom' the psyche is simply 'world'…. The more archaic and 'deeper,' that is the more *physiological,* the symbol is, the more collective and universal, the more "material" it is."[7]

As for Chardin so many reflections could summarize his studies of paleontology though this one is quite unique and parallels what Jung was intimating:

> Where are the roots of our being? In the first place they plunge back and down into the unfathomable past. How great is the mystery of the first cells which were one day animated by the breath of our souls! How impossible to decipher the welding of suc-

---

6 C.G. Jung, "On the Nature of the Psyche" in *The Structure and Dynamics of the Psyche,* CW 8, ¶ 764. (Note: CW refers throughout this publication to *The Collected Works of C.G. Jung.*)

7 C.G. Jung, "The Psychology of the Child Archetype," in *The Archetypes and the Collective Unconscious,* CW 9i, ¶ 291.

cessive influences in which we are for ever incorporated! In each one of us, through matter, the whole history of the world is in part reflected.[8]

For both Jung and Chardin, we as members of the present day human species, have our roots and heritage extending far back into prehistoric times. For them it was essential for the survival of the planet to not forget where we came from, that all things are interconnected, and come from the same Tree of Life.

The third reflection has to do with this interconnection. Here we have Jung's notion of the collective and cultural unconscious that connects everyone on the planet psychologically and Chardin's notion of the noosphere as the planetary thinking layer that all humanity is building up and upon. We are all connected today and seem to struggle with what consequences for good or bad that entails. There is no place on earth where a warring skirmish would take place that the rest of the world would not know of it within twenty-four hours though usually sooner. There is an emerging planetary mind; witness the place of the Internet a term that suggest the fabric in which we are all caught and held for better or worse. Today we speak of global economy, global markets, global finance, global terrorism, global environment, global communication, the World Bank, the World Trade Organization, and the International Monetary Fund. At the same time, and as seen in environmental movements throughout the world, a growing weariness of war, nations coming together as with the European Union, pushing against the local and national bullies, increase in local markets, attempts to find new forms of worship and the beginning of religions comingling and so forth. Evolution involves the entire human species just as the Jungian concept of individuation involves every human person and even nations. Both of these men looked at the "within" of things whether it be the within of the human psyche that awaits its fulfillment through the individuation process or the within of matter that demands its spiritual evolution.

Chardin and Jung put emphasis on a person taking up their moral responsibility to increase their conscious life, that is, their interior life leading to a greater spiritual elevation and furthering the world. Jung made it clear that it is one thing to understand what comes out of our unconscious; it is another to live the ethic it requires. Our worldview is different than our ancestors. We know the world is not flat and know as science and the atom bomb have demonstrated that matter is not dead. We have done more in the last 100 years than in the last 5000. The world is evolving faster

---

8 Teilhard, *The Divine Milieu*, p. 59.

than ever. Will we keep up with it? Will the individual soul keep up with the world soul? To know life demands growth/evolution, and that matter is not dead can help us endure the terrible things that happen. Evolution has intent as certainly as a person's individuation journey. That is the keyword; intent. That life, wherever it is found, has intention and is trying to take us somewhere is far different than any notion of randomness or survival of the fittest.

It is true that people are losing heart/trust in the work they do to help bring the world into the future. When I have asked people if they believe the human race is hardwired to advance to a higher level of life or if a person's individuation process is trying at all cost to fulfill itself, even when I have given the qualifying statement that I was aware we might not make it but that the energy force behind Life intended it, there was consistent hesitation and quietness; an uncertainty prevailed. All this is so understandable given the destruction being done to the planet and the peoples of it. To see the big picture, however, that is, to not forget that all of life descends and ascends, that it is bloody with war and birthing and to remember that, if we do not keep trying to bring the world into a new day, it is over today at least for ourselves. Chardin would say, "reflection," is the one gift with which the human race has to save itself, a concept with which Jung would certainly agree. Kathleen Duffy quotes Chardin as saying, "'…evolution is now busy elsewhere in a richer, more complex domain, constructing spirit, with all our minds and hearts put together.' This reassures him that not only is the cosmos complexifying but it also has a 'psychically convergent structure.' Teilhard concludes that 'Matter is the matrix of Spirit'."[9]

There is so much more that can be said, but I will leave it to the various contributing authors of this book. The reader will find a wonderful diversity of individuals and approaches to the relationship between Carl Gustav Jung and Pierre Teilhard de Chardin. There are very personal and academic oriented reflections. Sometimes, there will be more emphasis by a writer on Chardin, other times more on Jung. Of particular interest are three chapters dealing with the role women played in the lives of these two men. There are frequent references to the state of our environment and how the thinking paradigms Jung and Chardin offer can help all of us find a better way to do business. Though there will always be some overlap of information in a book like this, each author stands unique among the other.

---

9 Arthur Fabel and Donald St. John, editors, "The Texture of the Evolutionary Cosmos" in *Teilhard in the 21ˢᵗ Century*, p. 142.

I was amazed and pleased how quickly the initial stages of this undertaking developed. Invariably, I heard how glad the authors were to get reacquainted with Jung and/or Chardin again. This speaks, I believe, to just how important these thinkers are not only to the authors but to our world today. Understanding Jung and Chardin and their parallel lives along with the development of their independent intellectual inquiries and courageous researches, pushes the personal and collective soul forward and places both of them at the foreground of our need to understand and integrate on a planetary level the core values of their expansive work.

Bibliography

Fabel, Arthur and St. John, Donald, editors. *Teilhard in the 21st Century.* Maryknoll, New York: Orbis Books, 2007.

Jung, C.G. *Memories, Dreams, Reflections.* New York: Vintage, 1965.

Jung, C.G. *The Structure and Dynamics of the Psyche,* CW 8. New York, N.Y.: Pantheon Books, Inc., 1960.

Jung, C.G. *The Archetypes and the Collective Unconscious,* CW 9i. New York, N.Y.: Pantheon Books, Inc., 1960.

Teilhard de Chardin, Pierre. *The Divine Milieu.* New York: Harper & Row, 1960.

1

THROUGH DESCENT, TO ASCENT AND THEN TO THE FUTURE

The Parellel Journeys of Jung and Chardin

Richard W. Hanhardt

Introduction

Perhaps it is best to begin by acknowledging to the reader that I have bitten off more than I can chew by attempting to examine the descents and ascents of these complex men. But the attempt is worthy. So much was happening in these men outside of our awareness! I am left with the problem of focusing on the sun sparkling on a babbling brook. I will not be able to talk about the enormous forces underneath; new and ancient waters pummeling rocks into sand; fish barely able to maintain their strength in the current and at the same time foraging in a complete, self-sustaining ecosystem; fallen trees decaying and adding nutrients every second of every day; minute-by-minute stories of life and death. And so it must be with our look into the lives of these men. But hopefully a glimpse at the sparkling sun on the surface will be a window and encourage the reader to look deeper. Seeing deeper into this part of the descent and ascent of these men's lives takes great effort and study in *The Red Book* and *The Divine Milieu* first and then other subsequent gifts from their lives.

There are many parallels between the life paths of these gifted men, Carl Gustav Jung and Pierre Teilhard de Chardin. These parallels have become critically important for us because of the enormous importance of their contributions to our thought in the twenty-first century where so much is in flux, and where entire basis of our organized civilization, which we have trusted so much, is now in question. And this question is frightening but also exhilarating as we can now share their view of the enormous potential and evolution of human thought and action. Therefore I will end with a brief discussion of two important contributions for the future, Natural Mind from Jung and the Noosphere from Chardin.

They set off on their journeys to pioneer and discover the true soul within a twentieth century time of horrendous wars in Europe. Their outer-world home was under attack. Most readers of this chapter will not know of this experience in any but an academic way; we can only imagine the horror. But these men kept the inner-world life pristine and accessible through their personal courage and integrity; nothing else would have accomplished the separation from the outer pain of their times and it is this separation that allowed their journeys.

Therefore, we will discuss these two life-paths in three parts. First we will examine the descents of these men into a world as yet undiscovered in their lives, a diminishment, which was absolutely necessary despite important outer world success they had already achieved. Perhaps many of the readers have already experienced a descent of their own. If so, you will know about this journey. Secondly we will take a brief look at the discoveries that they brought forth and the process of their ascent in *The Red Book* and *The Divine Milieu*. Finally we will look briefly at what they thought their discoveries meant for the future of man and how man must approach the future with Natural Mind for Jung and in the Noosphere for Chardin. Despite this necessary division into three sections, it remains important to note that the processes were fluid and the phases flowed into each other. This kind of analysis does not do justice to a process that by its nature is outside our reductionist desires.

The Descent

It is a common motif in mythology for a hero to descend to the underworld in search of something precious that has been lost. The writers of both new and ancient stories wrote often and extensively about the descent often undertaken in desperate hope of discovering what was lost and returning it to a waiting world in pain. It is outside the scope of this writing to explore these descents but a momentary pause into your story-memory will suffice for examples.

Both men arrived at the choice of paths in their lives and they concluded that they must take the path of diminishment and descent. There was no other way, and they knew it. We can speculate on how much the outer world pressures precipitated the diminishment and descent, certainly they did not live in vacuums, but when any of us faces this diminishment (and we all have or will) we must enter the inner world defenseless and with great humility. St. Francis had to face the Bishop's court and his overbearing father and then tear off all his clothes because even the clothes of a rich man's son and especially the pretense of a bought-and-paid-for religious court blocked his descent into humility before his God. This descent became the basis for his celebrated life.

So Jung perhaps feared insanity and Chardin was terribly alone and depressed in his state of being all but banished from his home and from sharing his discoveries; inner and outer world defeats always open the potential for inner world descent in pursuit of healing. The journey is at times epic and captured in archetypal mythology and alchemy and in virtually every culture's story from the beginning of time. And so it was with Jung and Chardin. These two men wrote new stories for themselves but also for us. Their stories are inspiring, and a great legacy we need to understand for our time. Let us begin, then, with the diminishment and the descent. Even now, many decades after their deaths, we may be just beginning to tell the great myth of their descent, discoveries, ascent, and sharing of their gifts.

To become conscious we must all descend. And, if at all possible, we must do so with the same courage and integrity as these men. The most poignant example of human descent of course is how we face death. Can there be a complete personality without facing death? Here is what Chardin said:

> *The function of death is to provide the necessary entrance into our inmost selves.* It will make us undergo *the required dissociation.* It will put us into the state organically needed if the divine fire is to descend upon us. And in that way its fatal power to decompose and dissolve will be harnessed to the most sublime operations of life. What was by nature empty and void, a return to bits and pieces, can, in any human existence, become fullness and unity in God.[1] (Italics mine)

Here is the method of change for him: a return to the "bits and pieces" of our lives, and surrender to the decomposing of self and the dissolving of ego. A descent. And

---

1 Pierre Teilhard de Chardin, *The Divine Milieu*, p. 56.

even when our egos refuse to allow the descent, we will eventually face death, which forces our hand. God will have his way with most of us (the lucky are entrapped in his snare early in their lives). Both Jung and Chardin spoke directly to this issue of the death and transformation of the ego. For example, Jung spoke of the purpose of a descent into neurosis being to remove "the false attitude of the ego." This he saw as the purpose of our suffering.

Chardin spoke at length about what he called "diminishment." We must diminish and ego must die in order for God to make an entrance into our lives. These realities in our lives force us into the experience of living under the power of *the brutality of Natural Mind in the service of God himself.* We will explore Natural Mind (Jung's term) below, but for now we can take it to mean Mind *devoid of ego*. In Natural Mind we are left exposed to the pure and unfiltered forces of the creation as they manifest in both our inner and outer lives. The pathway to growth in the descent is our consciousness of our mortality (provided by Natural Mind) and the pain of our awareness of our personal diminishment and dying. Chardin stated:

> Uniting oneself [to God] means, in every case, migrating, and dying partially in what one loves. But as we are sure, this being reduced to nothing in the other must be all the more complete the more we give our attachment to one who is greater than ourselves, then we can set no limits to the tearing up of roots that is involved on our journey to God. ... There is a further step to take: the one that makes us lose all footholds within ourselves... What will be the agent of that definitive transformation? *Nothing else than death.*[2] (Italics mine)

Jung examined an alchemical drawing where King and Queen have died and are lying on a sarcophagus having been transformed into a single hermaphroditic form with two heads. The beginning of the caption reads: Here the King and Queen are lying Dead/In great distress the soul is sped. Jung's comment on the image:

> When the opposites unite, all energy ceases: there is no more flow. The waterfall has plunged to its full depth in that torrent of nuptial joy and longing; now only a stagnant pool remains, without wave or current. So it appears at least looked at from the outside. As the legend tells us, the picture represents the *putrefactio,* the corruption, the decay of a once living creature. Yet the picture is also entitled *"Conceptio."* The text says: ... "the corruption of one is the generation of the other, an indication

---

2 Teilhard, *Divine Milieu*, p. 55.

that this death is an interim stage to be followed by a new life. *No new life can arise without the death of the old.*[3] (Italics mine)

The descent is bound to death as much as it is to beauty, energy, abundance, power, and unceasing time because God lives in it. Here we also have the introduction of the opposites. The purpose of a descent can be described as a search for a way in which the opposites, (life and death in this example) which are tearing us apart, can be resolved. This resolution is healing and it is accomplished by learning how to find a way to live in the middle, or for the Taoists, discovering "The Way." The gifts from history of The Beatitudes of Christ, The Great Integrity (the Tao), The Noosphere of Chardin and the Natural Mind of Jung *all* draw from this integration of the opposites. The reason is that the achievement of any of these must follow a descent but also tremendous psychic energy when accomplished. Therefore just as descent and ascent are opposites that when united into a single whole release tremendous energy, so we live with a limitless number of opposites which require resolution before "The Way" of our lives can emerge. Do we all have a *Red Book* or *Divine Milieu* waiting to emerge?

What these men found was that a descent was necessary and that they could not grow (or stay sane) without this obliteration of ego. In so doing, they found diminishment and death and Natural Mind led them there. But it all had a remarkable purpose: the completion of their personalities and the awakening of Self. Further they found *raison de etre* in passing on this knowledge and writing for us how this work could benefit our lives.

In *The Divine Milieu,* Chardin pressed for the understanding that the diminishment and descent was purposeful in creating in us a new relationship with God. He was establishing a purpose for our suffering and looking at his own pain as the template for that paradigm. And what a fantastic purpose it is! It is nothing less than a deeper communion with God than we have had before. He calls it "Communion through Diminishment." These words are holy words and require some meditation; they should not be passed over intellectually. These words are a description of the pathway to healing and to a holy defeat of evil. Chardin said plainly that death was evil. To defeat it Chardin wanted first a Descent into Communion, and then the opening of the door to healing relationship with Christ. Here we have a reason for our suffering and for that of our clients, and the reason we will heal if we can allow the suffering to occur without blocking it with denial, ego, or even (at times) medication,

---

3 C.G. Jung, *The Practice of Psychotherapy*, CW16, ¶ 467.

just plain "noodling out," or other distractions. Suffering is communion, it is a holy event and must not be disturbed, if possible, but only understood and challenged for its meaning for us.

I have believed for a long time that humility is the key to the path of healing and health. Jung would say a descent is necessary and Chardin, I believe would concur, also adding the term diminishment. Whatever the terms, it seems clear that both men understood this need for the defeat of the human ego (humility); we cannot enter God's healing antechamber without first admitting to ourselves our utter humanness, which includes our ultimate death. It seems that for many (or all) acceptance of the loss of pride and what we cling to in a worldly sense (ego, title, role and other outer-world definitions of ourselves) can be the most painful part of the process. We must drink of this bitter cup and many of us wait until we are facing our own death or the profound loss of another is staring directly at us and defying our "strength." Often we wait until we realize that we cannot escape and that we must get close to this "right" level of humility to encounter the living God.

For example, the bulk of the Old Testament could be viewed as the struggle between human pride and the grace of God. It is clear that God detests our pride because it keeps us from communion with him. This eliminates our chance to receive healing grace. A study of the lives of Chardin and Jung will find this necessary diminishment of pride. I think this need is poorly understood in our culture. Other cultures have ceremonies and rituals to symbolically bring to the surface this understanding of the need for diminishment. In these cultures, temporary dissolution of ego is institutionalized and therefore recognized as essential for discovery. Through their studies and life experiences both Jung and Chardin also understood this, culturally, historically, and personally.

In application to our clients we must be prepared for the descent they will need to experience (or that they bring to us at the beginning). We will be asked deep questions. Hopefully our clients will find a place in us that resonates with their descent and reflects to them how the ascent is possible, yielding hope. Those of us who would work with others must understand diminishment at a visceral level; this understanding will be demanded of us. Further there is *meaning* in the descent and, as Jung and Chardin demonstrated, it is often this meaning that sustains us through the tough times. If we do not know how to respond we will not be able to help. Looking deeper at the holy descent and diminishment issues for Jung and Chardin may give us the answer to this essential question our clients will ask (and we may be continuously asking ourselves) about the descent of man: "What indeed does it mean?"

As we have seen, Chardin was clear in his experience that suffering is holy because it leads to a closer relationship with God. How many clients are bringing Holy suffering to their therapists only to find that the answers are only discovered by those willing to descend in their own lives and then, later, (often much later) to trust sharing their discoveries with others. I believe Jung's descent was required of him. He agreed. After discussing this a bit further we must then deal with the discovery recorded in Chardin's writing that God does not want us to suffer as the end point of this work. Rather He permits it to lead us to a place of *transformation*. Jung's descent was clearly about the same transformation. While injecting that brief note of optimism about the outcome, let me proceed further with the discussion of diminishment and descent.

Let us begin with an admittedly historical fictional look at the pictures:

In Europe we have Jung isolating himself from his practice, colleagues, and to a large extent his family, climbing to his third floor office space at Kusnacht alone each night. We might be able to look into the scene at dinner with his family where he will have again spent the meal in introversion and quietness. The family has felt his silence and withdrawal for many years. His wife Emma has dedicated herself to the home and to her own studies understanding intuitively that this absence of his former self somehow is necessary. The family knows he will leave and not return downstairs again that night choosing to remain in the secluded office where he now spends his life.

His climb up the steps into the study was again heavy, intentional and sole in purpose: he would again allow the images, whatever would come, to take over his psyche. And now we know that the images and symbols and memories came in powerful waves many of which must have been excruciating and terrifying. But night after night with great courage, like Jacob wrestling with God, he clung to the images and captured them. He brought them into the light and (as we would say in psychotherapy) he finally externalized (wrote about or painted) them. In this process he came to own them and then fear them no longer. Although we now have these recordings in *The Red Book*, we will never know the extent of the Suffering in the Upper Office at Kusnacht.

On the other side of the world in China we find Chardin working in archaeological expeditions. He sits on the edge of a dig whose bottom has by now disappeared from sight as evening approaches. He is covered in dust with mud up to his elbows and covering his boots. He holds in his hand a fossil skull of one of the ancient ones and again is lost in thought about what this incredible experience actually means for him and for the world. He allows the death of this ancient one to enter his emotional life and he feels tremendous sadness at the distance he has from this mysterious man. Intellectually, he wonders about all of the aspects of this one's life. He ponders the earth religion of this "primitive" one and wonders what this faith would have to teach us now. Although he is exhausted as the sun sets on this day of discovery, he knows he must keep digging; there might be answers to this essential question in the artifacts in the hole below his dangling boots. The intrigue is too great for him to ignore.

The exhaustion is from the work but also from the utter loneliness of this place so far from his home. For all practical purposes he has been banished to China and into silence by his own Jesuit brothers. They have refused to allow him to teach and he has also been refused to publish his written work. His world-enlightening thoughts are too controversial. But Pierre Teilhard knows at his core how important his teaching and his writings are and that they are not about furthering "him" as his brothers may have suspected.

The works are about a new vision for mankind emerging out of his understanding of paleontology, but more so from an intense love and fascination with the natural world. He knew from his observation and emersion into nature that we humans must also evolve and that, for him, this change must be through a relationship and knowledge of Christ. Being silenced with this terribly important message has been excruciating for him. Although this banishment is a great blow to him he has dutifully accepted the decisions of his brotherhood and left for China for an undetermined length of time. Perhaps this is the beginning of his descent (the necessary destruction of ego), initiated by inner and outer world events.

We can now deepen the understanding of the gift of the descent by expanding Chardin's concluding statement of his prayer entitled, "Communion through Diminishment": "Teach me *to treat my death as an act of communion* to include, and to treat my suffering and that of others as further communion with you while still alive."[4]

Here Chardin includes others in his prayer. Both men always had their eyes on the need for compassion in the modern world. This is a critical outgrowth of the descent of these men and it is the plan many of us have written for our life stories: to be a compassionate person for another and perhaps many others. It is an ultimate

---

4 Teilhard, *Divine Milieu*, p. 57.

and extremely important way to live. In Buddhism, for example, these extraordinary compassionate people are named Bodhisattvas and the Buddhists have an enigmatic belief to explain them. They are felt to be on their last incarnation or even to have surrendered the achievement of Buddha nature and to have reentered incarnation voluntarily (descended) to help others escape suffering. They are Holy men and women and they are thoroughly equipped to be compassionate.

A critical part of the story of Christ, of course, is his descent to live among us, and then (perhaps because of his descent) the activation in his work of acts of extraordinary compassion for the intense human suffering he found. We have then our perception of God wrapped in descent and diminishment, and compassion is interwoven in both the descent and the subsequent ascent. We will look at the descents of these two men but also take a brief look at mythology to examine that story of humans descending for a purpose: to reclaim something lost or something new and extraordinary for all of us. But to see this first hand in our current subject area, let us return to the lives of these men and further consider these events in their lives and development as compassionate and gift-bearing humans.

We realize that they both descended and these descents were profound. If we begin with the understanding that we all exist containing the attributes of soul, body and mind (a common motif) we quickly realize that they used their entire soul-body-mind structures to descend into vast unknown, wonderful, and dangerous areas of their own psyches. They risked careers, credibility and the psychic life itself in the descent and diminishment to a place they both knew they had to go to discover what had always been unconscious, looming, perhaps even horrifying. And they did it for us. We must note and be grateful for the complete *integrity and courage* with which these descents and diminishments took place. How easy it would have been for them to refuse this cup.

Both men sought an intellectual way to understand this descent before engaging the process personally. Jung's study into "descent" is extensive including mythology (the study of Demeter's descent), Native American stories (the story of the wandering, searching Hiawatha), many other mythologies and numerous studies in alchemy. Chardin's study in paleontology was similar with profound realizations that accompanied discoveries of minerals and the bones of ancient man. But both men found their greatest fulfillment in the study of the descent and diminishment of Christ.

Jung discusses Christ's equivalent descents but emphasizes (with the alchemists) Christ's final descent in the days after his physical death and before his resurrection. In that Christ is the ultimate defeater of evil. His work on the cross was enough for physical man, but Jung felt evil itself remained unredeemed. Therefore Christ descended now into hell. And he emerged as the *New Fire*: "Christ lay as one asleep or in the fetters of death during the three days of his descent into hell, when he went down to the *ignis gehennalis,* from which he rises again as the New Fire."[5]

We must see the many descents of Christ to fully understand His compassion and the deep attachment of Chardin especially but also Jung. They also help us to understand His many ascents and ultimate ascent in glorification. His initial descent of course was incarnation. Other descents could be described as "embodiment and pain," "betrayal," "humiliation," "suffering," "crucifixion," "death," and "descent into hell." The ascents and gifts are "compassion and healing," "the sermon on the Mount," "the parables and teachings," "the transfiguration," "resurrection," "ascension," and "glorification."

As we leave the discussion of the descent, it is useful to see the parallels and the gifts in the same structure as the above lists for Christ's life. Of course Christ is God and these Godly experiences are not available to any man, but similar lists with different names could be constructed for each of our subjects from the writings they have left us.

Part Two: The Ascent and the Written Gifts

Now we have the gifts of *The Red Book* and *The Divine Milieu*. Prior to their descents Jung and Chardin were already studying and writing about the descent but in the immersed reality of living through the process for each of them came the truth, which they have shared with those seeking the same awakening. The Buddhists would instantly recognize them as Bodhisattvas, their gifts are always written with a deep sense of compassion for the human race. In the descent they learned compassion for themselves, which always precedes the ability to be compassionate with another.

---

5 C.G. Jung, *Psychology and Alchemy,* CW 12, ¶ 451.

The ascent for them and for us is only possible with the constant presence of a vision for how life can be now or could be in the future. When we look closely at ascent it becomes immediately apparent that the requirement, aside from a substantial descent and subsequent defeat of the previously existing ego, is this vision for the outer world future and, more important, an understanding of the universe that transcends ego. Here lies the birth of the symbol, the myth, the story, the archetype, alchemy, all religions, all faith, etc. Here also is hope for the future and the ability to see the present with a new clarity and to immerse oneself in the world for positive reasons (for example, compassion) that transcend self. Let's take a brief look into the ascents as recorded for us in *The Red Book* and *The Divine Milieu* before proceeding in Part Three to a further look at two specific gifts, Natural Mind from Jung, and Noosphere from Chardin.

Jung and *The Red Book*

In looking into *The Red Book* for the first time my feeling was that I was intruding into the deepest part of a man's soul, what we may call The Essential Self. I was looking at the result of powerful alchemical processes, base metals had mixed and beautiful new images and substances had emerged. Some of them must have been won on emotionally bloody battlefields, some given as gifts in the heroic process of Jung's venturing forth into areas that he must have known were potentially dangerous to his psyche. I decided to stay with the images for a long time before dedicating myself to understanding their interpretation. The interpretation of symbols always puts us right into our heads, which has a nasty habit of taking away their power. I am still living with the images.

Similarly, I have learned, in practicing therapy for all these years that clients can be easily robbed of the value of their symbolic experience by another who immediately wants to make it into something that they might be able to understand intellectually. The power of the experience evaporates. Readers who would acquire this book might consider taking a similar approach to it.

Jung said that the value of *The Red Book* was that it formed the basis of all his subsequent works. From the back cover:

The years of which I have spoken to you, when I pursued the inner images, were the most important time of my life. Everything else is to be derived from this. It began at that time and the later details hardly matter anymore. My entire life consisted in elaborating what had burst forth from the unconscious and flooded me like an enigmatic stream and threatened to break me. That was the stuff and material for more than only one life. Everything later was merely outer classification, the scientific elaboration, and the integration into life. But the numinous beginning which contained everything was then.[6]

In this frame, then, we can begin to place the complexity and beauty of not only *The Red Book* but also all of his subsequent contributions. He wished it so. The ascent continued throughout his life with a fountain of works that took him to so many places, and left us with the Collected Works and other works of great value. One of these other works was *The Visions Seminars* in which he greatly expanded the concept of Natural Mind to which we will return in the next section.

Chardin and *The Divine Milieu*

The experience of *The Divine Milieu*, which I believe contains not only a summary of Chardin's diminishment and descent but also of his ascent is, like *The Red Book*, a very personal disclosure. And it is remarkable in its contrast between the opposites of his experiences. If you are a reader of *The Divine Milieu* and can take the writing very personally and try to join Chardin's emotional journey, which is documented therein, you will find yourself experiencing with him the most difficult of descents. But you will also join him in the remarkable beauty of the final section (named *The Divine Milieu*), which stands in such utter contrast to the section preceding it as to defy the thought they may have come from the same person.

Once again the similarity of the paths of these men is unmistakable. Pain followed by beauty and the stage set for a lifetime of contributions, which we are only beginning to understand. Chardin personally commented on his process:

…I took the lamp and leaving the zone of everyday occupations and relationships where everything seems clear, I went down into my inmost self, to the deep abyss

6 C.G. Jung, *The Red Book*.

whence I feel dimly that my power of action emanates. But as I moved further and further away from the conventional certainties by which social life is superficially illuminated, I became aware that I was losing contact with myself. At each step of the descent a ew person was disclosed within me of whose name I was no longer sure and who no longer obeyed me. And when I had to stop my exploration because the path faded from beneath my steps, I found *the current which I dare to call my life.*[7] (Italics mine)

By his own definition, then, the ascent for Chardin produced the current of his life. Once again we see the necessity of the descent and its gifts and purpose. We could end reading with the statement above and feel we had been in the presence of a great mind but, of course, as we have discussed, there was the need that emerged to promise a look at a compassionate future for mankind and so we have the end of the book discussing the divine milieu into which we are all invited to live.

Delving any further into the ascents and descents is beyond the scope of this writing, although there is a great deal more to say. We have only begun to describe the sparking sun on the stream. However, to be complete, this chapter needs a brief foray into two of the gifts from these men for a compassionate future for mankind. The descent and ascent processes were so shattering for them that we must know that they emerged strengthened and renewed knowing that the process had produced *hope* in them and for us, and our future.

The Natural Mind and the Noosphere

My conception of Natural Mind is a mind in an advanced state; mind as it is commonly defined but with the addition of the spiritual. The addition of the spiritual takes us beyond ourselves, beyond ego. There is no place for ego in Natural Mind, no room is left because Natural Mind expands to fill all of us, indeed all of Creation. It begins, of course, with nature; a relationship that both men loved. Thus my belief is that the natural world is the world of God, His Creation, and until we make it our own we cannot advance personally or as a species. Jung and Chardin would, I believe,

---

7 Teilhard, *The Divine Milieu*, p. 42.

agree and they mapped out how we might proceed to an evolved and more enlightened future.

Both men seemed constantly impressed (astonished?) by nature. At first glance it seems easy to state that Jung looked at nature primarily as it is reflected in the soul, even the inner recesses of the soul, and that Chardin looked at nature in its outer world manifestations and then was drawn into how this is reflected in the Christian soul. But it is clear that both men simply loved the Creation in all its beauty and were repeatedly drawn to time in nature. This simple characterization will serve to start this discussion, which will take us more deeply into Natural Mind for Jung and Noosphere for Chardin.

I believe that Jung was as aware of the beauty of the outer world and celebrated it as much as did Chardin. Even though he did not take up an outer world academic identity, as deeply as did Chardin (paleontology), he demonstrated his fascination through his travels and comments and he contributed substantially through his formulation of what he called Natural Mind. Natural Mind for him was the base metal required for the flow of dreams, symbols, stories, myths, alchemy, and understanding the daily events of power in our psyches. This concept had the brilliance of making understandable and useful the natural world in the thoughts of those who have lost this appreciation of a piece of themselves from which emanates vast stores of psychic energy. But even if one does not or cannot immerse oneself in nature it will make itself known in dreams and life events, over which we have no control.

Instead of its proper location in our relationship with the Creation, the energy is trapped deep in our psyches or it seeps out in intellectualization or other defenses. When we are separated from this energy we become emotionally ill; we need this energy. Yet it is discouraged; we are told we are better without it.

Once in the spring I was on a canoe trip where there were many bald eagles with nests located along the river. They had their nests high in the tallest and often dead trees. When they saw the canoe an adult would swoop down out of the nest past the front of the canoe and then take a perch in a tree downstream where it could see us approach again. When we drew near the new perch the eagle repeated this action and moved further downstream. After four or five times it then flew off back to its original nest. The flight of the eagle was majestic, commanding the airwaves, almost effortless. This was a very beautiful thing to witness. Of course what the eagle was doing was instinctual; it was protecting its nest (and eaglets) by leading us away. Jung would say both the eagle's actions and my witnessing of it are Natural Mind.

After a while farther downstream another eagle started the same pattern and when it was finished and started back to its nest, something different happened. It suddenly stopped and started hovering in mid-air along side a tall sandstone wall. Then with incredible force from two powerful wing strokes it launched itself forward, talons out and plunged the points of its talons into a duck that was emerging from the other side of the wall. The duck had no chance, barely even awareness of impending instant death. Raw power; brutal force. No mercy, no question, no hesitation. Jung would also say this is Natural Mind.

Notice that there is human judgment even in what I have written. In the two paragraphs there are these words: majestic, commanding, effortless, very beautiful, incredible force, instant death, raw power, brutal, no mercy, no question, and no hesitation.

Here is what nature cares about these human judgments: Nothing! This is Natural Mind and it is so utterly beyond us as to not even notice our pronouncements. This is the mind we have lost and the beauty has been lost with the brutality. This is what Jung learned in his exploration of Creation and more importantly in the descent. There is nothing separating us from Natural Mind in a descent. What happens, happens. Whatever images and emotions flow simply flow. Nothing is present to mediate or lessen the impact of these events. This is why both men described loss of self and even psychosis as fears in their descents. But Natural Mind can release tremendous energy for each of us if we are willing to find it. The trip may be difficult and the experiences on the journey raw.

Chardin also discovered this mind. His exploration was in paleontology and archaeology and his findings were in the work of eons of time that gave age and history to his discoveries. As he sat in the dust of a "dig," I must imagine that he had the same sense of the timelessness and the distance that nature has necessarily kept from our judgment over history as he held bones millions of years old in his hands. This is the same sense of incalculable distance and yet attachment with Natural Mind that Jung had in his observations in Africa, in the North American Southwest, in the dreams of his clients, etc. If they had communicated I suspect they would have had much to say to each other about this deep mutual understanding of this aspect of Natural Mind.

They both recognized that the correct attitude of our human approach was first to know of the presence of Natural Mind, then to know much about it including its life disregarding our judgment or pretense, but then to also know that we must *participate in it* and in so doing we must allow it to transform us. For both men to arrive at a compassionate future plan for man, they had to experience a breakdown of the flow of internal symbols and outer world Natural Mind. We have already discussed this as a descent.

Most of us do not want this and we try hard not to have to experience it. However, despite our arrogance derived from our ability to control many aspects of nature, Natural Mind lives in each of us. If we don't live Natural Mind consciously we will not achieve the highest level of consciousness available to us. Jung pointed to it coming to life in the unconscious as found in dreams in powerful animistic forms. Chardin centered Natural Mind in the Trinity arguing that the Creation has a true home in the human heart where Christ lives and reigns. Note that both men each in their own way *elevated* the natural to the level of the spiritual. This would have been another dramatic discussion between them to listen to if it could have happened. It has important material for how we now consider the future.

By way of providing an example here is one reason why we must bring this discussion to our hope for the future: I believe that the answer to our destruction of the planet will only be achieved from atop this mountain. The natural world must be viewed from the view of Jung and Chardin: with the utmost of spiritual reverence and knowing that *we must be materially and personally changed by the Creation in the process*. I'm not sure we can change the downward spiral of our planet any other way. Jung's concept of Natural Mind demands that we would adopt a love and respect for nature, as would Chardin's belief in the preeminence of the Creation of God. Even though our earth is in worse shape than it was when they lived, they laid the groundwork through Natural Mind for how we could have avoided being where we are and how we might fix it now.

The Noosphere

Chardin defined the Noosphere as the thinking envelope of the Earth.[8] As he introduced the concept he immediately made it clear that the Noosphere is in a process of

---

8 Pierre Teilhard de Chardin, *The Future of Man*, p. 125.

change and the change is vitally important for the future of man. The change is also evolutionary and positive. We must evolve and this movement in consciousness is remarkably hopeful. Like Jung with Natural Mind he begins with the Earth, with the whole Creation, and he does not separate our consciousness from the consciousness at play every second in nature. However he does differentiate in his hope (expectation?) that we will take our role, the development of human awareness, in this change with great hope but also seriousness. Our consciousness is to Chardin: consciousness to the second degree. He stated:

> The Earth could more easily evade the pressures, which cause it to contract upon itself, the stars more easily escape from the spatial curve, which holds them on their headlong courses, than we men can resist the cosmic forces of a converging universe![9]

The converging universe is Chardin's desire for our future. Into this convergence he sees the hope of the blurring into extinction of our separations, prejudices, un-aware hatreds, abuse of the Earth, major conflicts and wars. If we can become close enough to the needs of the other, no matter whom or where, our (sometimes quite inert) compassion can be resurrected. He also believed that because this convergence is evolutionary, this change is certain to occur. The Noosphere is the container of this change in the entire human consciousness, like the force of gravity assures us the containment of oxygen near to the planet for us to breath. The Noosphere enlists certain laws about the growth of our consciousness as the Earth "deploys" the law of gravity.

Perhaps we could wonder where this incredibly positive hope for our future emerged for him. I believe he wanted to make a case for it being a scientific formulation from his studies in paleontology. And it may well be so. My thought is that it transcends science (without ignoring its rigors) and moves us into the realm of the Spirit. And here we have entered the most powerful healing force ever known: the Christian Trinity. Chardin brings to life his vision of the members of the Trinity in the future of the Noosphere in fascinating ways:

> And since Christ was born, and ceased to grow, and died, *everything has continued in motion because he has not yet attained the fullness of his form.* He has not gathered about Him the last folds of the garment of flesh and love woven for him by his faithful. *The mystical Christ has not reached the peak of his growth...* and it is in the continu-

---

9 Teilhard, *The Future of Man*, p. 125.

ation of this engendering that there lies the ultimate driving force behind all created activity…Christ is the term *of even the natural* evolution of living beings.[10]

Here we may have one of the items that may have been so hard for Chardin's colleagues in the Jesuit order to read: Christ himself evolving! And doing so *with us* with an end in mind. Further Chardin comes very close to a pantheistic position with his final statement, "Christ is the term *of even the natural* evolution of living beings." As dangerous as this may sound to orthodoxy, it is important to remember that Christ described himself returning to us in a much different form than the depictions of him we currently live with:

> …one like a son of man, clothed with a long robe and with a gold sash around his chest. The hairs of his head were white, like white wool, like snow. His eyes were like a flame of fire, his feet were like burnished bronze, refined in a furnace, and his voice was like the roar of many waters. In his right hand he held seven stars, from his mouth came a two-edged sword, and his face was like the sun shining in full strength.[11]

However, interjecting a personal note again, this heresy of the evolution of Christ (if it was judged to be so) has a strong ring of truth and hope for the future attached to it. I want so much for Chardin's future to be true for us and for us to witness this new Earth and for a Noosphere to which we all belong, personally and collectively. Chardin has given us a plan for how it could be, and how it must be. The path that many of us have planned for our lives reflects the enormous possibility and responsibility of this world yet to emerge.

Summary

We have, then, two extraordinary and compassionate men with very similar paths of descent and ascent leading to their gifts for the future. They suffered and bore their suffering, capturing for us, and for our planet, a new plan which is hopeful and which we must take very seriously if we are to survive personally and as a species. This brief

---

10 Teilhard, *The Future of Man,* p. 307.
11 Revelation 1: 13-16 English Standard Version.

foray into this subject will be served well if it stimulates others to look deeper into their own personal descents, ascents, and hopes for the future.

Bibliography

Foote, M. (Ed.). C.G. Jung. *The Visions Seminars: Book One, Parts One-Seven*. New York: Spring Publications, 1976.

Foote, M. (Ed.). C.G. Jung. *The Visions Seminars: Book Two, Parts Eight-Thirteen*. New York: Spring Publications, 1976.

Jung, C.G. *Psychology and Alchemy,* CW 12. Princeton, N.J.: Princeton University Press, 1968.

Jung, C.G. *The Red Book*. New York: W.W. Norton and Company, 2009.

Teilhard de Chardin, Pierre . *The Divine Milieu*. New York: HarperCollins, 1960 and 2001.

Teilhard de Chardin, Pierre. *The Future of Man*. New York: Random House, 1959 and 2004.

2

TEILHARD, JUNG, PATRIARCHY, AND THE MATERNAL PRINCIPAL

Contexts for Understanding Good and Evil Especially in Jung's View of Job in Jung's *Answer to Job*

John Giannini, MBA, MA, M.Div.

There are two kinds of intelligence: one acquired as a child in school memorizes facts and concepts from books and from what the teacher says, collecting information from the traditional sciences. With such intelligence you rise in the world.... You stroll with this intelligence in and out of fields of knowledge getting always getting more marks on your preserving table.

There is another kind of tablet, one already completed and preserved inside of you.... This other intelligence does not turn yellow or stagnate. It's fluid, and doesn't move from outside to inside through the conduits of plumbing-learning. This second knowing is a fountainhead. From within you move out.

–Rumi[1]

---

1 Coleman Barks, "Two Kinds of Intelligence" in *The Essential Rumi*, p. 178.

Introduction

I first learned of Teilhard de Chardin in the 1980s. At that time I was teaching Carl Jung's psychology to students enrolled in Matthew Fox's Creation-Centered Spirituality MA program. Fox holds that there is a balance and inner harmony between science and religion. Fox also awakened us to the feminine in psychology and theology. The cultural historian Thomas Berry taught us his and Teilhard's understanding of the cosmic mother, an understanding which was shared by Jung. Both Jung and Teilhard also suffered from a patriarchal pathology which has dominated our civilization for five thousand years. Patriarchy is pathological only when it excludes any viewpoint and class of people different than its own. It has fostered misogyny, the fear and hatred of femininity and of Mother Nature. Finally, this ideology has fomented endless wars between nations and within groups. Rumi's "Two Intelligences" gives us a lyrical view of the content of our two archetypal principles, first as patriarchy within our Learned Historical Self and, secondly, the maternal principle as the ground of the Natural Essential Self.

Patriarchy as damaged and already three thousand years old caused the Greek and Roman republics to yield to tyrannical leaders. In Jesus' time the Pharisees lived this ideology with their rigid laws, in contrast to Jesus' message of love, community, care for the needy, reverence for creation, and self-empowerment. Then, a Christianity as a community of equals changed into an exclusive hierarchy. Sophia's cosmic presence in the Wisdom literature, which Jesus would have known and which told us that "Yahweh created me...before earth came into being..." and that she was "at play everywhere in his world..."[2] gave way to a male-based religion and way of life. This latter mindset led, as Gary Wills tells us, into a "long process of leaching women out from the gospel story."[3] A patriarchal view was further intensified by Augustine who developed the idea of original sin attributed mainly to Eve. This doctrine meant, as Elaine Pagel tells us, that "through an act of will Adam and Eve *did* change the structure of the universe; their single, willful act permanently corrupted human nature as well as Nature in general."[4] Finally, this alienation from Nature changed Christology, wherein Jesus was viewed as more divine than human, according to historian

---

2 Proverbs 8:22-31.
3 G. Wills, *Papal Sin: Structure of Deceit*, pp. 117-118.
4 E. Pagel, *Adam and Eve and the Serpent*, p. 133.

Joseph Jungmann, S.J.[5] In turn, a lay peoples' spirituality aligned lovingly with Jesus as brother was replaced by a passive obedience to a priest-based society. This is the Christianity that Teilhard and Jung knew in the last quarter of the nineteenth century.

Patriarchy and the Maternal Principle in the Life and Thought of Teilhard and Jung

Teilhard as a child had sensed a feminine "universal being" in Nature. As a science professor, this awareness developed into a theology of Nature that he describes as a "divine milieu." The French bishops declared his idea that the sacred existed also in nature so dangerous that they ordered him exiled from France.[6] In 1947 he was forbidden by Rome authorities to write or teach philosophy and to publish books. Even his most important work, now *The Human Phenomenon*, suffered initially from an editing conforming to a male-based orthodoxy. For example, the exclamations: "Demeter! Mother Earth! a fruit? What kind of fruit? Is it seeking to be born on the tree of life?" were totally eliminated.[7]

As to parenting, Teilhard had enjoyed a loving relationship with his father. Jung, in contrast, had suffered an early loss of trust in his, a Christian minister who espoused a blind faith.[8] As compensation, Jung early felt he was two personalities: as an obedient little boy and as a wise old man who lived in the eighteenth century.[9] He experienced a father-son relationship with Freud until the latter, seemingly afraid of Jung's "unconscious religious factors," demanded that Jung embrace Freud's "dogma of sexuality" as a "bulwark against occultism."[10] In turn Jung was rebelled when, offering to interpret Freud's dream, Freud refused, saying "I have to protect my authority."[11] Much of the professional and social opposition to Teilhard and Jung had to do with their experiencing and writing about the great mother. As a child, Teilhard loved rocks. Jung as a

---

5 J. Jungmann, *Pastoral Liturgy.*
6 J. Skehan, *Geology and Grace: Teilhard's Life and Achievements*, p. 8.
7 Pierre Teilhard de Chardin, *The Human Phenomenon*, p. xxi.
8 C.G. Jung, *MDR*, pp. 42, 52.
9 Jung, *MDR*, pp. 33-35.
10 Jung, *MDR*, pp. 150-1.
11 Jung, *MDR*, pp. 152-158.

boy experienced a deep affinity with a rock on which he often sat. Ironically, he feared black-frocked Jesuit priests, the order to which Teilhard belonged. He dreamt of being in a cave in which a huge phallus topped by an eye paralyzed him with fear, especially, when his mother cried out, "That is the man-eater." Paradoxically, he realized that this grave-like interior with its frightening male figure had green curtains, which "symbolized the *meadow,* in other words, the mystery of Earth…."[12]

In Teilhard's *Hymn of the Universe*, he wanders in the desert like Jung in *The Red Book.* Suddenly he is aware of a powerful mother figure who says, "Son of earth, steep yourself in the sea of matter" and her matter is the "essence which penetrates to the innermost depth of all things."[13] Jung writes in *The Red Book* that Philemon "showed me the immeasurable mystery…I saw that the sky had the form of a woman…." Philemon then says to her, "he wants to become your child."[14] In another event, Jung stands before an old woman, who "throws her veil back" revealing a "beautiful maiden…." Finding her strangely familiar, he asks, "Who are you?" She responds," I am your soul."[15]

Both men were steeped in quantum physics. Teilhard refers early in *The Human Phenomenon* to the influence of such physicists as Poincare, Einstein, Sir James Jean and others.[16] Jung personally met with Einstein, acknowledges he influenced his later ideas on synchronicity, and led to his long relationship with the physicist Wolfgang Pauli. These scientists understood that the universe is informed with mind as stated by Sir James Jean in 1937: "…the universe begins to look more like a great thought than like a great machine."[17] Teilhard called this cosmic mind the "noosphere" and as the force "driving all living beings toward a higher consciousness."[18] Jung describes the same as the collective unconscious that "is more like an atmosphere in which we live than something that is found *in* us," and that does not "behave merely psychologically; in the case of synchronicity it proves to be a universal substrate present in

---

12 Jung, *MDR,* pp. 12-13.

13 Pierre Teilhard de Chardin, *Hymn of the Universe*, pp. 61, 63-65.

14 C.G. Jung, *The Red Book*, p. 355.

15 Jung, *The Red Book*, p. 29.

16 Teilhard, *The Human Phenomenon*, p. 2.

17 A. Koestler, *The Roots of Coincidence*, p. 58.

18 Teilhard, *The Human Phenomenon*, p. 122.

the environment."[19] Finally, both held, contrary to many scientists, that Nature has an inward purpose.

The Problem of Evil in Teilhard and Jung: Jung

Rumi's "The Two Intelligences" have significance in considering this issue. Rumi's first intelligence describes what I call the "Learned Self," such as when a "child in school memorizes facts and concepts." This "Self" includes damaging family influences as well as a patriarchal pathology. However, as Jung writes, patriarchy's positive task is to realize "logos," that is, a consciousness that knows a "discrimination of opposites" as it "extricates itself…from the maternal womb," that is "the unconscious," which becomes the ego's necessary opposite.[20] Then humankind must realize the other intelligence, which Rumi describes as "already complete" and a "fountainhead from within you moving out" that is the "Essential Self" in the unconscious. This Self, as Jung writes, "carries for us that inborn image of the mater natura and mater spiritualis, of the totality of life…."[21] This "Self," like all archetypes, remains substantively hidden, and yet she is the "fountainhead" of our entire existence and our deepest connection with the Universe.

Teilhard first points to the evil we all know in our "Learned Self," which he describes as "physical suffering and moral wrong" which he experienced from church authorities. Yet, Teilhard said little about evil in his private life nor about Nature's violence we humans often experience. This lack of focus on evil was deliberate, because as he writes "my purpose has been solely fixed on isolating the *positive essence of the biological process of hominization*" (his emphasis) rather than "to develop the negative aspect of the image." This cosmic "positive essence" is in us as the "The Essential Self." Teilhard then gives us his view of original sin: "The Fall is not an isolated fact but a general condition affecting the whole history."[22] This outlook was condemned by Christian authorities. Teilhard held that, along with our free-will capacity for moral evil, ontological or natural evil is the resultant of many factors in Nature, such as "trial

---

19 Jung, C.G., *Letters*, Vol. 1, p. 433.
20 C.G. Jung, *The Archetypes and the Collective Unconscious*, CW 9i, ¶ 178.
21 Jung, *Archetypes and the Collective Unconscious*, CW 9i, ¶ 172.
22 Teilhard, *The Human Phenomenon*, pp. 224-5, 268.

and error… decomposition" and so death, and finally "*evil is in the form of growth*" that spans a spectrum from "the throes of child birth" to "a universe that toils, that sins, that suffers." He ends his book with a remarkable statement: "In one way or another, even in the eyes of a mere biologist, it is still true that nothing resembles the way of the cross as much as the human epic."[23] In my view, he means that we humans are the universe conscious of itself not only as creative but as suffering. We thus participate in Teilhard's Christology that is cosmically oriented, so that in Jesus, Divinity "is aggregating the entire psyche of the earth to himself."[24] Furthermore, "the cross would appear as symbolizing not just the expiation of sin, but the upward and laborious rise of all creation."[25] This view is in line with the early Christian understanding that humankind lives in an Easter condition, not in a fallen state. So there was then no body on a cross but rather a jewel, symbolizing Nature's and the Soul's sacredness.

Jung's overall ideas of good and evil meshes well with Teilhard's, but Jung's *Answer to Job* raises problems. Jung's Job version tackles one of the most crucial puzzles in religious thought, since all of us, as in the Biblical Job, know innocent suffering. The *Jerusalem Bible* editors note that "The main character, Job, is a famous figure in ancient history" among other cultures.[26] A modern version of such suffering is Harold Kushner's *When Bad Things Happen to Good People*.

The Job story in scripture is as follows. God, meeting with his "sons" including Satan who walks the earth, praises Job as a good man. Satan holds that he has never been challenged. So God allows Satan to test Job. Satan calls on storms to destroy his crops and buildings and kills his children and then afflicts Job with ill health. Teilhard would see these as the vicissitudes of life that innocent persons experience. In Rumi's terms, Job knows these pains as aspects of the Learned/Experiential Self. Job's four friends hold to an old patriarchal view that such havoc means Job has sinned. Job, insisting that he has not, challenges God's justice.

The fourth and youngest friend, Elihu, introduces us to the unconscious depth of the Essential Self when he tells Job that God "speaks by dreams, and visions that come in the night," that tell him "to turn away from evil-doing and make an end of

---

23 Teilhard, *The Human Phenomenon*, p. 226.
24 Teilhard, *The Human Phenomenon*, p. 21.
25 R. Faricy, *Teilhard's Theology of Redemption*, p. 554.
26 A. Jones, *The Jerusalem Bible*, p. 726.

his pride."[27] Jung's ideas are identical. He holds that dreams, in their deep wisdom, often contained "an ethical obligation" that, if not obeyed, causes one "to fall prey to the power principle" that damages self and others.[28] Then consistent with the unconscious and Nature's cosmic mind, Elihu sings of Divinity's creative wonders. The Jerusalem Bible commentators call this sublime section "A hymn to God's wisdom and omnipresence."[29] Before Job can respond, God, continuing the same theme, speaks from "The heart of the tempest," that is, Job's unconscious. The text reads: "*Yahweh gave Job his answer*" (my emphasis), that Job must bow to the creator's wisdom.[30] The divine answer, present in the unconscious depth of each of us and resonating with the Wisdom Literature's Sophia, is that innocent suffering can be endured when we ponder the wonder and mystery of our cosmic existence.

Another modern retelling of the Job story is the movie, "The Tree of Life," by Terrance Malick. Unlike Harold Kushner's book, which minimally gives an answer to the problem of innocent suffering, this movie gives one comparable to the scriptural story. The movie begins with a quote from Job when God says to our archetypal protagonist, "Where were you when I laid the earth's foundations? When all of the stars of the morning were singing with joy, and the Sons of God in chorus were chanting praise?"[31] Malick then tells the story of the O'Brien family in which the marine-sergeant-like father afflicts his three sons with his endlessly critical authority. Later, this family mourns the death of the gentle second son who has been killed in war. As the sensitive and Nature-loving mother grieves while in a forest, she experiences a long vision of the wonders and powers of a beautiful, wild evolving Nature. This echoes God's response to Job. Continuing this theme, the oldest son and narrator, Jack, asks, "Where were you when I needed you. You spoke to me in the trees." Malick writes in the movie's script, "The whole of creation is in the image of a tree, all parts feeding on the same sap," that is, the hidden cosmic unity of Mother Nature.[32] Later, Jack reflects: "Nature is dying….What is despair but to lose the eternal."[33] Finally, in an after life vision, he experiences a reconciling family harmony. There, he has this sense

---

27 Job, 33:15-17.
28 Jung, *MDR*, pp. 192-3.
29 Job, 36:22-33-37:1-24.
30 Job, 38:1-41:25.
31 Job, 38: 4-7.
32 T. Malick, Script of the movie, *The Tree of Life*, p.124.
33 Malick, *The Tree of Life*, p. 11.

of his mother as "his mysterious guide" and the carrier "of his moral being. She is the Mother of all Creation...she is the gateway, the door." Malik adds in the script her final words: "Know that I am."[34]

Jung's *Answer to Job,* on the other hand, gives us a view of Job as the dominant wise consciousness and Divinity as the miserable, inept unconscious. This book is totally at odds with his entire corpus. Jung's overall view is evident in the opening sentence of his autobiography: "My Life is the story of the self-realization of the unconscious," that is his individuation. Then he writes: "Life has always seemed to me like a plant that lives on its rhizome...What we see is the blossoms which pass. The rhizome remains."[35] The blossoms symbolize our Learned Self and the rhizome the Essential Self. More importantly, Jung repeatedly holds that moral evil comes from humans[36] and especially self-hatred.[37] That is why the *Answer to Job* is so seemingly astounding. Here, Jung stubbornly holds to the idea of the substantive character of good as well as evil even in God, the thought of which "We naturally boggle at ...."[38]

However, Jung does say in his Introduction that he is talking "in a world of images that points to something ineffable....so that none of my reflections touches the essence of the Unknowable."[39] So Jung images a view of God which is certainly not in the Biblical Job: "God is eaten up with rage and jealously...." and so reveals his "divine darkness" because "Job in a human awareness...had secretly been lifted up to a superior knowledge of God which God himself did not possess."[40] "God's problem is that he is too unconscious to be moral. Morality presupposes consciousness."[41] Recall Jung's contrasting view that dreams reveal Divinity's moral wisdom! Teilhard would have understood Jung's need to vent, but would have found, I hold, his raging tone appalling or certainly problematic.

The problem with Jung's Job–and I believe Teilhard would agree–is that Jung too readily enters into "the Unknowable" and so into the realms of metaphysics and faith. So, for example, he writes that "To believe that God is the *Summum Bonum* is impos-

---

34 Malik, *The Tree of Life*, p. 125.

35 Jung, *Memories, Dreams, Reflections*, pp. 3-4.

36 C.G. Jung, *Psychology and Religion*, CW 11, ¶ 247.

37 Jung, *Psychology and Religion*, CW 11, ¶ 133.

38 Jung, *Psychology and Religion*, CW 11, ¶ 291.

39 Jung, *Psychology and Religion*, CW 11, ¶¶ 555-6.

40 Jung, *Psychology and Religion*, CW 11, ¶¶ 560-1, 583.

41 Jung, *Psychology and Religion*, CW 11, ¶ 547.

sible for a reflective consciousness."[42] Yet, at the end of his autobiography, he holds that "we are in the deepest sense the victims and instruments of cosmogonic 'love'." So in the face of this "mystery of love," he adds, "Like Job, I had to lay my hand on my mouth."[43]

When Victor White, a noted theologian, an analyst, and a friend of Jung, read the manuscript, he saw it as an active imagination through which Jung had experienced recovery from a physical ailment. However, White urged Jung not to publish it. He felt that its wild and injudicious rhetoric, while understandable as a therapeutic, would damage White's attempt to bridge Jung's psychology with Christian theology. Jung, however, published the manuscript, the upshot of which was the temporary loss of their strong friendship in the 1950s. Also, White was removed from important professional assignments because of his involvement with Jung. Fortunately for me and for many associates, White was "banished" to our Dominican monastery in Oakland, where he changed many of our lives. As my first analyst, he helped me to value the unconscious and so realize a life-long turning point.

Discerning people know the Old Testament Deity is like an angry tyrannical King dispensing his will for good or ill. The Job story was the first to question this picture of God. For this reason the compilers of the Old Testament were reluctant to include the book in the scriptures. They did so, however, since it belongs to the Wisdom Tradition in which Divinity is a sacred true, good, and beautiful force in Nature whose power and presence finally spoke to Job from the depth of his own unconscious. The bible commentators entitle this section, "Job must bow to the creator's wisdom." This is not the "God who is eaten up with rage and jealousy," as Jung describes the Deity. In the Book of Job, Divinity speaks authoritatively, "Who is this obscuring my designs with his empty-headed words? /Brace yourself like a fighter; /now it is my turn to ask questions and yours to inform me."[44] God is saying, you've laid out your thoughts; now hear mine. God's answer was not to leave Job "trembling in every limb with the terror of almost total annihilation," as Jung writes, but to lay out the wonder and mystery of existence as the only answer to life's innocent sufferings. Job surrenders with humility and discernment, not out of fear and trembling: "I knew you then only by hearsay, but now, having seen you with my own eyes, / I retract all I have said, / and in dust

---

42 Jung, *Psychology and Religion*, CW 11, ¶ 662.
43 Jung, *MDR*, pp. 353-4.
44 Job 38: 2-3.

and ashes I repent."[45] Then, contrary to Jung's holding that "Yahweh has no interest whatsoever in Job's cause…"[46] Yahweh rebukes Eliphaz and friends, requires them to offer up sacrifices for the sake of Job, and points to their folly "in not speaking of me properly, as my servant has done." Then God in her maternal wisdom and largess not only enriches Job again with property and sons but for the first time with three beautiful daughters to whom Job grants an inheritance equal to their brothers.[47]

Now, Jung was, of course, familiar with the psychological and spiritual elements in the story, such as the fourth friend, not only as the young one but also as the transcendent fourth dimension as understood in his vast study of quaternity. Further, he knew the unconscious as wise and as united with all of Mother Nature. So why did he write the *Answer to Job* in a way which seems antithetical to his overall work? I think the answer resides in the recognition that Jung had suffered in so many ways from patriarchal domination beginning early in his life, as in the phallus dream, the sight of black-robed Jesuits, his break with his father and, later, with Freud. He also endured the horror of World War I and World War II, with the unbelievably vicious behavior of Hitler, and then Stalin's purges in which he murdered millions. So Jung, when he wrote Job, had experienced in the last century's first fifty years the most violent period in human history which is now called "The Blood Flood." For all these reasons he began *Answer to Job* with the empathic biblical passage expressing his concern for his fellow humans: "*I am distressed for thee, my brother….*"[48] Because of this cumulative patriarchal nightmare, Jung projected this historical male cruel horror on an Old Testament masculine Deity who, as we noted above, functioned like a "tyrannical king." Jung reminds us that patriarchy's one-sidedness, like all such pathologies, becomes "barbaric."[49] After this first part's almost endless tirade against a monstrous maleness that Victor White called his *Sturm and Drang*,[50] Jung turns to the Essential Self and its relationship with mother earth and the archetype of the universal mother. He acknowledges the "cosmic Sophia" as "God's self reflection."[51] Then, he devotes an entire section to the 1950 papal proclamation of Mary's assumption into Heaven.

---

45 Job, 42:5-6.
46 Jung, *Psychology and Religion*, CW 11, ¶ 588.
47 Job, 42:7-17.
48 II Samuel, 1:26.
49 C.G. Jung, *Psychological Types*, CW 6, ¶ 118.
50 Victor White, *Soul and Psyche*, p. 240.
51 Jung, *Psychology and Religion*, CW 11, ¶¶ 714, 727.

He reminds readers that "Sophia was with God before the creation." Jung then writes that Mary as being in the godhead is "the most important religious event since the Reformation."[52] He writes: "We cannot tell whether God and the unconscious are two different entities. Both are borderline concepts for transcendental contents."[53] Finally, in his concluding sentence he declares, Job-like, that "even the enlightened person … is never more than his own limited ego before the One who dwells within him, whose form has no knowable boundaries, who encompasses him on all sides, fathomless as the abysms of the earth and vast as the sky."[54] As a great teacher of the maternal principle, he returns to her and so grounds himself again in her cosmic wisdom in this most powerful and controversial of all of his books.

Bibliography

Barks, Coleman. *The Essential Rumi*. Edison, N.J.: Castle Books, 1997.

Faricy, R. *Teilhard's Theology of Redemption*. Washington, DC: Catholic University Press, 1981.

Jones, A. *The Jerusalem Bible*. New York: Double Day and Company, 1966.

Jung, C.G. *The Archetypes and the Collective Unconscious*, CW 9i. Princeton, N.J.: Princeton University Press, 1969.

Jung, C.G. *Psychology and Religion: West and East*, CW 11. Princeton, N.J.: Princeton University Press, 1958.

Jung, C.G. *Memories, Dreams, Reflections*. New York: Vintage, 1965.

Jung, C.G. *Letters: Volume 1 1906-1950* and *Volume II 1951-1961*. Princeton, N.J.: Princeton University Press.

Jung, C.G. *The Red Book*, ed. Sonu Shamdasani. London & New York: W.W. Norton and Company, 2008.

Jungmann, J. *Pastoral Liturgy*. New York: Herder and Herder, 1962.

Koestler, A. *The Roots of Coincidence*. New York: Random House, 1972.

---

52 Jung, *Psychology and Religion*, CW 11, ¶¶ 748, 752.
53 Jung, *Psychology and Religion*, CW 11, ¶ 757.
54 Jung, *Psychology and Religion*, CW 11, ¶ 758.

Kushner, H. *When Bad Things Happen To Good People.* NY: Random House, 1978.

Malick, T. Script of the movie, "The Tree of Life. 1979/2011.

Pagel, E. *Adam and Eve and the Serpent.* NY: Random House, 1988.

Skehan, J. *Geology and Grace: Teilhard's Life and Achievements.* NY: American Teilhard Association, 2006.

Stein, M. *Jung's Treatment of Christianity.* Chicago, Illinois: Chiron Publications, 1986.

Teilhard de Chardin, Pierre. *The Human Phenomenon.* Portland, OR: Sussex Academic Press, 1999/2003.

Teilhard de Chardin, Pierre. *Hymn of the Universe*. New York: Harper and Row, 1961.

White, V. *Soul and Psyche.* London: Collins and Harvill Press, 1959.

Wills, G. *Papal Sin: Structure of Deceit.* New York: Doubleday, 2000.

3

A VIEW FROM GRANITE POINT

The Unfinished Work of C.G. Jung and Teilhard de Chardin

Jon Magnuson

"Our blue tents are pitched at the edge of a fossil-bearing cliff, looking out over the immense flat surfaces of Mongolia; the terraced levels, uniformly grey with a tinge of delicate green, have a magic when the rays of the setting sun skim over them."

Teilhard de Chardin[1]

"The rocks are alive. The only difference is they breathe slower than the rest of us."

C.G. Jung[2]

Along with seven other kayakers, I've pulled my 18-ft sea kayak onto the beach of a small sandy cove. We're cautiously making our way now, through a swarm of mosquitoes, up a gently sloping, uneven rock face four billion years old. This is the third day out on a 50-mile trip along the shores of Lake Superior. We've stopped for a break at an outcropping of granite cliff, perched out from a forested shoreline, in order to catch an overview of the horizon. In my daypack I'm carrying a crumpled copy of Teilhard de Chardin's prayer "Hymn to Matter."[3]

---

1 *Teilhard de Chardin Album*, (on an expedition in 1930 to the Gobi Desert) p. 52.
2 The reader is referred to C.G. Jung's *Man and His Symbols*, especially pages 204-217.
3 Pierre Teilhard de Chardin, *Hymn of the Universe*.

This morning a member of our group mentioned during a casual conversation she is a distant relative of Davidson Black, once Chairman for the Geological Survey of China, who worked with Teilhard de Chardin on an expedition to China in the 1930s.[4]

Now an Anglican priest in Montreal, she's traveled to join us for this five-day retreat on spirituality, symbol, and landscape sponsored by the small nonprofit institute with which I'm now affiliated. Awaiting me at our next campsite is a personal duffel bag in which I've packed, thanks to the influence of Carl Jung, a tattered dream journal.

The spirit of Chardin and Jung continue to influence the Cedar Tree Institute's mission here in the Upper Peninsula of Michigan, silently imprinting varied projects and programs. For sixteen years the Institute's annual summer kayak retreat has been described to prospective participants as "encounters with both inner and outer land-scapes."

Critics and scholars agree both Teilhard de Chardin and Carl Jung significantly shaped the foundations of psychology, anthropology, and theology as we know them today. Though contemporaries, Jung (1875-1961), the founder of Analytical Psychology, and Chardin (1881-1955), a Jesuit priest and world-respected paleontologist, never had a face-to-face encounter, none-the-less they shared common ground. Creative, prophetic individuals, they were both admired but marginalized by authorities in their respective disciplines. Even their fiercest critics regarded them as intellectual giants. Now thanks to the increasing influence of conservative religious voices in popular culture and the dominance of pharmaceutical-driven paradigms shaping psychiatric practice, Jung and Chardin are regarded by most conventional medical and religious institutional settings as respectable outlaws.

On a personal note, Jung's and Chardin's views of the human condition have continued to shape my interior life. In the 1950s, as a young boy I stumbled upon a copy of Chardin's *The Phenomenon of Man.*[5] The moment remains clear for me. It was a summer afternoon in our family's parsonage in Minneapolis. I remember its pages lying open on my father's bedside bookstand. Years later, Fred Gustafson, recently ar-

---

4 Davidson Black was a Canadian paleoanthropologist who spent years with Chardin in China searching for early human fossils. He's best known for his discovery of *Homo erectus pekinensis* or the "Peking Man." In 1934, Black died at his desk in Beijing from a heart attack, working late at night over the skeletal remains of his discovery. He was 49 years of age.

5 Pierre Teilhard de Chardin, *The Phenomenon of Man.*

rived back in Wisconsin with his wife Karen from studies at the C.G. Jung Institute in Zurich, introduced me to Carl Jung's world of depth psychology during a retreat in Northern Michigan. Fred became my respected colleague and mentor.

There were consequences. In the decades that followed, sometimes to the bewilderment and frustration of both secular and ecclesiastical authorities, I've subsequently but willingly found myself engaged in a shifting multi-dimensional approach when dealing with various levels of subjective and "objective" worlds in which I've come to find myself. Carl Jung and Teilhard de Chardin have left their marks.

For me, facts will never be simply "facts" thanks to Jung and Chardin. Instead, I've now come to believe they are phenomena constructed out of personal projections, collective fantasies, and socially sanctioned expectations, supported by selected sets of evidence, but all ultimately driven by a deep hunger of the human heart. What I've also come to believe, thanks to Jung, is that those respective "facts" pull us into the future. Psychologically, we move forward, step-by-step, building our personal identities on what actually are relative and competing views of realities. The personal challenge for many of us is how, then, do we navigate through such dream worlds? Where do we find a reliable compass? Who can best serve as guides? What will anchor and ground us as we seek to live out lives of integrity, and modicums of hopeful purpose?

We've reached our temporary destination atop a rugged 40-foot granite precipice overlooking Lake Superior, facing the Eastern horizon. It's time to drop our daypacks and relax for awhile. Below us, directly below the cliff's edge, lies the shoreline of largest body of fresh water by area in the world. Lake Superior's depths plunge 1300 feet below sea level, her temperature off the bottom of her shoals holding to a constant 37 degrees Fahrenheit. Author Philip Caputo writes that peering into the depths of this Great Lake's cold, crystal-clear waters is "looking into the eye of God.[6]

No doubt that Chardin would have loved this fierce landscape. Geologists travel here from around the word to examine the basalt, greenstone and granite formations that majestically frame the Lake's 1500-mile shoreline. I've learned the granite formation we're standing on is part of what geologists call the pre-Cambrian Shield, dating back billions of years. It's a sample of the oldest exposed rock left on the planet.

Old Carl Jung would be smiling as well. Five American Indian Reservations are located within a hundred and fifty miles of this afternoon's resting place. Their communities are broken with unemployment, domestic violence, and alcoholism but remnants of their

---

6 Philip Caputo, *Indian Country*.

Mediwiwin religion (dreamer societies) still are practiced with drums and sacred fires, deep within forests inside the boundaries of their treaty lands.

Our group spreads out over the expansive granite rock face, some choosing to make their way down to the water's edge for a swim. Others take advantage of our break to examine lichen and moss. Still others choose to find knoll and spend time staring off into the horizon. A few lie on large, sun-kissed granite slabs and close their eyes in rest.

Over the years, when guiding groups in such settings, I've come to find it a challenge to creatively balance an intersection of spirit and place, a religious sensibility and a world of hard science. There are always participants eager to learn about the specific geology and history of Michigan's Upper Peninsula. They come to learn as much as they can about our forgotten landscape's ecological map, its remote geography, its shifting climate, diverse wildlife. I've discovered others prefer, during our days together, to move more toward the internal and subjective. They are looking for experiences that might lead to insights around vocation and relationships or more personal emotional matters.

This division, often surfacing as a subtle, creative tension in our group dynamics, reflects, I've come to believe, a larger, broader fracturing of Western consciousness which we all share. The rise of individualism and science during the Enlightenment and the resulting challenges to formal authority (both secular and ecclesiastical) we know contributed to the success of the 16th century Protestant Reformation. Reason and autonomy were victorious. It's important to remember those values still dominate, at least in the collective consciousness, the spirit of Europe and North America's ruling classes. "I think, therefore I am," wrote René Descartes (1596-1650).

We are awakening now. We are recognizing there has been a cost. Our modern Western world is one in which religious ritual and ceremony are increasingly threatened (ask any priest or clergy) and one for which the dominant, unspoken religion can be understood as innovation, speed, specialization, and efficiency.

Evidence suggests that Jung and Chardin understood this problem clearly and struggled against living in an ever-encroaching secularized universe. Both attempted to integrate, intellectually and spiritually, lessons of history, science, and medicine with their own experience. Both suffered the consequences, professionally and personally, of trying to expand narrow, dogmatic, and limiting worldviews dominant in the psychology, science, medicine, and theology of their times.

For Chardin, the tension manifested itself as he navigated the worlds of science and religion in which he traveled and balanced, as best he could, his personal identity. On one hand, he was highly respected by his colleagues as a researcher and paleontologist. He regularly published his research findings in scientific journals. His contribution as a scientist was valued by his peers. Chardin was promoted, in 1947, to the rank of Officer of the Legion of Honor by France's Ministry of Foreign Affairs with the following citation:

> For outstanding services to the intellectual and scientific influence of France through a body of work mostly written and published in China, which has established him as a leading authority in international and particularly English-speaking scientific circles. He may now be regarded in the field of paleontology and geology as one of the chief ornaments of French Science.[7]

At the same time, despite his public recognition, we know that most of his professional scientific colleagues had little interest in his more mystical writings as a theologian and priest. This was a disappointment for Chardin. And another shoe was also about to drop. Two months following the French government's commendation, he wrote to his colleague Abbe Breuil:

> A week ago I had a letter from my General (Rome) forbidding me (in a perfectly courteous way) from publishing anything that involved philosophy or theology. And that neatly cuts out a large part of the activity still left open to me. It isn't making life any brighter.[8]

The power of Chardin's thought threatened, of course, the religious institution that provided him both his priestly authority and personal identity. The Vatican has continued to regard Chardin's theological contributions with suspicion. In 1962 and in 1981 The Sacred congregation of the Holy Office issued a ban on his writings. It still remains.

> For this reason, the most eminent and most revered Fathers of the Holy Office exhort all Ordinaries as well as the superiors of Religious institutes, rectors of seminaries and presidents of universities, effectively to protect the minds, particularly of the youth,

---

7 *Teilhard de Chardin Album*, Auboux, 1966, p. 176.
8 *Teilhard de Chardin Album*, 1966, p. 178.

against the dangers presented by the works of Fr. Teilhard de Chardin and of his followers.[9]

Carl Jung's struggle to find a respected voice in his time can be seen, in some respects, as similar to Chardin's. Jung's break with Sigmund Freud in 1912 set Jung apart, alienating him from many of his colleagues in the emerging International Psychoanalytic Association (IPA). We know from personal correspondence that initially Freud and Jung held each other in high esteem. Freud, in fact, was grooming Jung for a key leadership role in the prestigious IPA. But that hope was soon to be dissolved. Jung's insistence of a broader, deeper understanding of the meanings of symbols and archetypes threatened the core of Freud's theoretical framework. His mentor perceived the human psyche as a closed system, rooted in primal drives, shaped by childhood experiences buried deep within the unconscious. Jung's emphasis on the potential healing power of religion, his conviction of a deeper Self, and his belief in a collective unconscious brought them into bitter conflict.

Deirdre Bair, in a biography of Jung describes how these two personalities and Freud's rigid ideology led to a shattered relationship between two of the Western world's most prominent thinkers and analysts. She documents how Jung frequently remembered how passionately Freud implored him "Promise me one thing: look after sexuality!" There would be no room for compromise on Freud's end. Jung, in turn, dismissed Freud's dogmatic position as "scientific materialism."[10]

Although a respected physician and the son of a Swiss Reformed pastor, Jung was, during his lifetime, only hesitantly embraced by a few theologians, clergy, and priests. Some believe many religious leaders dismissed his appreciation for symbol and ritual because it required, ironically, a descent into the inner life. Dogmatic, one-dimensional guardians of church doctrine saw his emphasis on the role of the unconscious as heretical.

Jung's view of the psyche, in contrast to Freud's, was that it was an "open system," swirling with archetypes, fantasies, and dreams. Jungian-oriented therapists will remain a minority. It's been my experience that the current majority of cognitive-oriented, task-centered therapists generally regard Jungian perspectives as off the radar. Medication reviews, 20 minutes or less with a psychiatrist, are currently the accepted

---

9 (Monitum Concerning the Writings of Fr. Teilhard de Chardin) "America Magazine," December 4, 2010.

10 Deirdre Bair, *Jung: A Biography*, p. 227.

gold standard for most mental health clinics and hospitals. A colleague of mine, a respected psychiatrist, recently retired from her private practice, telling me: "No one wants to talk about his or her inner life. They want to feel better, quickly. That means medication. I can't with good conscience do this anymore."

I'm standing barefoot on a granite cliff 3 billion years old, staring off into Lake Superior's vast cloud-framed horizon void of any sign of human life. The moment is mesmerizing. In such settings nature unfolds to us her mystical patterns: cycles of light and darkness, shifting winds, sounds of thunder. Chardin noted that observations of the natural world elicit a basic human need for order and purpose. Classification of species, identification of plants and animals point to a need for some underlying unity. Jung's Analytical Psychology uses its own theoretical framework. Both science and religion, at their best, seek to meet such a hunger for meaning. Both long to meet in the other.

Chardin searched for an integration of evolutionary biology and geology. He came to believe the whole of the universe was moving toward an Omega Point. Carl Jung carried a parallel conviction that each human psyche was involved in, as part of musical-like score, an unfolding Magnus Opus (Great Work). From a psychological perspective, Jung believed there existed in each of us a powerful drive for wholeness, seeking to integrate, directly or indirectly, the psyche both in its collective and individual expressions. In that respect, both Chardin and Jung were, with certain qualifications, optimists. But their visions were imperfect, incomplete. And as with all great thinkers, by their own admissions both of them knew that as well. It leaves for us, in our own time, an invitation to take another step in a great Unfinished Work.

We can begin with respectful recognition of both Jung's and Chardin's limitations. Although disconcerting to some, it's important to recognize both Jung and Chardin were part of the embedded European aristocracy of their times. In Chardin's case, it was the French upper class. In Jung's case, the privileged Swiss elite. The consequences of this social identification were, disappointing but perhaps not surprisingly, reflected in their positions on the horrific politics of racism and war that defined their times. Around them the world was bleeding. Both Jung and Chardin were both quietists. Evidence from personal correspondence suggests they both saw themselves, for better or worse, as "above" (or "beyond") the fray.

In Jung's case, the biographer Dierdre Bair states Jung's ready excuse for ignoring social responsibilities was his extensive travel connected with lecturing and receiving honorary degrees. She notes that he would also mention that upon returning home to

Zurich, his energy was often too weakened by amoebic dysentery to become involved in public affairs.[11] In Chardin's case, Claude Cuenot, a colleague and admiring Chardin biographer, suggests, and I think unconvincingly, that Chardin's philosophical positivism encouraged him to seek to accept social movements, however horrific, as part of a larger, complex movement toward integration.[12]

Even more significant, it is important to recognize that neither Jung nor Chardin lived to experience the remarkable revolution in thinking about the natural environment (air, water, forests) that generations born in the last quarter of the 20th century have began to accept as normative. Neither witnessed the birth of the United States' Environmental Protection Agency in 1968 nor did Jung nor Chardin experience the impact of social media, the Internet and the exponential growth of the world's population.

What we know now, in the beginning of the 21st Century, is that the carrying capacity of the earth (in terms of natural resources) has exceeded its limits. We are living on borrowed time. To engage in designing complex strategies to ensure social justice and sustain positive cross-cultural dialogues between nations and corporations will necessarily demand high levels of self-awareness. This heightened psychological self-understanding along with the hard work of building resilient, eco-sensitive human communities will most probably become two critical lynchpins for rescuing a tottering fossil-fuel dependent global economy and ensuring realistic hopes for a relative, peaceful international co-existence. And there have been signs of hope.

Both Chardin's and Jung's groundbreaking contributions to science and psychology begin to be first integrated into practical theology in the thinking of Joseph Sittler (1904-1987), a protestant theologian at the University of Chicago Divinity School. Sittler was one of the first voices that addressed the need for anchoring theology in science, psychology, and the natural world.

In the year of Jung's death, Sittler addressed a World Council of Church's meeting in New Delhi. He made the pivotal observation, at that time a radical one, that the medieval church made the error of institutionalizing and mechanizing grace through the practice of indulgences, annulments, rituals, and intercessions. Reformers, on the other hand, he asserted, made the equally problematic mistake of reducing religious experience to exclusively human interactions. In his New Delhi address, he opened a

---

11 Bair, *Jung: A Biography*, pp. 455-463.
12 Claude Cuenot, *Teilhard de Chardin*, p. 258.

door to what my clergy colleague Bruce Heggen calls "the ancient rubrics of nature and grace." At that theological presentation, Sittler referred to the natural environment as "God's Haunted House," inviting the human community to behold that natural world as a "Garden of the Lord."[13]

Thomas Berry (1914-2009), a Roman Catholic theologian, took another step forward on this same path a few years later with his invitation to "The Great Turning." In *The Dream of the Earth*, Berry encouraged readers to turn and bless the natural environment with a new empathy, respect, and compassion. He believed that a healing of the environment will carry alongside it a healing of the human spirit. Berry invited people of faith to engage the best of our religion and science to help build a new way of living with the planet.[14]

The Unfinished Work for the followers of Jung and Chardin's, if we choose to participate, will involve a very practical commitment to our neighborhoods, to specific landscapes where we live, to our watersheds, our rivers, lakes and streams. It will also involve exploring an interior ecology, discovering ways of living with each other that are measured by a different kind of prosperity than an economic Gross National Product.

The Unfinished Work for us will involve a nurturing of the inner life while rejecting disembodied, untethered spirituality. It will mean recovering an ancient language of prayers and liturgies to bless our gardens and our food. It will mean slowing down, listening to our dreams, and living out the wisdom of poets like Mary Oliver who mystically invite us: "Do not hurry. Bow often."[15]

We still have another hour or two on the water to reach tonight's campsite, a cabin where a sauna and dinner await us. It's time to move back to the beach and our kayaks. As we gather our daypacks, water bottles and put on boots and sandals, I notice a weather front coming in; the wind has picked up, clouds, tinged by darkening billows, loom with a warning across the afternoon sky.

We stand upon the granite cliff now, forming a circle around a small cedar surrounded by patches of lichens and moss clinging to the hard rock face. In the distance, an eagle sits high upon the limb of a white pine. In the dim shadows of the tree line Carl Jung hammers

---

13 Bruce Allen Heggen, *A Theology for Earth: Nature and Grace in the Thought of Joseph Sittler*.

14 Thomas Berry, *Dream of the Earth*.

15 Mary Oliver, "When I am Among the Trees," in *Spiritus: A Journal of Christian Spirituality*, Vol. 6, Num. 1, Spring 2006. p. 93.

away at the stones that he will use to build the tower at Bollingen. Next to him another figure, tall, gaunt, wearing a French beret kneels on a rock face, pondering the imprint of a million year old fossil.

We're ready to move on. Before we leave, as is the tradition on these trips, we bless this place. I read from a crumpled paper that I've carried here, one of Chardin's prayers to the earth.

> Blessed be you, harsh matter, barren soil, stubborn rock; you who yield only to violence, you who force us to work if we would eat.
>
> Blessed be you, perilous matter, violent sea, untamable passion: you, who unless we fetter you will devour us.
>
> Bless be you, mighty matter, irresistible march of evolution, reality ever newborn; you who, by constantly shattering our mental categories, force us to go ever further and further in our pursuit of truth…
>
> I acclaim you as the divine *milieu*, charged with creative power, as the ocean stirred by the Spirit, as the clay molded and infused with life by the incarnate Word…
>
> Raise me up then, to those heights through struggle and separation and death; Raise me up until, at long last, it becomes possible for me to embrace the universe.[16]

Bibliography

Bair, Deirdre. *Jung: A Biography*. Boston, MA: Little, Brown and Company, 2003.

Berry, Thomas. *Dream of the Earth*. Sierra Club Books, 1988.

Caputo, Philip. *Indian Country*. New York: First Vintage Contemporaries Edition, 2004.

Christianson, Drew. "On the Slope with Teilhard." America Magazine, December 13, 2010.

Cuenot, Claude. *Teilhard de Chardin*. Baltimore, Maryland: Helicon Press, Inc., 1958.

Heggen, Bruce Allen. *A Theology for Earth: Nature and Grace in the Thought of Joseph Sittler*. Montreal, Canada: McGill University, 1995.

---

16 Teilhard, *Hymn to the Universe*, Chapter III, pp. 65-8.

Jung, C.G. *Memories, Dreams, Reflections.* New York: Vintage, 1965.

Mortier, Jeanne and Auboux, Marie-Louise, designed and edited for publication by *Teilhard de Chardin Album.* Teilhard de Chardin Foundation, 1966.

Oliver, Mary. "When I am Among the Trees," in *Spiritus: A Journal of Christian Spirituality*, Vol. 6, Num. 1, Spring 2006.

Teilhard de Chardin, Pierre. *Hymn of the Universe.* New York: Harper and Row, 1961.

Teilhard de Chardin, Pierre. *The Phenomenon of Man.* New York: Harper & Row, 1960.

4

JUNG, TEILHARD, AND THE PSYCHOLOGICAL PROBLEM OF DUALISM

Stan V. McDaniel

In his 1941 essay "The Atomism of the Spirit," Teilhard made this far-reaching observation:

> Ever since man reflected, *and the more he reflected*, the opposition between spirit and matter has constantly risen up as an ever higher barrier across the road that climbs to a better awareness of the universe: and in this lies the *deep-rooted origin* of *all* our troubles.[1] (My emphasis)

Paying close attention to Teilhard's wording, we see that by *all* he infers a universal malady that is "deep-rooted," running far back in the sweep of time, and which increases as the degree of reflection increases. It is a generalized malady of consciousness: a worm in the apple of increasing awareness. As such it must be fundamental to the very existence of psychology.

The philosophical name of this human problem is *dualism* in all its many forms, foremost of which is mind-body dualism: the perception of an irreconcilable schism between consciousness and the material body. As a philosophical problem, metaphysical dualism has manifested from Plato to Descartes and even to contemporary Cognitive Science under the aegis of Neuroscience: the materialistic reductionism which dominates the latter is actually a form of closet dualism (denial of one factor is a tacit assumption of division rather than reconciliation).[2] The result is a one-sided monism which divests the world of consciousness and all that consciousness entails. And in-

---

1 Pierre Teilhard de Chardin, "The Atomism of the Spirit" in *Activation of Energy*, p. 23.
2 H. Jonas, *The Phenomenon of Life*, p. 129.

deed in Cognitive Science today we see denials of the existence of consciousness, despite the obvious contradictions involved.[3]

Almost 60 years ago, I encountered the question of dualism in quite a different context. In the halls of academia I was exposed favorably to a number of western philosophers who do not adopt a cavalier attitude toward dualism but, like Teilhard, treat it with utmost seriousness. These included Kant, Nietzsche, Bergson, and the Pragmatists Peirce, James, and Dewey. At about the same time I was confronted with the depression and suicidal tendency of a close friend. I had the strong intuition, which emerged from my philosophical studies, that mind-body dualism lay at the heart of his psychological state. I found that to speak to him about such a strange thing as "dualism" was a useless endeavor. You cannot heal dualism as a psychological problem by discussing metaphysics philosophically, however correct the etiology may be. It was then that I understood dualism as a problem of the psyche. I came to agree with Teilhard that it is a universal problem of consciousness – a kind of "original sin" one might say.

So this is my initial premise: Dualism is a universal psychological problem. Those who deny the existence of selfhood, intentionality, belief, value, and consciousness under the hypothesis that the mind is the brain and the brain is a computer (which I call the mind-brain-computer identity hypothesis or MBCI), are rejecting what John Dewey called *Experience* in his seminal book, *Experience and Nature* (1929). Dewey denied a schism between the two and analyzed the many philosophical and logical errors implicit in dualism. But in the MBCI view, there is only "nature" and no such thing as experience. Computers have no experience; they can only "process." Ergo, that is all "we" can do (except that there can be no "we").[4] Nothing could be farther removed from Teilhard's vision of humanity in *The Phenomenon of Man*.

How does the quest for a non-dualistic framework capable of transmission into human culture as a whole involve a comparison of Jung and Teilhard? Teilhard's concept of evolution and particularly of the orthogenetic complexity-consciousness evolutionary axis is a powerful cosmological architectonic arguing for an expansion of physics into "hyperphysics." On the other hand, Jung's theoretical framework involves the architecture of the psyche, where concepts such as the collective unconscious, the

---

3 R. Tallis, *Aping Mankind:Neuromania,Darwinitis and the Misrepresentation of Humanity*, pp. 55-56, 261.
4 See Tallis, *Aping Mankind* for details on this syndrome.

ego, the Self, archetypes, and the psychological role of dreams are uppermost. Where do the cosmological and the psychological intersect? Exploring that question from a philosophical perspective, I turn first to Jung.

> There is in the analytical process, that is to say in the dialectical discussion between the conscious mind and the unconscious, a development or an advance towards some goal or end, the perplexing nature of which has engaged my attention for many years.[5]

Jung refers of course to the process he called individuation, whose goal is "the ultimate integration of conscious and unconscious."[6] In the patient's initial situation there is a schism in the psyche between the unconscious mind, particularly the collective unconscious, and the conscious mind. The ego is cut off from the collective and the subject is in a divided condition. As Jung has often expressed, such division is also a *general* pathology of ego-consciousness. So we may imagine, at the very least, an analogue here to the universal pathology of dualism. Further, healing the rift involves the initiation of a natural teleology, brought about by the pressure of activated archetypes upwelling from the collective unconscious, whose *telos* is reconciliation of the ego with the collective – just as for Teilhard the *telos* of evolution, Omega, is a collective unification, a "mega-synthesis" of humanity.[7]

It is this analogy that interests me. Many questions may arise when considering it. One is whether unification of the ego with the collective unconscious, if carried out on a worldwide scale, would result in some sort of Teilhardian mega-synthesis. A related question is whether the evolutionary process as Teilhard conceives it may result in a "universal individuation" in the Jungian sense: a community of realized selves.[8] Do the two teleologies converge?

My approach to such questions here is to focus on the nature of non-dualistic systems of thought or of personal transformation as they may assist my inquiry: systems which perforce contradict the lopsided paradigm of MBCI. I believe the Teilhardian and Jungian systems, one cosmological, the other psychological, belong to such a

---

5 C.G. Jung, *Psychology and Alchemy,* CW 12, ¶ 4.

6 C.G. Jung, *The Structure and Dynamic of the Psyche*, CW 8, ¶ 557.

7 Pierre Teilhard de Chardin, *The Phenomenon of Man*, p. 244.

8 See Dunlap, P., "Generational Attention: Remembering How to Be a People." *Journal of Jungian Scholarly Studies*, Vol. 8, No. 1.

group. But what criteria should be used to identify and evaluate such systems generally?

Over years of researching this topic I have developed a sort of template as an indicator of non-dualistic systems. Here I will use that template, which looks for a specific kind of organization applied to groups of elements, understood as functions of larger wholes. The various elements so arranged in different systems may be thought of as the "clothing" in which the template is "dressed." This organization must involve a teleological thrust and requires the presence of five parameters, which I will define in context as we proceed.[9]

In today's scientific milieu, those who challenge the reductionist-materialist paradigm are swimming against the current. Recently however the noted philosopher Thomas Nagel has severely criticized MBCI. He is not alone, but in his case he has made a move in a direction seldom found in such criticism. Assuming the general outlines of human evolution, Nagel favors a teleological option, and cites three types of theories which attempt to integrate consciousness and matter within an evolutionary process. Two of these he calls external theories, which he rejects. In those theories the direction of evolution is determined by an external factor: either the operation of chance mutation under physical laws, or the will of a divine creator. In contrast, the internal theory asserts that the teleology in evolution belongs *internally* to the natural world since the origin of the universe.[10] We might say that instead of mechanism or theism, it is a kind of non-mechanistic naturalism. "A naturalistic teleology would mean that organizational and developmental principles of this kind are an irreducible part of the natural order, and not the result of intentional or purposive influence by anyone."[11]

So Nagel differs from Teilhard on specifically the theological interpretation of the *telos*. In Teilhard's view theology and evolution meet within "the Christian Phenomenon."[12] For Nagel, no such theological factor is involved, and he offers no idea as to what the ultimate direction of evolution may be, except that increase of

---

9 For more detail see McDaniel, "Models of Development in Esoteric and Western thought," http://www.stanmcdaniel.org/pubs/development/modelsofdevelopment.pdf.

10 T. Nagel, *Mind and Cosmos: Why the Neo-Darwinian Conception of Nature is Almost Certainly False,* pp. 32-3.

11 Nagel, *Mind and Cosmos,* p. 91.

12 Teilhard, *The Phenomenon of Man,* p. 298.

consciousness is implicit in the otherwise undefined telic impulse. But on the o
hand, Nagel agrees with Teilhard with respect to his affirmation of the *continuity*
the consciousness-matter nexus.[13] "In the world, nothing could ever burst forth as
final across the different thresholds successively traversed by evolution...which has not
already existed in an obscure and primordial way."[14]

We uncover here a further requirement of the template: In addition to having a
teleological thrust, any non-dualistic system will embrace *continuity of development*.
Indeed, the defining core of such systems is the assertion of continuity. John Dewey
affirmed what he called the "principle of continuity," which was a foundation of his
philosophy. In his discussion of the origin and nature of logic, he articulated this
principle in a way Teilhard himself might easily have done.

> The primary postulate of a naturalistic theory of logic is continuity of the lower (less
> complex) and the higher (more complex) activities and forms. The idea of continu-
> ity...excludes complete rupture on one side and mere repetition of identities on the
> other; it precludes reduction of the "higher" to the "lower" just as it precludes com-
> plete breaks and gaps. The growth and development of any living organism from seed
> to maturity illustrates the meaning of continuity.[15]

Teilhard, Jung, and Dewey have in common a sense of this continuity. And in all
three cases it originates from an integration of the physical and psychological with
the biological. To reduce any organism to a mechanism is to fail to comprehend the
nature of *biological time*. Development within biological time is not a mechanical sequence of change from discrete moment to discrete moment, but a continuous flow.[16]
Continuity is not a simple linear idea. A complex system is required. The complexity
is a result of the simultaneous presence of the five parameters of the template (which I
will describe in just a moment), and especially in the way these relate to one another. I
identify such systems in a small core of western thinkers, in the much larger spread of
eastern religio-philosophical systems, and to differing degrees in western esoteric systems such as Alchemy, Cabala, Hermeticism and the inner tradition of Ritual Magic.

---

13 See O'Manique, J., *Energy in Evolution*, p. 40.
14 Teilhard, *The Phenomenon of Man*, p. 71.
15 J. Dewey, *Logic: The Theory of Inquiry*, p. 23.
16 See Bergson, *Creative Evolution*, pp. 3-5.

But the conscious acknowledgment of these parameters in any system as an application of a generalized ideal form is never the case. It appears instead to be a kind of unconscious guiding image underlying the manner in which the system is presented. And the various "contents" which eastern and esoteric systems organize are typically represented in the system as occult or metaphysical fact. The significance of this particular point will figure importantly in my concluding remarks.

Where is the sense of continuity in Jung? Jung does not mount a cosmology of evolution as does Teilhard. But continuity lies in his identification of the symbols employed by non-dualistic systems as archetypes; particularly in his identification of the mandala, which in its deepest meaning expresses continuity of all functions of consciousness; and also in the "discussion between the conscious mind and the unconscious" which he refers to as "dialectical."[17]

In eastern philosophy, particularly in Buddhist Tantra,[18] the developmental sequence of the psyche in yoga involves a series of stages, the so-called chakras, or psychic "wheels." To the uninitiated these are commonly understood to be localized as bodily organs, or at the very least organs in a set of "etheric bodies" visible to clairvoyants. But at the deep esoteric level they are not "things" but *complex systems of functions*, represented graphically as "petals" of a flower-like mandalic form, increasing in complexity along the developmental chain of yogic transformation: an esoteric complexity-consciousness axis.[19]

Well, now we have run directly into Jung. Any developmental system which embraces continuity takes so-called "entities" such as the ego not as "things" but as dynamic spatio-temporal complexes of functions. For Jung, the ego is such a complex, not a substantive "soul" or entity. Specifically the ego is a complex of the ectopsychic functions. Similarly the self is a greater complex of functions, many of which are unconscious (endopsychic functions). At the deepest level of the endopsyche lie the archetypes, which play a functional role in the teleology of the psyche (Jung 1935: 10-21, 49). And Teilhard agrees. In *The Phenomenon of Man* he says "from the phe-

---

17 See my discussion of the Mandala in Genetti, *The Wheel of Change Tarot*, Epilogue.

18 The terms "Continuity" and "Tantra" are etymologically related.

19 The energy is Kundalini. See Avalon, A. (Sir John Woodroffe), *The Serpent Power*, pp. 474-75.

nomenal point of view... 'consciousness' [is] not a sort of particular and subsistent entity, but...the specific effect of complexity."[20]

We may at last, then, fill out the non-dualistic template. It represents a teleological system of developmental continuity having a specific arrangement of "contents" which are functions, and which have a functional relationship to one another and to the whole. What functions are chosen, how many, and how they are named varies from system to system. What matters is not the particular set of functions chosen in a given system, or their number, but the mode of their organization. For example, in the Tantric system mentioned, as in the derived system of Theosophy, we find the series of chakras along with a parallel series of "etheric bodies." These functional divisions of the psyche are presented in terms of four of the five parameters: simultaneously developing *serially* in a temporal sequence, *hierarchically* in an ascending sequence, in functional *complementarity* in a mandalic sequence, and having a particular *analogy* as the basis for this complex relationship.[21] Dewey expresses this analogical connection as an analogy of "pattern." "Organic acts are a kind of fore-action of mind...intelligent action in utilizing the mechanisms they supply, *reproduces their patterns*."[22] (My emphasis)

This "analogy of pattern," is a fundamental trait of the relationship between functions in any non-dualistic system of development. The reader will recognize it in the dictum of Hermetic philosophy, "as above, so below." And in all such systems we find that the analogue is that of synthesis, the bringing together of opposites, presented generally using the image of a "triangle of synthesis" whose center expresses the birth of the next level of development.[23]

Western texts seldom use diagrammatic representation. In those cases the unifying image must be inferred from textual analysis. As an example of how the image of synthesis is extracted from a text, we may cite this passage from Teilhard: "Object and subject marry and mutually transform one another in the act of knowing."[24] Here the dualism of "object" (*without*) and "subject" (*within*) is reconciled. The relationship of complementarity lies in the expression "mutually transform." The agent of synthesis is

---

20 Teilhard, *The Phenomenon of Man*, p. 308. See also McDaniel, "The Coalescence of Minds" in *Philosophers Look at Science Fiction*.

21 This set of relationships is implicit in de Chardin, *The Phenomenon of Man*, p. 290.

22 J. Dewey, *Experience and Nature*, p. 282.

23 Figures 1, 2, and 4 copyright by S.V. McDaniel, 2013.

24 Teilhard, *The Phenomenon of Man*, p. 32.

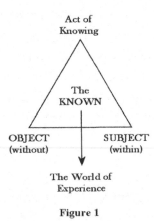

Act of
Knowing

The
KNOWN

OBJECT
(without)   SUBJECT
                  (within)

The World of
Experience

Figure 1

the act of knowing. The role played by the analogy is that each "higher" function develops from the "lower" ones by the action of synthesis, and the totality is related by the same analogy to its functional elements (Figure 1). This relationship, which is echoed in the classic mandala, is specific in Teilhard.[25]

In Tantric yoga, each move from a lower to higher chakra is the result of a "crossing" (a unifying synthesis) of "solar" and "lunar" (active and passive) energies, which weave up the psychic nerve channels ida and pingala. Figure 2 on page 59 shows examples as are found in Cabalistic Magic, Tantra, Jung, and Teilhard.[26]

Especially enlightening is Teilhard's use, in the preceding quote, of a marriage analogy for this process. The male-female embrace is a central emblem of creative synthesis in Tantric yoga, as it is in Alchemical symbolism. One example is the great mandala of the Dhyani-Buddhas in which the four functions, distributed evenly around the circle, are represented as different archetypal couples in yab-yum, sexual embrace, while associated with each couple are multiple series of qualities, all of which are represented according to the template parameters of serial, hierarchical, complementary, and analogical relationship. In Alchemy, we have the copulating male-female principles in the "alchemical vessel" (Figure 3). The energy of synthesis is the fire of the alchemist's oven (not shown here but inferred; often the heat of the Sun). Above the couple is the child, the fruit of their union, the fourth factor in the center of this triangle. This dynamic process is one of creation and movement "upward."

The most important message behind this archetypal image is that because of the possibility of creativity, *freedom* results. Freedom in the image is represented by the

Figure 3

25 Teilhard, *The Phenomenon of Man*, p. 260.

26 See McDaniel, S. V. (2010a). "The Transactional Developmental Model: Part 2" at http://www.stanmcdaniel.org/pubs/development/tdm2.pdf, Section 5, "Dynamic Networks." For the Cabalistic version, see Sadhu, M., *The Tarot*, pp. 36, 46, 58.

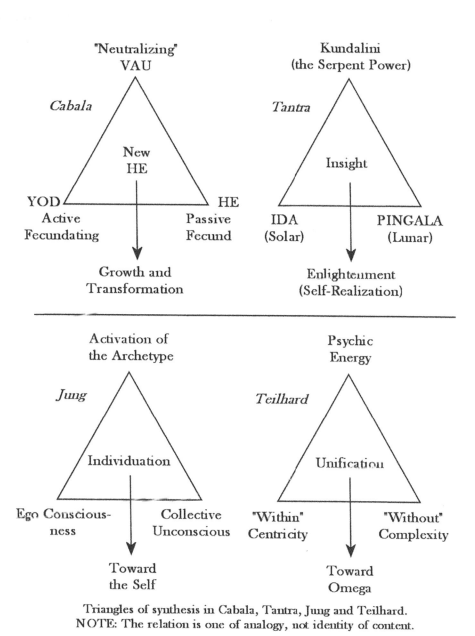

Triangles of synthesis in Cabala, Tantra, Jung and Teilhard.
NOTE: The relation is one of analogy, not identity of content.

Figure 2

open mouth of the vessel showing seed-pods or buds, living things, emerging out of the enclosure. In other alchemical images these are replaced by birds whose flight can take them upward to the freedom of the open sky.

We now turn to the significance of the concept of freedom in synthesis, particularly as this relates to Jung and Teilhard. The overall direction of development in a non-dualistic system is toward a given telos, which may be defined differently in different systems; but in order for the system to be fully non-dualistic the telos must not be a final end-point. Instead it is a directionality whose trait is precisely that it remains open, like the indefinite and "empty" void, Sunyata, "Great Space" in Buddhism.[27] The reason for this is that true creativity requires something new, and abrogates the confinement of a mechanical view of the world. The five parameters of the non-dualistic template are therefore Sequence, Hierarchy, Complementarity, Analogy, and Freedom. Applied to Teilhard's complexity-consciousness axis, the result is that this is not a linear axis, but a vector, we might say, of three axes, whose relationship is that of analogy (the analogy of synthesis), and whose telic impulse lies in the direction of freedom. The three axes and their relationships are present in Teilhard although he does not explicitly model them, as I have here, but leaves the axis to appear as a single line of sequence.[28]

In Teilhard's Omega, there has been a persistent ambiguity as to whether it embodies that fifth parameter, or instead is a final term or closure. In his Introduction to *The Phenomenon of Man*, Huxley raises just that issue. "Presumably, in designating this state Omega, he believed it was a truly final condition. It might have been better to think of it merely as a novel state or mode of organization, beyond which the human imagination cannot at present pierce."[29]

Teilhard does refer to Omega as a "closing" of the noosphere.[30] Does Teilhard's system fail at just this point or is it truly non-dualistic? Looking again at the triangular images of synthesis, we see that the arrow emerging from each triangle represents its opening, its transcending of the constraints imposed by dualism. Noting the resemblance of the triangle of synthesis to a bow and arrow, we find the symbolism of

---

27 Also the meaning of "The Fool" card in the esoteric Tarot. See Genetti, A., *The Wheel of Change Tarot*, p. 26.

28 This three-axis vector represents an image of what is referred to above as biological time.

29 Teilhard, *The Phenomenon of Man*, p. 18.

30 Teilhard, *The Phenomenon of Man*, p. 291.

an arrow in a drawn bow as a catapult to liberation or freedom in this passage from the Upanishad: "Having taken as a bow the great weapon of the secret teaching, one should fix in it the arrow sharpened by constant meditation...The OM is the bow; the arrow is the self; Brahman is said to be the mark." Here the OM is associated with liberation "either as a means to it, or as a symbol of its attainment," leading to Brahman, "the experience of the infinite within us."[31]

Thus any system which embraces synthesis as the connecting analogy must accommodate the fifth parameter. To assist our discussion at this point, I provide Figure 4 on the next page, a comparison of the Tantric and the Teilhardian developmental systems under the parameter of hierarchy, along with a brief explanation.[32]

In these two schemas, the sequence of development is from bottom to top. The hierarchical relationship is understood by the vertical arrangement and by the increase of complexity. Complementarity is represented by the inferred overlapping of the functions upon one another: If the images were three-dimensional, a cross section at the top would reveal the functions arranged in a series of concentric circles, a graphic device used ubiquitously in eastern texts and also frequently by Jung. The functions chosen in each system are in each case the "clothing" of the template.

Our focus of interest is the final term. On the left we have Sunyata, "Great Space" of no definition, the Void, wherein all possibility lies latent. Liberation and freedom are inherent in this concept. Continuity is expressed in two ways: the first is that the transition from each stage to the next is understood to be accomplished by the action of synthesis, and the second is that each stage is not simply replaced by the next, but is carried along in equal status, complementary to the rest, from the moment of origin. At the converging point is bindu, "the point from which inner and outer space have their origin and in which they become one again."[33]

On the right we have the Teilhardian sequence, where Omega stands at the point of convergence. Is it, like Sunyata, infinitely open? Teilhard seems to say so in this observation: "Is not the end and aim of thought that still unimaginable farthest limit

---

31 Lama Anagarika Govinda, *Foundations of Tibetan Mysticism*, pp. 23-4.
32 See McDaniel, S. V. "Models of Development in Esoteric and Western thought: A Brief Summary," (2010) diagrams 7, 8 & 9.
33 Govinda, *Foundations of Tibetan Mysticism* p. 117.

of a convergent sequence, propagating itself without end and ever higher? Does not the end or confine of thought consist precisely in not having a confine?"[34]

The perceived ambiguity of Teilhard's view arises, I think, with his emphasis on the theological and specifically Christian interpretation of Omega. On the one hand, he argues that "space-time is necessarily of a convergent nature";[35] on the other, he seems to make the course toward Omega dependent on human resolve.[36] But neither directly addresses the nature of Omega itself. If the opposites under synthesis in evolution are universal cosmic antagonists (as are consciousness and matter), then their reconciliation *necessarily* has cosmic significance. It represents a move out of a world-space of division into a space beyond division. The arrows in the triangles of synthesis are loosed in the direction of freedom. In the present analysis, this would define Omega as the *freedom of humanity*, freedom from the bondage of division.

To the extent that Teilhard embraces continuity and its analogy of synthesis, and affirms and uses the template of non-dualism, Omega cannot be limited by closure. But to cast the cosmological necessity in terms of any specific doctrinal context utilizes the contents of that doctrine as the "clothing," just as such contents as the chakras are another set of "clothes." But there is a difference between the two. In esoteric Tantra, the final goal moves beyond the "clothing" of the path. This is the meaning of Sunyata. In Figure 4 the implied closure surrounding Omega may be seen as demanding that the "clothing" of Christianity be worn and not discarded at the summit. Any attempt to free the top of that image would have to open the door to all the other representations of the non-dualistic template. If Omega is the parameter of Freedom, then it must imply freedom from doctrinal Christianity, as well as from all other such contents and forms. The pointing finger, as the Zen saying goes, is not that at which it points. I believe that Hermetic philosophy, for example, in its interpretation as *esoteric* Christianity, incorporated the necessary opening.[37]

How then might we judge *Jung's* concept of individuation with respect to freedom? For Jung, the myriad forms taken by archetypal symbols of multiple cultures are equally "clothing" whose common role is the dynamic one of activation. The marriage

---

34 Teilhard, *The Phenomenon of Man*, p. 231.
35 Teilhard, *The Phenomenon of Man*, p. 259.
36 Teilhard, *The Phenomenon of Man*, p. 230.
37 See McDaniel, S. V. Review of *Western Esoteric Traditions* by Nicholas Goodrick-Clarke in the *Journal of Scientific Exploration*, Volume 25, Number 3, Fall 2011: 590-600.

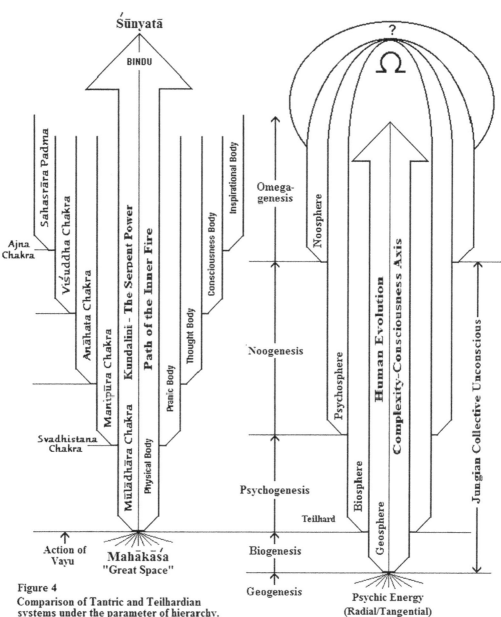

Figure 4
Comparison of Tantric and Teilhardian
systems under the parameter of hierarchy.
NOTE: Correlations represent analogies,
not identities.

of conscious and unconscious by the synthesizing agent of the activated archetypes, must have as its child freedom from projection of one's shadow-traits onto the "other." If accomplished on a worldwide scale, this would, in Jung's view, contribute to freedom from the madness of war and social strife, a kind of human unification.

If we go on to consider Omega from a Jungian standpoint as the God-image, as the archetype of the self and a function of the psyche, then reaching Omega is tantamount to individuation, and the answer to our question as to the relation between Jung's and Teilhard's *teloi* is that they merge; but only if the clothing of Christianity is understood as just one among the vast wardrobe of symbolic archetypal forms.

There is much more implied by an identification of the Jungian and Teilhardian *teloi* than one might think. Omega has the position of the evolutionary *telos*, and the teleology of Teilhard's philosophy is oriented toward the reconciliation of consciousness and *matter*. So if Omega is understood as the archetype of the self, then the goal of individuation is at once unification of conscious/unconscious but also unification of mind and body. If so, then Jung's teleology of individuation "solves" the problem of dualism – provided everyone on the planet reaches that ideal, which as things stand does not seem very likely (unless, perhaps, under an immediate threat of the liquidation of humanity, a miraculous mass activation of the archetype might occur). Nevertheless, the interpretation of the relationship between the two systems given above suggests a deep idea, which I will frame as a double-barreled hypothesis. And with this highly speculative hypothesis as food for thought I end this chapter.

1. At the far right of Figure 4 is a reference to the collective unconscious. Under the principle of continuity, consciousness must extend to the beginning of the cosmos, the bindu of origin. The synthesizing action of the "Big Bang," in Teilhardian terms, is the action of the fundamental energy, which he called "psychic energy" and whose aspects are the twin energies, tangential (without) and radial (within). This would place the collective unconscious back in time into biological and physical history. That is to say, the collective unconscious is the memory of that history carried forward in biological time. The result is that the collective unconscious would be both "matter" and "consciousness" at once. The outburst into time and space of the original unified energy, as the energy of synthesis, then gives rise to the myriad archetypes of synthesis.[38] That is why synthesis is the fundamental analogy. So it is the reason that

---

38 In *Activation of Energy* Teilhard suggests that gravity is the first force of synthesis. The very recent confirmation of the existence of the "Higgs Field" immediately after the "Big

Jungian "activation" of the archetypes initiates the synthetic process of individuation: Activation is the synthetic force present in the potentiality of the bindu of origin, and this governs the teleology leading to the bindu of unification, which, as the result of the entire synthesis, gives the gift of freedom.

2. Given the hypothesis of (1), a derivative hypothesis is that the template of non-dualism utilized in this chapter is itself an archetypal image: a generalized pattern of the organization of contents open to a multiplicity of choices of such contents. But then, because of its endless generality, the template acts as an archetype of archetypes. If this is the case, it would explain why it is that the template persists, and has persisted, over many centuries in all the concatenations of contents and archetypal symbolic forms, but its role as underlying the physical and metaphysical claims made by those who, in mystical visions or in profound philosophic contemplation have put it forward again and again, is not acknowledged even by them as a guiding image. It is an unconscious driving force. Jung and Teilhard would then be placed prominently among those whose systems developed under the activation of that archetype of archetypes, from the depths of the collective unconscious – the bindu, the core of consciousness/matter unity.

Bibliography

Avalon, A. (Sir John Woodroffe). *The Serpent Power.* Madras: Ganesh & Co., 1964.

Bergson, H. *Creative Evolution.* Translated by Arthur Mitchell, Foreword by Erwin Edman. New York: Random House, Modern Library edition, 1944.

Dewey, J. *Logic: The Theory of Inquiry.* New York: Henry Holt and Company, 1938.

Dewey, J. *Experience and Nature.* New York: Dover reprint edition, 1958.

Dunlap, P. "Generational Attention: Remembering How to Be a People." *Journal of Jungian Scholarly Studies*, Vol. 8, No. 1, 2012.

Genetti, A. *The Wheel of Change Tarot.* Rochester, Vermont: Destiny Books. 1997.

Bang" as initiating mass in particle fields (since gravity is a phenomenon of mass) would agree with this assessment. See McDaniel "Models of Development in Esoteric and Western Thought," Diagram 9 ff.

Greenway, R. Interview in *Ecopsychology*, March 2009, p. 47.

Govinda, Lama Anagarika. *Foundations of Tibetan Mysticism*. New York: Samuel Weiser, 1974.

Jonas, H. *The Phenomenon of Life*. New York: Dell publishing, 1966.

Jung, C.G. *The Structure and Dynamics of the Psyche*, CW 8. New York, N.Y.: Pantheon Books, Inc., 1960.

Jung, C.G. *Psychology and Alchemy*, CW 12. Princeton, N.J.: Princeton University Press 1980.

Jung, C.G. The Tavistock Lectures, published as *Analytic Psychology, Its Theory and Practice*. Vintage Edition, 1968.

Leadbeater, C.W. *The Chakras*. Adya, Madras 20, India: The Theosophical Publishing House, 1927.

McDaniel, S.V. "The Coalescence of Minds" in *Philosophers Look at Science Fiction*. Nicholas D. Smith, editor. Chicago: Nelson-Hall, 1982.

McDaniel, S.V. "Models of Development in Esoteric and Western Thought: A Brief Summary" at http://www.stanmcdaniel.org/pubs/development/modelsofdevelopment.pdf

McDaniel, S.V. "The Transactional Developmental Model: Part 2" at http://www.stanmcdaniel.org/pubs/development/tdm2.pdf

McDaniel, S.V. "Transactional Analysis of Esoteric Systems" at http://www.stanmcdaniel.org/pubs/development/transactionalanalysis.pdf

McDaniel, S.V. Review of *Western Esoteric Traditions* by Nicholas Goodrick-Clarke. Journal of Scientific Exploration, Volume 25, Number 3, fall 2011, pp. 590-600.

McDaniel, S. V. Review of *Mind and Cosmos: Why the Neo-Darwinian Conception of Nature is Almost Certainly False* by Thomas Nagel (Oxford University Press, 2012) in Journal of Scientific Exploration, Volume 27, Number 2, Summer 2013, pp. 339-347.

Nagel, T. *Mind and Cosmos: Why the Neo-Darwinian Conception of Nature is Almost Certainly False*. Oxford University Press, 2012.

O'Manique, J. *Energy in Evolution*. New York: Humanities Press, 1969.

Rockwell, W.T. *Neither Brain nor Ghost: A Non-Dualist Alternative to the Mind-Brain Identity Theory*. Cambridge: MIT Press (A Bradford Book), 2007.

Sadhu, M. *The Tarot: A Contemporary Course of the Quintessence of Hermetic Occultism*. London: George Allen & Unwin Ltd., 1968.

Teilhard de Chardin, P. "The Atomism of the Spirit." In *Activation of Energy.* New York: Harcourt Brace Jovanovich, Inc., 1971.

Teilhard de Chardin , P. *The Phenomenon of Man*. New York: Harper & Row. Harper Torchbook TB383, 1965.

Tallis, R. *Aping Mankind: Neuromania, Darwinitis and the Misrepresentation of Humanity*. Durham, NC: Acumen Publishing, 2011.

Wehr, G. *Jung: A Biography*. Trans. Weeks, D.M. Boston & London: Shambhala, 1987.

Whitney, M., (producer). "Matter of Heart," a motion picture documentary of the C.G. Jung Institute of Los Angeles, 1983.

Acknowledgements

I wish especially to thank the assistance of my wife, Sally, whose sharp eye and depth of understanding was of inestimable help in the polishing of this manuscript. Also I express my gratitude to my friend, former student and colleague-in-spirit, Peter Dunlap, whose encouragement has kept me focused on my work over many years.

5

C.G. JUNG AND TEILHARD DE CHARDIN

Peacemakers in an Age of Spiritual Democracy

Steven B. Herrmann

It is not always recognized that in 1912, with his seminal two part monograph *Wandlüngen und Symbole der Libido* (translated into English from German as *The Psychology of the Unconscious*) Jung took this occasion to outline the structure of the modern American psyche. He did this by advancing a brilliant psychological analysis of the fantasies of a young American woman who had published them under the pseudonym Miss Frank Miller in an essay that had attracted the attention of Jung's Swiss mentor and colleague Théodore Flournoy. Taking his cue from Flournoy that here was a pure example of "the mythopoetic imagination," Jung amplified Miss Miller's visions and her poetry with lengthy literary analysis of Longfellow's 19th century narrative-poem, "Hiawatha," which had been published in 1855, the same year Walt Whitman published *Leaves of Grass*. Miss Miller, like all Americans of her generation had read Longfellow, and Jung himself is certain to have read at least a few lines by and about Whitman in William James' classic *The Varieties of Religious Experience*. (Jung met James twice, and late in life says that in his formative years between 1909 and 1921 when his own understanding of depth psychology was consolidating, Flournoy and James were the only figures in the new science of the mind with whom he could have an uncomplicated conversation).

In describing the process of writing *Wandlüngen,* over a decade later, in a 1925 seminar given to an audience now committed to Jung's own analytical psychology, Jung said that when he had surveyed the American psyche, through his study of the Miller fantasies, he had turned her mythopoetic products into pure *gold*, put a lump of bullion in his pocket, and walked away with it.[1] America at that time had not yet gone off the gold standard, so this was politically still apropos, but Jung was also channeling an alchemical metaphor for the quintessential goal of spirituality in the West: the lapis, or philosopher's stone. Jung's work with the Miller fantasies gave his psychology of the individuation of consciousness out of an unconsciously mytho-poetic base a distinctly American accent. It marked the beginnings of his break with Sigmund Freud, who had still been developing 19th century medical psychology when he invited Jung to accompany him on his first trip to America, in 1909. It is inter-esting to note, therefore, that the case Jung had begun to study was of an American woman who, at the beginning of the twentieth century, was searching for her purpose and meaning in life: a *vocation* to live by. It is not surprising that her psyche, appear-ing to her in hypnogogic imagery, relied upon a Native American Indian myth for its exegesis.

In turning to America, Jung's own unconscious has formed a shamanic well of energizing vision through which to envision the psyche's task in the face of modernity in the very country that would soon weigh in on the world stage as the new cen-tury's defining power. Elsewhere, I have emphasized how much the great 19th century shaman-poets, Melville, and Dickinson, anticipated this development, and I have advanced the view that Whitman, as a poet-shaman was the first to formulate the notion of Spiritual Democracy as the instinctive contribution of America to world religion.[2] Whitman realized, I believe, that he was the successor of a totemic lineage that goes back to the shamanic ancestors on the North American continent, and even further back, to Cro-Magnon times in Europe. He understood that he belonged to the spiritual articulation of the meaning of what the great Alexander von Humboldt, friend of Goethe and Schiller and Jung's grandfather Carl Gustav Jung, and mentor to William James' great teacher, Louis Agassiz, had called *Cosmos*.[3] But Whitman was far from alone in seeing America as heart of the New World of Cosmic Consciousness. Longfellow, who published "Hiawatha" in 1855, a year before Sigmund Freud's birth, was also writing in this democratic tradition. Each of the American poet-shamans I have written about, Whitman, Dickinson, Melville, Everson, and Jeffers, contributes something unique to the American myth of Spiritual Democracy, a notion Whitman

---

1 C.G. Jung, Analytical Psychology: Notes of the Seminar Given in 1925, p. 31.
2 Steven Herrmann, *Walt Whitman: Shamanism, Spiritual Democracy, and the World Soul.*
3 A. von Humboldt, *Cosmos: A Sketch of the Physical Description of the Universe*, Vol. 1.

named for us. Longfellow was writing out of this tradition too, as was Jung from the moment he first encountered the American continent. How can we relate what emerged here with what was also happening on the other side of the world in the country destined to become the 21ˢᵗ century's emerging power? Let us turn now to examine this connection in the life and works of the French Jesuit priest and mystical visionary Teilhard de Chardin (1881-1955). We will return to Jung's vision of Spiritual Democracy later.

Chardin spent twenty years in China doing paleontology, and he had a wide view of history and culture. He sought to blend science and religion into a single unitary theory of evolution, with the early post-modern insight that a scientific study of nature and psycho-spirituality cannot be separated. In *The Future of Man,* he wrote for instance that "what will finally crown and limit collective humanity at the ultimate stage of its evolution, is … the establishment of a sort of focal point at the heart of the reflective apparatus as a whole."[4] This reminds me of what Whitman said in a conversation with Horace Traubel in old age: "I don't want the brotherhood of the world to be so long a-coming. I can wait till it comes—it is sure to come—but if I can hurry it by a day or so I am going to do so."[5] Chardin, no less than Whitman and Jung was to hurry the myth of Spiritual Democracy along from a different cultural base, but it was essentially the same vision. In 1949, for the United Nations, now a world peacekeeping power, Chardin began an essay called "The Essence of the Democratic Idea," in response to a questionnaire by UNESCO: "What exactly is hidden behind the idea of Democracy?"[6] Two years earlier he had stated in an essay "Faith in Peace" that "Mankind is not only capable of living in peace but by its very structure cannot fail eventually to achieve peace" and the "soul of Mankind" is "resolved at all costs to achieve, in its total integrity, the utmost fulfillment of its powers and destiny."[7]

We all know the degree to which American politics has returned to national interests and to resisting the idea of a United Nations authority over its selective use of aggressive tactics to settle disputes. Chardin's vision would not have felt too advanced, however, for the 19ᵗʰ century American poets. American poet-shamans like Whitman and Longfellow, are Peacemakers. Their primary purpose is to work towards a

---

4 Pierre Teilhard de Chardin, *The Future of Man*, p. 185.
5 see *Walt Whitman in Camden* under Traubel in Bibliography at end of paper.
6 Teilhard, *The Future of Man*, p. 248.
7 Teilhard, *The Future of Man*, pp. 157, 160.

common brotherhood of the world. Whitman was the first to say so, but Longfellow too attempted this in his own way by immortalizing a poem that would be read by American school children. Jung was well aware of this archetype of the Peacemaker too, for he had read and commented on the meaning of "Hiawatha," the 14th Century Iroquois chief who was named the "Peacemaker." In a 1928 *Dream Seminar* Jung told participants that he had smoked the pipe of peace[8] and in 1948 he too, like Chardin, was asked by UNESCO to give his specific thoughts and recommendations on what is required to avert Wars in an essay "Techniques of Attitude Change Conducive to World Peace."[9]

How does peacemaking relate to American Democracy, which had so often chosen leaders who were willing to wage war to secure its ends? We need to remember that the mythology of the Peacemaker is a very old image in the history of religious ideas. It is found in a passage in Isaiah, in the second chapter of the *Bhagavad Gita,* and in the saying of Jesus: "Blessed are the Peacemakers." We find it in Hinduism, Buddhism, Islam, and Sufism alike. It is a very old archetype. Its origins are, of course, everywhere evident in shamanism, which is concerned primarily with healing the human tribe.

In *The Sacred Pipe,* Black Elk speaks about the seven rites of the Oglala Sioux and the destiny of America. The disunity of disharmonized nations finds a spiritual center of peace through the rite of vision. The sacred pipe was given to the people by Wakan Tanka. The tomahawk pipe is a living symbol of peace shared by Ishmael and his Polynesian husband, or wife, Queequeg, in Herman Melville's masterpiece *Moby-Dick.* The two men smoke the pipe of peace before they are ritually "married."

In *Black Elk Speaks* the old shaman says to John Neihardt that we are all related; all of us are the same really. (One often hears just this rhetoric in the speeches of Barak Obama). All religious faiths, all nations must live in harmony together with the Great Spirit. Black Elk was a carrier of the sacred pipe. He sends up his voice, at the beginning of his narrative, to the "Spirit of the World."[10] As a prayer to all nations, he calls for world peace. The holy pipe is offered to all nationalities, including, not incidentally, the "star nations all over the universe," for the Great Spirit dwells in all things.[11]

---

8 C.G. Jung, *Dream Analysis: Notes of the Seminar Given in 1928-1930*, p. 35.
9 C.G. Jung, *The Symbolic Life,* CW 18, ¶ 1390.
10 John Neihardt, *Black Elk Speaks*, p. 2.
11 Neihardt, *Black Elk*, p. 5.

In 1931, Black Elk traced his notion of Spiritual Democracy in his Great Vision to a moment when he found himself standing on the highest mountain on the earth. This happened to be Harney Peak, in the Black Hills, South Dakota. Around and beneath him, he says, there appeared before his mind's eyes "the whole hoop of the world." In his vision a nine-year-old boy, Black Elk was seeing in a sacred manner the shapes of all things of the spirit world living together like one universal being. Then, Black Elk says: "I saw that the sacred hoop of my people was one of many hoops that made one circle… But anywhere is the center of the world."[12]

The center of the world is everywhere, as Humboldt would have argued. Cosmos is here. Consciousness is now. In a spiritually democratic world, the cosmic consciousness of everyone's religious equality is taken for granted, and becomes a vocation, something we are all called to live up to. It is our life-task to discover what our vocation is and offer it as a gift for the betterment of the world. The personalization and Divinization of the universe is what Jung and Chardin agree on: a vehicle of "vocation" is the way Cosmic Consciousness may be ushered in.[13] Central in this vision is the realization of an ultimate point upon which "*all realities converge*"[14] a creative vocational channel carved in the collective psyche (Jung) or noosphere (Teilhard) to which every individual has access. The main difference between Chardin and Jung however is that while Chardin places Christ at the center of a divine milieu, anthropogenesis, hominization, or Omega point, Jung hypothesizes that Christ is only a symbol for the Self, not the other way around. Chardin writes for example: "Christ–for whom and in whom we are formed, each with his own individuality and his own vocation–Christ reveals himself in each reality around us, and shines like an ultimate determinant, like a centre, one might almost say like a universal element."[15] Nevertheless, the divine milieu is not a fixed point in the universe, in Chardin's view, but a moving center that we each, in our own individual ways, have to follow like a loadstar, and to this end: "That star leads each man differently, by a different path, in accord with his vocation."[16]

---

12 Neihardt, *Black Elk*, p. 43.
13 Pierre Teilhard de Chardin, *The Divine Milieu*, p. 46.
14 Teilhard, *The Divine Milieu*, p. 114.
15 Teilhard, *The Divine Milieu*, p. 125.
16 Teilhard, *The Divine Milieu*, p. 139.

In the fall of 1947, fifteen years after Black Elk narrated his story to John Neihardt (at a time when Chardin was beginning to articulate his own vision of a cosmic ethic that "The mystical Christ has not yet attained its full growth; and therefore the same is true of the cosmic Christ")[17] he recorded an account of the seven rites of the Oglala people, where the focus of the narrative is centered on the sacred pipe, and its importance to Lakota people. At the age of eighty-five, three years before his death, Black Elk reported to Joseph Epes Brown a vision that places a Feminine symbol of Christ at the center of Spiritual Democracy:

> We have been told by the white men, or at least by those who are Christian, that God sent men His son, who would restore order and peace upon the earth; and we have been told that Jesus the Christ was crucified, but that he shall come again at the last Judgment, the end of this world or cycle. This I understand and know that it is true, but the white men should know that for the red people too, it was the will of Wakan-Tanka, the Great Spirit, that an animal turn itself into a two-legged person in order to bring the most holy pipe to His people; and we too were taught that this White Buffalo Cow Woman who brought our sacred pipe will appear again at the end of this "world," a coming which we Indians know is now not very far off…. There is much talk of peace amongst the Christians, yet this is just talk. Perhaps it may be, and this is my prayer that, through our sacred pipe, and through this book in which I shall explain what our pipe really is, peace may come to those peoples who can understand, an understanding which must be of the heart and not of the head alone.[18]

This extension of the global consciousness towards a point of world peace is what Chardin calls the "critical point of species-formation"[19] and it has been in the process of progressive psychosocial evolution during the "whole process of hominization."[20] In *The Phenomenon of Man* he traces the origins of this formation of thought in the noosphere in a chapter "The Homo Sapiens Complex" to the Neolithic age of the reindeer, when "a definitely liberated thought explodes, still warm, onto the walls of the caves" of our ancestors.[21] This is the central impulse at the heart of the human

---

17 Pierre Teilhard de Chardin, *Hymn of the Universe*, p. 133.
18 Joseph Epps Brown, *The Sacred Pipe*, pp. xix, xx.
19 Teilhard, *Hymn of the Universe*, p. 110.
20 Teilhard, *Hymn of the Universe*, p. 116.
21 Pierre Teilhard de Chardin, *The Phenomenon of Man*, p. 202.

psyche that I have called the enduring *shamanic impulse*: the impulse towards healing, poetry, science, and art.

The notion of vocation pervades the great vision of Black Elk, the Oglala Sioux shaman.[22] I first realized this in a tutorial accompanying the course "Birth of a Poet," taught by the poet-in-residence, William Everson, at UC Santa Cruz, where I spent my undergraduate years. It has formed a palimpsest for much of my writing and teaching ever since. Everson served as faculty advisor for my thesis, "Meister Eckhart on the Recollection of the Self: A Jungian Perspective." From the fall of 1980 to the winter of 1981, I also worked for Everson in his course, introducing students to the art and science of dream interpretation from a Jungian point of view. The call from the shamanic archetype is, as Jung was able to document, a summons from a central archetype of order and totality in the human psyche; the transpersonal Self acted in a powerful way at this time, drawing me inward, like a magnet. I had a dream in 1980, at around this time when I was trying to decide whether to change my major from experimental psychology to a new one I would call "Depth Psychology and Religion." In my dream, I was constructing a wooden cross for my younger sister, who at the time was also an inner anima figure for me.

I had this dream on January 8, 1980, just after the fall quarter of "Birth of a Poet" had ended. "*In the dream I find myself with my sister at the center of an old Christian town in a round building, with seats that spiral toward a center, and where standing in front of a golden altar is an energetic, religious man, a magnetic personality, delivering a Sermon. I have the distinct feeling: this is what Meister Eckhart might have been like.*" What a wonderful play on words—Everson to Eckhart. Eckhart, a 14th century German Dominican Catholic, as Anglican priest Matthew Fox can attest, was no doubt a shaman in the sense Everson used that term. You can read for yourself what he meant in the book I co-authored with him, *William Everson: The Shaman's Call*. This dream pulled me towards my destiny like a lodestar, by drawing great stores of encoded information out of long and short term memory banks into my lower brain stem, where excitatory phenomena and instinctual processes were suddenly released. Something got "switched on" through evocation: the call to write and to teach. The moral injunction in my dream to move towards my inner center, and to listen to Eckhart's sermons allowed dreams with deep vocational significance to surface; it made the world open up to me, as a Cosmos within: a microcosm, spiraling towards a center, and mirror-

---

22 Steve Herrmann, personal experience in 1980.

ing our spiraling Galaxy, with the shaman, or mystical preacher of the Word at its spiritual center. What is most important to add here is that it was at this time that I discovered the writings of Teilhard and Matthew Fox.[23] Over a decade later, in a Festschrift for Everson's 80th birthday, in 1991, I gave a paper in which I mentioned the vision of Fred Gustafson an American Jungian analyst who dreamed he was in a Protestant church wearing a vision quest blanket.

In these two papers along the way to my own appreciation of the emerging global vision of an environmentally sensitive Spiritual Democracy, I was reviewing as a contemporary American, what Cosmos requires of us, and accepting that vocation. In so doing, I was also heeding the essentially Taoist vision of Chardin, who had realized similar ideas through his study of Chinese thought (including, of course, Confucianism and Buddhism, both of which recognize the interdependent, ecological nature of compassionate spiritual awareness, an attitude designed to benefit everyone). What I want to emphasize here is the democratic idea that appears in Gustafson's dream. The dream appears in his chapter "Fathers, Sons, and Brotherhood."[24] There he gives a full description: he was wearing deer antlers in a church, wrapped in a vision quest blanket. The Lutheran pastor of the church came to Gustafson and told him that he was angry at him, that he wanted him to change his dress right away. Fred woke up from the dream, saying to himself: "He is not my boss and I must indeed tell him that!" In his own interpretation of this dream, Gustafson writes: "This dream reveals the collision of two forces within my psyche: collective western Christianity and natural, inherent spirituality. Although I was identifying with the latter, I was trying to align with both in the dream, i.e., a vision quest blanket in a Christian church. The dream task was not to let either force dominate the other but to bring together the truths of what both systems represent. The Native American blanket, a symbol of that part of the psyche that is 'wild' is redeemed from the forest of the unconscious and given royalty, a place of honor in church, that is, given a place in the individual and collective psyche."

This dream and its interpretation struck me as containing the same kind of spiritual gold Jung had put in his pocket when he analyzed the visions of Miss Miller, with Longfellow's "Hiawatha" by his side, the gold of Spiritual Democracy.

---

23 Matthew Fox, *Breakthrough: Meister Eckhart's Creation Spirituality in New Translation.*
24 Fred Gustafson, "Fathers, Sons, and Brotherhood" in *Betwixt and Between: Patterns of Masculine and Feminine Initiation,* p. 163.

Books have a way of finding their way into a person's hands at significant moments, and for Everson and myself as his teaching assistant at UC Santa Cruz, one such book was Ira Progoff's book *Jung, Synchronicity, and Human Destiny.* This is one of the classic texts on the notion of the archetype of vocation in post-Jungian thought, and it is not surprising that Progoff opens this masterpiece, which lay in his desk drawer for twenty years, with a chapter called "Interpreting the Multiple Universe: Jung and Teilhard de Chardin."

Experience shows, by way of empirical amplifications with the mythologies of the world a sequential patterning of the stages of the expansion of human consciousness existing in potential in each individual through instincts of vocational activity, or, what C.G. Jung termed "instincts as impulses to carry out actions from necessity, without conscious motivation. In this 'deeper' stratum [of the unconscious] we also find the *a priori,* inborn forms of 'intuition,' namely the archetypes of perception and apperception, which are the necessary *a priori* determinants of all psychic processes. Just as the instincts compel man to a specifically human mode of existence, so the archetypes force his ways of perception and apprehension into specifically human patterns. The instincts and the archetypes together form the 'collective unconscious.'"[25] That there is an archetype for a new world religion is a fact of human knowing based on a pattern of behavior intrinsic to evolution, and as Chardin and Jung both showed, this movement in increasing psychic and cosmic energy tends towards Spiritual Democracy. In other words, all world religions have known that there is an archetype of order that can unite the world and lead to world peace. Events such as we have been experiencing across the globe since the Arab Spring, in many nations of the world, suggest that the archetype of Spiritual Democracy is in the process of becoming conscious of itself as a "miracle" of reflective consciousness. Such a transformation in human consciousness was foreseen half a century ago by Jung and Chardin. While the two men never met, Miguel Serrano reports in his book that when he visited Jung shortly before his death:

> "On the small table beside the chair where Jung was sitting, was a book called *The Human Phenomenon* by Teilhard de Chardin. I asked Jung whether he had read it."

---

25 C.G. Jung, *The Structure and Dynamics of the Psyche,* CW 8, ¶ 270.

"It is a great book," he said. His face was pale, but seemed strangely illuminated by an inner light.[26]

Jung was well aware of the impact of the earth on the evolution of the human mind. In the *Vision Seminars*, for instance, the subject of Jung's study, the American psychoanalyst Christiana Morgan, has a vision of an "old Indian woman" and Jung refers to her as an "ancestral figure." He adds: "She would be the essence of the American character, a living thing most adapted to the special nature of the American soil… this old squaw, this exceedingly earthly being, holds the germ of spiritual life peculiar to that soil…. There is a piece of the old religion still alive."[27] The old religion alive in Morgan, Miss Miller, Whitman, Jung, and Teilhard, is the religion of Spiritual Democracy that we also find in Taoism and Zen.

I read a footnote to Chardin's thoughts on spiritual-cosmic energy "I am dreaming to write since some time under a name which occurs to my mind in English (untranslatable into French): "The Golden Glow" (meaning the appearance of God from and in 'The Heart of Matter')."[28]

There's something about all these notions moving towards a critical mass of species-formation, a critical point, a center that interests me. What's the critical point going to be in world events in history; is it going to be some big spark, or coming together of the human heart, or an increase in vision that is about to happen? Some synthesis of Eastern and Western religions? This question is not unique to Jung and Chardin. "Are all nations communing?" Whitman asks, "Is there going to be one heart to the globe? / Is humanity forming en-masse?"[29] Both Jung and Chardin were interested in Democracy as a unitary notion.

Although Teilhard's writings were suppressed by his Catholic superiors and he was forbidden from teaching and publishing his major masterpieces, many volumes were made available to readers in the years following his death on Easter Sunday, 1955. A new era of a uniquely global vision of transcendent cosmic spirituality emerged within five years, and as we have seen, Jung was reading him on his death bed in 1961. His vision can be seen as an evolving union of human consciousness with the divine

---

26 Miguel Serrano, *C.G. Jung & Hermann Hesse: A Record of Two Friendships*.
27 C.G. Jung, *The Visions Seminars*, p. 396.
28 Pierre Teilhard de Chardin, *The Heart of Matter*, p. 77.
29 Walt Whitman, *Leaves of Grass*.

Light. But this is not the same metaphor of the Cosmic Christ we see in "New Age"[30] spirituality that is typically unaware of its own shadow; for Teilhard the Divine is the "combined essence of all evil and all goodness," filled with compassion as well as with "violence."[31]

Chardin was one of the first researchers to excavate Peking man in China. He was dazzled by a grand vision of the Cosmic Christ in China in 1916.[32] "The Whole Universe is aflame,"[33] he wrote, "Blazing Spirit, Fire… This is my Body…This is my Blood."[34] Chardin's view of the mystical body of Christ extends from the wafer of the consecrated host to the entire "cosmos itself."[35] This is a highly personal, psychological, and mystical vision, one that sees the very purpose of your being, my being, and all of your love and life, and mine, and his, as dependent on an inter-relatedness of "the union between yourself and the universe."[36]

In "Hymn to Matter" Teilhard acclaims further the "melodious fountain of water" and the "limpid crystal" from which the "new Jerusalem" or *divine milieu* of the Cosmic Christ springs[37] to be a living fountain of our common origination in anthropocentric cosmogenesis. This is also a shaman's crystal: an object of clear light that shines at the heart of every religion, in every culture on earth from the radiating heart of spirit and matter. Significantly, Teilhard refers to such a crystallizing prism as a "psychic cosmic center" or "supreme pole of consciousness" towards which all of the "elementary consciousnesses of the world shall converge" towards the "rising of a God."[38] And the only way such a critical point in the evolution of human consciousness is going to be achieved is through the vehicle of individual vocations working together through what Jung called the individuation of humankind.

Cosmic Consciousness is, therefore, a world-phenomenon that is in the process of becoming. This is not the Christ of the "old cosmos" only "but also of the new

---

30 W. Hanegraaff, *New Age Religion and Western Culture.*

31 Teilhard, *Hymn of the Universe*, pp. 60-1.

32 S. Herrmann, (2014). "Teilhard de Chardin: Cosmic Christ" In *Encyclopedia of Psychology and Religion.*

33 Teilhard, *Hymn of the Universe*, p. 78.

34 Teilhard, *Hymn of the Universe*, p. 22.

35 Teilhard, *Hymn of the Universe*, p. 14.

36 Teilhard, *Hymn of the Universe,* p. 36.

37 Teilhard, *Hymn of the Universe*, p. 70.

38 Teilhard, *Hymn of the Universe*, p. 90.

cosmogenesis."[39] In "The Religion of Tomorrow" Chardin adds: "*In a system of* cosmo-noo-genesis, the comparative value of religious creeds may be measured by their respective power of evolutive activation."[40] What Chardin actually means by evolutive is that "sooner or later there will be a chain-reaction."[41] This chain-reaction is the spirituality of the earth's peoples that is coming.

"The Transcendent Function" (the seminal essay written in the same year, 1916, Chardin had his great vision of the Cosmic Christ in China) formed the backdrop for Jung's mature reflections on "active imagination," his technique for interacting with the unconscious. In his Prefatory Note to "The Transcendent Function," Jung advanced towards an answer to the perennial question: "How does one come to terms in practice with the unconscious?"[42] This question, Jung argues, is the question posed by the philosophies of India, particularly by Buddhism and Zen. Jung's belief is that this question is *the* fundamental question in theory and practice of all religions and philosophies. His answer may be found in his method of "active imagination"[43] that he experimented with in his *Red Book.*

Active imagination is Jung's answer to the problem posed by all religions; Jung's individual way, his teaching, his personal solution, to religion the world over. In a world enlightened by Spiritual Democracy, the images of a "God yet to come" would appear to take an individual form in every individual who, through his or her spiritual calling, can make the supreme meaning of the Self conscious by means of a vocation. Jung articulated the cornerstone for this personal myth in the following passage:

> But the supreme meaning is the path, the way and the bridge to what is to come. This is the God yet to come. It is not the coming of God himself, but his image which appears in the supreme meaning. God is an image, and those who worship him must worship him in the images of the supreme meaning.[44]

Meaning is supreme. It is microcosmic and macrocosmic. Thus, as we have seen for Chardin, Christ is everything and all religions point to this final Light, which is nevertheless in the process of increasing complexification and species-formation. Jung,

---

39 Teilhard, *Hymn of the Universe,* p. 139.
40 Teilhard, *Heart of Matter,* p. 97.
41 Teilhard, *Heart of Matter,* p. 102.
42 Jung, *The Structure and Dynamics of the Psyche,* CW 8, p. 67.
43 Jung, *The Structure and Dynamics of the Psyche,* CW 8, p. 68.
44 C.G. Jung, *The Red Book,* p. 67.

however, is articulating a way of direct religious experience of the Self, which exists in the foundation of the human psyche, in each person, and Christ is only one symbol for this cosmic center of unity and peace in the personality: "In order to discover the uniformity of the human psyche, I have to descend into the very foundations of consciousness. Only there do I find that in which we are all alike. If I build my theory on what is common to all, I explain the psyche in terms of its foundation and origin."[45] In a sense, Jung who would realize the essence of his personal myth as the "miracle of reflective consciousness" on the Athi Plains of East Africa in 1926 is speaking a similar language as Chardin who said that "the heightening of consciousness in the universe" is a "function of complexity"[46] that is tending towards "new dimensions of cosmic reality."[47] This similarity in thought is, as I have said, based on a Humboldtian vision of the Cosmos although Jung had encountered it earlier, in Meister Eckhart. When Jung first read Meister Eckhart is unclear, although he is sure to have known about him as early as his primary school-years, when he was reading Pythagoras, Heraclitus, Empedocles, Kant, Hegel, and especially Schopenhauer, who was one of the first great thinkers to see the parallels between Eckhart and Hindu and Buddhist thought. Meister Eckhart filled Jung with a profound experience of divinity even though he claims in his youth "not" to have "understood him."[48] It was not until 1921 that Jung published his important piece on Eckhart in *Psychological Types,* where he says Eckhart's "painstaking exposition of the relativity of God to man and the soul seem to me one of the most important landmarks on the way to a psychological understanding of religious phenomena."[49] "In Europe," Jung wrote in a letter: "as far as I can make out, Meister Eckhart is about the first where the self begins to play a noticeable role."[50] Thus, it was Eckhart, in Jung's view, who relativized God in such a profound way that the distinctions between Christ, as a symbol for the Self, and the Self as a symbol for Christ, was completely obliterated, in the ultimate realization of the meaning of the interconnectedness of the entire Cosmos. Today, no one can proclaim to have discovered *the* Truth, only a "truth" to a Universal way that exists as a spiritual possibility

---

45 C.G. Jung, *Psychological Types*, CW 6, ¶ 852.
46 Teilhard, *The Future of Man,* p. 181.
47 Teilhard, *The Future of Man,* p. 175.
48 C.G. Jung, *MDR*, pp. 68-9.
49 C.G. Jung, *Psychological Types*, CW 6, ¶ 411.
50 C.G. Jung, *Letters*, Vol. 2, pp. 453-4.

inside each of us. The goal of analytical psychology is to re-unite the mind with what Jung, echoing Eckhart and his follower Jacob Boehme, had called the "eternal Ground of all empirical being"[51] the same cosmic divinity Chardin experience in his great vision of Christ in China. This divine Ground of being can be accessed directly by anyone who comes to "know beyond all doubt, that empirical reality has a transcendental background"[52] and finds a way through traditional teachings of any religion to the spiritual path of oneness, that will eventually lead, hopefully, to world peace. The greatest spiritual teachers of humanity have always taught that the way to God can be arrived at through many mystical paths, which all lead to the same foundation and source. This source is called the Godhead by Eckhart, Cosmic Christ by Chardin and Fox, or Collective Unconscious by Jung. All religions in other words have an *equal* model in God; all are divine; and all are ways to the divinization of humanity on earth and in the noosphere.

Like the American poet-shamans, Whitman, Melville, and Dickinson, Jung teaches that the supreme meaning is found in a cosmic Meaning that is transcendent of any creeds, denominations, or any one religion, because it is a meaning "common to all." In 1927 Jung obtained confirmation for his ideas about the Self by way of a dream. He represented it in a beautiful mandala called "Window on Eternity."[53] Out of this dream, Jung realized that everything is directed towards the center:

> Through this dream I understood that the self is the principle and archetype of orientation and meaning. Therein lies its healing function… Out of it emerged a first inkling of my personal myth.[54]

By May 1928, Jung coined the word "synchronicity." He used the word *synchronicity* in his *Dream Seminars* and mentioned it later in his memorial address for Richard Wilhelm in Munich, May, 1930, when he sought to explain the Chinese divinization method described in the *I Ching, or Book of Changes,* dating back to the fourth millennium B.C.[55] By 1932, Jung embraced a world-transforming vision of an interconnectedness of all the world religions. Meaning became the main thing in Jung's psy-

---

51 C.G. Jung, *Mysterium Coniunctionis,* CW 14, ¶ 760.
52 Jung, *Mysterium Coniunctionis,* CW 14, ¶ 768.
53 Jung, *MDR,* pp. 196-7.
54 Jung, *MDR,* p. 199.
55 C.G. Jung, *The Spirit in Man, Art, and Literature,* CW 15, ¶¶ 74-96.

chology by this time. The premises of nineteenth century science "do not give enough meaning to life. And it is only meaning that liberates."[56] He had found his way to the meaning of Spiritual Democracy, articulated by this time in his dream of the Self. Meaning becomes for Jung a transcendent state of fictional-healing, or meaning-cure. Jung's "healing fiction" becomes a "meaning that quickens"[57] Jung cites Chapter 25 of the *Tao Te Ching* as an example of what he means: "One may think of it as the mother of all things under heaven. / I do not know its name. / But I call it 'Meaning'."[58]

Jung began his studies of Chinese wisdom texts as early as 1927, yet by 1932, he was extending the concept of meaning to an international audience and his aim was to reach the world by becoming a bridge between Western and Eastern religions. Everything begins to converge by 1932 for Jung on the particular psychic state in the doctor that heals, and meaning becomes his cornerstone: the discovery of a healing fiction, a myth to live by. Meaning becomes the main thing from this point onward. Jung defines what he means by "religion" when he asserts it as a state of oneness that "will give meaning and form to the confusion" of the patients "neurotic soul."[59]

It is important to note that Jung's psychology of religion is not a doctrine. It is a science; an empirical method of observing and interacting with the psyche: a gateway to personal religious experience. As such, analytical psychology concerns itself, first and foremost with problems centering on meaning and meaninglessness during mid-life and beyond. This includes:

1)   The conflict of vocation (from the Latin root *vocare*), vs. career.

2)   Conflicts of conscience, the moral confrontation between good and evil.

3)   The discovery of a religious attitude and personal myth.

4)   The solution to problems of neurotic suffering and mental illness through a path to meaning: the chief concern of world religions and Jungian psychotherapists.

---

56 Jung, *Psychology and Religion*, CW 11, ¶ 496.
57 Jung, *Psychology and Religion*, CW 11, ¶ 498.
58 Jung, *The Structure and Dynamics of the Psyche*, CW 8, ¶ 918.
59 Jung, *Psychology and Religion: West and East*, CW 11, ¶ 498.

Jung makes clear in *Memories, Dreams, Reflections* that he realized that there were "certain objective problems" that called him to closer examination and analysis. These objective problems are central to his vision of Spiritual Democracy. Analytical psychology is spiritually democratic in the sense that it concerns itself with the discovery of images of the supreme meaning in a patient's life and not with God as a metaphysical reality. Its aim is to relativize God as a path of consciousness emanating from the human heart, from the Self, as the spiritual center that can be located in all religions. This meaning can only be conveyed through myth, or fictions that liberate. "What we are to our inward vision, and what man appears to be *sub specie aeternitatus*," Jung says "can only be expressed by way of myth" (see number three above).[60] *Memories, Dreams, Reflections* is Jung's confession of faith, his experience of God, a subjective confession revealed through the language of myth. Such a story is limited by the subjective factor of Jung's being-in-the-myth when he is creating it. "Thus it is," he writes that "I have now undertaken, in my eighty-third year, to tell my personal myth" (see number three above).[61] Jung's solution to the problem of neurotic suffering came to him through his discovery of vocation as a healing path in 1932:

> Behind the neurotic perversion is concealed his vocation, his destiny: the growth of personality, the full realization of the life-will that is inborn with the individual. It is the man without *amor fati* who is neurotic; he, truly, has missed his vocation.[62]

In his autobiography, he takes these ideas further:

> Meaninglessness inhibits fullness of life and is therefore equivalent to illness. Meaning makes a great many things endurable—perhaps everything. No science will ever replace myth, and a myth cannot be made out of any science. For it is not that 'God' is a myth, but that myth is the revelation of the divine life in man. It is not we who invent myth, rather it speaks to us as a Word of God.[63]

As Jung said to Max Zeller, moreover, while discussing the dream of a Jungian analyst: "Yes, you know, that is the temple we all build on. We don't know the people because, believe me, they build in India, and China and Russia and all over the world.

---

60 Jung, *MDR*, p. 3.
61 Jung, *MDR*.
62 C.G. Jung, *The Development of Personality,* CW 17, ¶ 313.
63 Jung, *MDR,* p. 340.

That is the new religion. You know how long it will take until it is built? - about six hundred years"[64] Jung means the world, the globe here; he means the place in the psyche where we are all the same. We are all building on it. One difference between Jung and Chardin that must be noted is their experience of Divinity in light of the church.

There was no sense of "union" in church for Jung, no exaltation, no vista, where cosmic consciousness could be experienced. Traditional Christianity was for Jung an experience of the "absence of God" and the church was a place where he realized he "should not go," for there was only "death."[65] Jung says: "My 'religion' recognized no human relationship to God, for how could one relate to something so little known as God?"[66] "Only in Meister Eckhart" Jung says "did I feel the breath of life."[67]

In "The Symbolic Life" Jung responded moreover to a question asked by the group leader about the "next step in religious development." He turned the discussion to a series of stories from his clinical and personal experiences, and I outline a few of them here: the meditation practices in India;[68] a personal story of his talks with the Taos Pueblo Holy Man, Mountain Lake, whose ritual of praying to the sun gave him a sense of cosmic meaning;[69] a case of a Jewish girl from a Hasidic family, whose anxiety neurosis was cured in one week when he directed her to return to her ancestral forms of worship, as a true child of God;[70] a story from Rasmussen's experiences with Polar Eskimos; a medicine man became leader of his tribe on account of his visions.[71] The list goes on. Jung concludes: "I am only concerned with the fulfillment of that will which is in every individual."[72] "Religion," he writes "is careful observation of the data."[73] Finally, Jung calls "synchronicity"[74] a "coincidence in time of two or more

---

64 Max Zeller, "The Task of the Analyst." in *Psychological Perspectives* 6, 1975.
65 Jung, *MDR*, p. 55.
66 Jung, *MDR*, pp. 56-7.
67 Jung, *MDR*, pp. 68-9.
68 Jung, *The Symbolic Life*, CW 18, ¶ 626.
69 Jung, *The Symbolic Life*, CW 18, ¶ 626.
70 Jung, *The Symbolic Life*, CW 18, ¶ 635.
71 Jung, *The Symbolic Life*, CW 18, ¶ 674.
72 Jung, *The Symbolic Life*, CW 18, ¶ 639.
73 Jung, *The Symbolic Life*, CW 18, ¶ 673.
74 Jung, *Structure and Dynamics of the Psyche*, CW 8, ¶ 958.

unrelated events which have the same or a similar meaning."[75] The element of meaning is crucial here. Reflective consciousness is a miracle of human life. But, "Today," writes Jung "we are obliged to view the miraculous in a somewhat different light."[76] Jung asserts, "I believe that, after thousands of millions of years, someone had to realize that this wonderful world of mountains and oceans, suns and moons, galaxies and nebulae, plants and animals, exists."[77] This is essentially a vision he brought back with him to Switzerland from his trips to Taos and Kenya at the age of fifty.

In his last essay written in fluent English shortly before his death, Jung wrote (perhaps more critically than Chardin ever did?) that we have stripped the sacred of its mystery and numinosity and "nothing is holy any longer."[78] More: "I know that the Buddhists would say, as indeed they do: if only people would follow the noble eightfold path of the Dharma (doctrine, law) and had true insight into the Self, or the Christians: if only people had right faith in the Lord; or the rationalists: if only people could be intelligent and reasonable—then all problems would be manageable and solvable. The trouble is that none of them manages to solve these problems himself." Jung continues:

> We are so captivated by and entangled in our subjective consciousness that we have simply forgotten the age-old fact that God speaks chiefly through dreams and visions. The Buddhist discards the world of unconscious fantasies as 'distractions' and useless illusions; the Christian puts his Church and his Bible between himself and his unconscious.[79]

Because the world's religions have not retained much of their "original numinosity," Jung insists that we must return to our "original revelations" to uncover the truths of our own individual Selfhood. By this, Jung means that "infantile memories" still contain imprints of "archetypal modes of psychic functioning" that are primary channels or psychic gateways for "a greater extension of consciousness."[80] Jung is at pains to point out: "Man today is painfully aware of the fact that neither his great religions nor his various philosophies seem to provide him with those powerful ideas that would

---

75 Jung, *Structure and Dynamics of the Psyche,* CW 8, ¶ 849.

76 Jung, *Structure and Dynamics of the Psyche,* CW 8, ¶ 995.

77 C.G. Jung, *The Archetypes and the Collective Unconscious,* CW 9i, ¶ 177.

78 Jung, *The Symbolic Life,* CW 18, ¶ 582.

79 Jung, *The Symbolic Life,* CW 18, ¶ 601.

80 Jung, *The Symbolic Life,* CW 18, ¶ 595.

give him the certainty and security he needs in face of the present condition of the world."[81] As any change must begin somewhere, Jung concludes, it is only the single individual who will undergo it, and carry it through. The change must begin with one individual; and it might be any one of us.

> Nobody can afford to look around and wait for somebody else to do what he is loath to do himself. As nobody knows what he could do, he might be bold to ask himself whether by any chance his unconscious might know something helpful, when there is no satisfactory conscious answer anywhere in sight.[82]

The question of whether there will be a new religion has long shaped the imaginations of many nations. I believe the world religions are yearning for Spiritual Democracy. Spiritual Democracy is an archetype of peace. Jung advises us to look to our dreams, to an *experience* of the unity of the Cosmos and for an experience of the Peacemaker that dwells in the human heart.

It is perhaps on this point that Chardin offers a vision that complements Jung in a way that reflects a subtle difference between their psychological (Jung) and priestly (Chardin) vocations. This delicate difference may be found in Chardin's faith in the evolution of the planetary layer, or "envelope of thinking substance" that he names the "Noosphere"[83] as being oriented towards an apex of super-consciousness or "super-Brain" that is ultimately Christ-centered, as opposed to Self-centered. That is his calling as a priest and it prevailed to the very end for him, even to the moment of his death. Three days before his death, he wrote on Good Friday two articles of his credo to confirm his belief in God: 1) "The Universe is centered—Evolutively," and 2) Christ is its Center."[84]

It would appear that Chardin's vision is more sourced, therefore, in the Christian incentive as the ultimate point of evolution towards which everything in Space-Time turns, whereas for Jung, the ultimate point of centralization and complexification is the Self that subsumes, but does not supersede the Christ-image, for while Jung saw Christ as a center that is everywhere when he wrote in *Answer to Job* of the "Christi-

---

81 Jung, *The Symbolic Life*, CW 18, ¶ 599.
82 Jung, *The Symbolic Life*, CW 18, ¶ 599.
83 Teilhard, *The Future of Man*, p. 163.
84 Teilhard, *The Future of Man*, p. 324.

fication of many,"[85] this vision did not supersede other dispensations (in the sense of being superior to them).

Where the two authors agree is on the primacy of Cosmic Consciousness, vocation, and religious conscience as the apex of evolution and on an urge in humanity to transcend itself. In an Address to the World Congress of Faiths (French section), on March 8, 1947, for instance, Chardin took his belief in Christ to a point of objective, scientific reflection, when he spoke of the uniting force in humankind as an evolutionary force of the Universe that is becoming increasingly aware of itself as a unity-in-thinking, an urge upwards towards inter-planetary union, or what today we would call globalization. While addressing the world's faithful he added: "A tendency towards unification is everywhere manifest, and especially in the different branches of religion." Citing Aldous Huxley's abstract propositions about the "basis of a common philosophy" across the globe Chardin added: "We believe this to be helpful, and moreover we are persuaded that gradually, in religious thought as in the sciences, a core universal truth will form and slowly grow, to be accepted by everyone. Can there be any true spiritual evolution without it?"[86] Finally, he asked his audience, as if intending to reach the world's future: despite all ideological differences, will the world "eventually, in some manner, come together on the same summit?"[87] For Chardin the summit was Christ. For Jung the summit was the Self. For Whitman, the summit was Spiritual Democracy. The common way to the "Christification of many" is for Jung the continuing indwelling of the "Holy Ghost, the third Divine Person, in man," but by "many" Jung does not mean that all will become "complete God-men," or God-women. For every person, no matter how enlightened one might be, suffers from mortal sin, and we all have a human shadow. "That is to say," Jung concludes humbly that "even the enlightened person remains what he is, and is never more than his own limited ego before the One who dwells within him, whose form has no knowable boundaries, who encompasses him on all sides, fathomless as the abysms of the earth and vast as the sky."[88] We find the same basic teaching in Meister Eckhart, who said about the infinite depths of the feminine Godhead: "The innermost and highest realms of the soul—these two are one. There where time never penetrates, where

---

85 Jung, *Psychology of Religion*, CW 11, ¶ 758.
86 Teilhard, *The Future of Man*, p. 198.
87 Teilhard, *The Future of Man*, p. 199.
88 Jung, Psychology and Religion, CW 11, ¶ 758.

no image shines in, in the innermost and highest aspects of the soul God creates the entire Cosmos."[89] This Humboldtian vision is a common thread that unites the psychological with the religious paths in Chardin's and Jung's writings; it is a spiritually democratic way to arrive at world peace.

Bibliography

Brown, Joseph. *The Sacred Pipe.* New York: Penguin, 1971.

Hanegraaff, W. *New Age Religion and Western Culture.* New York: SUNY Press, 1978.

Herrmann, S. *William Everson: The Shaman's Call.* New York: Eloquent Books, 2009.

Herrmann, S. *Walt Whitman: Shamanism, Spiritual Democracy, and the World Soul.* Durham, CT: Eloquent Books, 2010.

James, W. *The Varieties of Religious Experience.* New York: Image, 1978.

Jung, C.G. *Memories, Dreams, Reflections.* New York: Vintage, 1965.

Jung, C.G. *The Visions Seminars,* in Two Volumes. Zurich: Spring Publications, 1976.

Jung, C.G. *The Red Book.* New York/London: W.W. Norton and Company, Philemon Series, 2009.

Jung, C.G. *Psychological Types,* CW 6. Princeton, N.J.: Princeton University Press, 1971.

Jung, C.G. *The Structure and Dynamics of the Psyche,* CW 8. New York, N.Y.: Pantheon Books, Inc., 1960.

Jung, C.G. *The Archetypes and the Collective Unconscious,* CW 9i. Princeton, N.J.: Princeton University Press, 1969.

Jung, C.G. *Letters* in 2 Volumes from Volume 2, edited by Gerhard Adler. Princeton: Bollingen, 1953.

Jung, C.G. *Psychology and Religion: West and East,* CW 11. Princeton, N.J.: Princeton University Press, 1958.

Jung, C.G. *Mysterium, Coniunctionis,* CW 14. New York, N.Y.: Pantheon Books, 1963.

Jung, C.G. *The Spirit in Man, Art, and Literature,* CW 15. New York, N.Y.: Bollingen Foundation, 1966.

---

89 Fox, *Breakthrough: Meister Eckhart's Creation Spirituality in New Translation,* p. 65.

Jung, C.G. *The Development of Personality,* CW 17. New York, N.Y.: Bolligen Foundation, 1954.

Jung, C.G. *The Symbolic Life,* CW 18. Princeton, N.J.: Princeton University Press, 1976.

Jung, C.G. *Dream Analysis: Notes of the Seminar Given in 1928-1930.* Princeton: Bollingen.

Jung, C.G. (1989). *C.G. Jung: Analytical Psychology: Notes of the Seminar Given in 1925.* Princeton: Bollingen, 1989.

Neihardt, John. *Black Elk Speaks: Being the Life Story of a Holy Man of the Oglala Sioux as Told through John G. Neihardt.* Lincoln: University of Nebraska Press, 1961.

Raubel, H. *With Walt Whitman in Camden.* 7 Volumes. New York: Rowman & Littlefield, 1961.

Serrano, Miguel. *C.G. Jung & Hermann Hesse: A Record of Two Friendships.* New York: Schocken, 1966.

Teilhard de Chardin, Pierre. *The Phenomenon of Man.* New York: Harper & Row, 1960.

Teilhard de Chardin, Pierre. *The Divine Milieu.* New York: Harper & Row, 1960.

Teilhard de Chardin, Pierre. *The Future of Man.* New York: Harper, 1964.

Teilhard de Chardin, Pierre. *Hymn of the Universe.* New York: Harper & Row, 1965.

Teilhard de Chardin, Pierre. ed. "Fathers, Sons, and Brotherhood," published in *Betwixt and Between: Patterns of Masculine and Feminine Initiation.* La Salle, Illinois: Open Court, 1987.

Von Humboldt, A. *Cosmos: A Sketch of the Physical Description of the Universe, Volume 1.* Baltimore: John Hopkins, 1997.

Whitman, Walt. *Leaves of Grass.* New York: Library of America/Vintage, 1962.

Zeller, M. "The Task of the Analyst." In *Psychological Perspectives* 6, 1975.

6

SMATTERINGS, SCATTERINGS, AND GATHERINGS

Sr. Barbara Faris

Dear Reader,

The question came from a long time friend, "Would you be willing to write an article about how Teilhard de Chardin and Carl Jung come together in impacting your life?" I responded immediately, "Yes."

Now I look back and wonder, "Whatever possessed me to reply with such sure affirmation?" I see now that it is my desire to "pay back," to hopefully honor the memories of these two great men, simply because they have done so much to ground my spirit in the mid 20th and beginning 21st centuries.

I have chosen to attach a list of the books that were referenced for this article. Where quotes of the authors' are within the text, it will be appropriately noted. So I invite you to trek along with me, inward, onward and upward where Jung and Chardin converge in my story, my myth.

I was born a neighborhood barkeeper's daughter into the time of a mid-century era which was crusted with generations of either/or, good/bad, right/wrong, and inclusive/exclusive worldviews; my father, full blooded Lebanese, my mother Austrian-Swiss. As such, my young life was spent pulling together a vision of the universe as seen through the eyes of the Near East and Germanic cultures spiced with eastern and western histories of Catholicism. A dichotomized notion of heart/soul, body/spirit, mind/will, light/dark, good/bad, created a brand of perfectionism which fed upon my super sensitive emotions and nursed abundant fears. Add to the mix, my life choice to become a Franciscan woman religious. Over the years, these blended one fine cocktail of guilt, fear, and burnout due to frenetic overwork. However, this state of affairs changed when midlife crisis shattered the idol of my rigid self image and I asked in the words of the popular song: "Is That All There is, my Friend?"

My early life as the daughter of a barkeeper brings back memories of my dad sharing a dream that he had of his own deceased father appearing to be suffering and in pain. When I asked what this meant, my father said, "It means that I must fast and pray for grandpa." A few weeks later my six-year-old ears perked up as dad told mom that he had another dream which showed grandpa peaceful and content, therefore he could stop his fast. This is the earliest memory I have that dreams could be taken seriously. This belief went underground as academics developed its discipline of rational thought.

It is during the bleak midyears of busy ministry among Native Americans when the world of dreams resurfaced from my depths. People would come to me sharing their dreams and sometimes visions, hoping to find someone who could help them decipher the contents. I needed more education in this realm of spirituality. I heard of a School for Spiritual Directors in New Mexico whose teachings broke through the bonds of an extreme rationality by using the world of dreams to open vistas into the realms of the spirit.

Enter Carl Jung

I enrolled in the Spiritual Directors' School at Pecos, N.M. when I was in my late 40s. The depth psychology of Carl Jung and his extensive research on human spirit and behaviors fused with the Gospel, forming a program of studies of the human spirituality.

Guadalupe Abbey in Pecos, New Mexico introduced me to the psychology of Carl Jung. It uncovered a method of listening which we students were challenged to experience ourselves before practicing on others. Its teachings emphasized a balance between mind and heart. In the words of the monastery abbot, "Just because the heart is turned on does not mean that the mind must be turned off." I learned that symbol systems are found not only in the world of psychology and mythology, but within each person as well. Dreams were seen as revealers of the unconscious level of personality. As such, we students were offered a method of interpretation (not analysis) which could be used in ferreting out and developing our personal dream symbolism in order to build a bridge between the conscious and unconscious realms. Jung's teachings helped me to be not afraid of the dark but to use it to find my way into deeper awareness of my place in the world around me. His approach toward individuation led me to see that everything in the world speaks on its own terms and is therefore much more than meets the eye – in the words of James Hillman; I was taught to "see-through" what is in front of my face and in my mind. Drawn to a wider view of being, I realized that all has its unique reason to be.

The little world of "me" blossomed into the world of "us." The Myers-Briggs Personality Inventory, based upon Jung's findings, gave us a tool for engaging our personal "blind spots" in the arena of human relationship, and taking a dive into the personalities of others in order to better communicate. These were not the only gifts of Pecos. It led me to a love for mythology. However, it was another seven years before the thought became action when I was given an advertisement by one of my sisters.

Pacifica, a university accredited Institute in Carpinteria California, advertised that it included in its fields of study both MAs and PhDs in Mythological Studies with Emphasis on Depth Psychology. Its motto "to tend the soul of the world" added to its personal appeal. My interest in mythology reawakened. After discerning with my religious community, it was decided that I return to academic studies. Pacifica accepted me as a student at age sixty.

The Institute's curriculum compacted the history of humanity into story (mythology) and psychology, based upon the contributions from cross-cultural secular, religious, and nonsectarian scholars of the past, present, and future. Professors came from a diversity of educational institutions and disciplines; students, from a mixture of spiritual beliefs and various professions, and from the US and foreign countries. By age sixty-seven I completed an MA and PhD while working part time as a hospital chaplain. Equipped with a solid education set in the human history of ancient, medieval, and present day mythologies and the fundamentals of depth psychology, I set out to conquer the world! As one job after another escaped my grasp, I returned to chaplaincy using my skills to accompany many people who walked through sickness, death, and dying. I was able to give them tools for facing the dark and the frightening aspects of their dreams, hallucinations and, at times, visions. Due to my studies, I felt more capable of offering some consolation and hope to families of the sick who floundered in darkness, fear, and helplessness. I was able to help them "see through" the suffering and touch upon their deep inner strength to carry them through the pain. Hopefully they would stand more firmly before the unexplainable. This did not necessarily alleviate the suffering but urged them forward to courageously embrace the inevitable.

Now at seventy-six, I have chosen to retire. I live with sixty-five sister religious at various stages of aging, some of whom volunteer outside of the house and others who are too fragile to do so. One of my sisters, Sister Lucille Walsh, led me back on the road to Teilhard de Chardin. She is an avid advocate for his teachings and previously engaged in a rich and active life. Sister was our religious community's dentist, having been the first woman religious to graduate from Marquette's School of Dentistry. In mid-years, due to a medical problem, she found it necessary to change professions and proceeded to study theology. She was hired to teach at the present Cardinal Stritch University where she was instrumental in developing the Department of Theology of which she became the head. Sister Lucille with Sister Jessine Reiss entered a dialogue with the Moslem community in 1980 helping to spearhead other such dialogues. At Sister Lucille's 100th birthday celebration, when asked of what she thought of aging she responded, "I don't think of aging. I just think 'onward and upward'." I speak of sister in this article because she credits Chardin with "giving a foundation for my spiritual life journey." Sister gives me courage to continue my pilgrimage into the future.

Teilhard de Chardin

I was first introduced to the works of Chardin in my early forties. I read and consumed *The Divine Milieu, Letters from a Traveler, Mass on the World, Hymn of the Universe* and with much less enthusiasm, *The Phenomenon of Man.* I sensed an affinity of heart and spirit with this man whose vision of a world on-fire-with-motion connected with my own love for this world. Love for matter shone through his works as living and beautiful, not as a threat to the human spirit and an "occasion of sin." The brilliance of his intellect and the depth of his vision demanded longer life experience and less absorbing ministry on my part. I needed time to focus. However, a new found hope for the future geminated within me. His wedding of matter to spirit grounded my love for this world. The faith/science historical conflict faded for me into a situation which just needed more time and new thought in order to see that they need one another. A new vocabulary flooded my mind: biogenesis, cosmogenesis, pleroma, hominization, planetization, cosmic evolution. However, ministry needed tending and Teilhard went to the back burner of my mind as I was enveloped in the activities of pastoral ministry.

A stormy period followed, as disenchantment with the behaviors of the administrative Catholic Church dampened the growth of a mature faith among the laity of the church, who desired to live out post Vatican II teachings. How could I model behaviors and sentiments in which I did not believe? How could I be steeped in constant struggle of Old and New Catholicism and remain true to what I was being drawn? I simply did not do so, and ministry took on the form of confrontations with the powers that be. I found that it no longer sufficed to stretch traditional religious teaching to its limits. I broke through the bonds and opted for cosmic theology with its embracing of the evolution of humanity and all of creation. I left direct ministry in the Church. Education in hospital and hospice chaplaincy ensued.

Thomas Berry, Brian Smiley, Judy Cannato, Barbara Marx Hubbard, Ursula King, and others accompany my mind and heart on the same cosmic journey. Serving the sick and dying allowed me to pass on whatever I had comprehended of Carl Jung's psychology and Teilhard de Chardin's philosophy and theology. They offered a vision of hope for the future of humankind which moves the universe closer to wholeness. Individually and collectively evolving into a new creation filled with hope, the movement forward continues unending for the individual and the communal collective. However, it was just beginning for me.

Confusion, frustration, and disillusion marked the last twenty years of my experience in the Church. I see now that much of my difficulty with the traditional Catholic views and the persons who propagated them sprang from an unconscious assimilation of Chardin's ideas. Integration demanded much disintegration. An arduous and lonely journey proceeded onward and upward as I struggled to see the connections among mythology, spirituality, cosmic theology, Catholicism, Franciscan tradition, and the modern world. Sciences marched on, leaving religion behind. Chardin's views made more and more sense to me that, first, organized religions (including Christianity) need to renew and re-found themselves in order to meet the movement forward in and with the evolution of the universe; second, cultures and spiritual traditions unite with one another in the endeavor to establish in this world a new order of love and cooperation; third, an invitation to call a truce between science and religion that together they may guide the world into an ever unfolding future; and, fourth, call with a renewed urgency to formulate new understandings of a mysticism that is inclusive of all humanity. These can be accomplished only through the energy of love.

Where to Now?

I believe that Jung's and Chardin's understandings connect where time and space evolve and converge. What does this look like to me?

Jung accumulated stories of early humankind, using the mythologies of many cultures to come to understand that these myths touched a level where the conscious and unconscious converge. A notion of soul beckoned him throughout his life, as he mentions in his autobiography *Memories, Dreams, Reflections*. Mythology drove the engine of Jung's study of human personality. He brought the past into the present, giving an expanded insight into a level of truth where fact meets fiction, intuition connects with rationality, and the unconscious enlightens the conscious. In the journey from "the me, of me" into the odyssey "of us," Jung bridges the gap between "then and now," a "now" which holds within itself the promise of a more conscious future founded upon reaching beyond self-centered egotism.

Jung's concept of individuation still challenges me daily to seek my whole self, able to differentiate that self from the collective mores. Jung makes a clear distinction between individualism and individuation. As proposed by Jung, individuation leads outward toward the world from within a deeper understanding of one's personal journey into the unconscious and out toward self-knowledge. Thus the individual and the collective unite as partners in their movement into wholeness. The one needs the other.

My choice to be in solidarity with the poor steers me into the ministry of social justice and peace. This preference calls for the courage to speak out when faced with unjust systems which discriminate against peoples according to their race, creed, culture, or sexual orientation. In order to do this work effectively, it is strategic to "know thyself" and come to understand how to communicate with others. Jung gives the tools to work with these necessities. I consider Jung as my guide to Chardin. I love this world that I live in. It is here where Jung has helped me to move "onward and upward" into the cosmic vision of Chardin.

Chardin and "The World"

The gift of meeting the right people at the right time carried me through to age seventy-six. I am aware of the volumes of writings that both Jung and Chardin have left to this world. That I should have been privy to some few of them gives me cause to be grateful because they facilitated my own challenge to listen to my heart. I have been proffered the privilege of experiencing a full and challenging life. Writing this article has encouraged me to resurrect writings which will hopefully assist in continuing to "age well." There remains more in my saga of individuation and evolutionary cosmology. Perhaps it just might continue after I die!

In my chosen Catholic faith tradition, the mystics reiterate the belief that one finds oneself by moving beyond and outward from a solid base of self-knowledge. Jung offered me self-knowledge. Chardin buttresses my faith in this world's wild evolutionary journey into the future. Cosmogenesis, Chardin's word for bringing together the cosmos plus its evolutionary propensity, has revitalized my once static faith which now explodes with meaning beyond the bounds of dogma and demands. Chardin further stretches his understandings toward a Christic Omega point, where all creation seems to be heading. Since I am a believer in Christ, this affirms my own thought that this Christ is beyond religion and inclusive of all creation. Other faith traditions may call it by another name.

Science and religion remain the challenge of the 21st century. Science opens realities to the human mind which are known to exist, however, cannot be "sensed" in common parlance. Chardin suggests that there is another sense which lifts human thought to a higher level of knowing, into the consciousness that all of creation is a living organism of which the apex, thus far, is human. The challenge and the choice to move the "now" into an ever evolving beyond remains with humanity. As for me, the choice is made.

Bibliography

Campbell, Joseph, editor. *The Portable Jung*, (Translated by R.F.C. Hull). New York: Viking Press, 1971.

Jung, C.G. *Memories, Dreams, Reflections* (recorded and edited by Aniela Jaffe, translated by Richard and Clare Winston). New York, N.Y.: Vintage Books, 1989.

King, Ursula. *Spirit of Fire, the Life and Vision of Teilhard de Chardin.* Maryknoll, New York: Orbis Press, 1996.

Samuels, Andrew; Short, Boni, and Plant, Fred. *A Critical Dictionary of Jungian Analysis.* New York: Routledge, 1986.

Teilhard de Chardin, Pierre. *The Phenomenon of Man.* New York, N.Y.: Harper & Row, 1959.

Teilhard de Chardin, Pierre. *The Heart of Matter*, (translated by René Hague). New York, N.Y.: Harcourt Brace Jovanovich, 1978.

Teilhard de Chardin, Pierre. *Writings in Time of War.* (translated by René Hague). New York, N.Y.: Harcourt & Row Publishers, 1916-1919.

Teilhard de Chardin, Pierre . *Writings Selected by Ursula King,* (Modern Spiritual Masters Series). Maryknoll, New York: Orbis Press, 1999.

7

C.G. JUNG AND
PIERRE TEILHARD DE CHARDIN

Is There a Border Between Psychic and Evolutionary Energy?

John Dourley

A Brief Biography of Pierre Teilhard de Chardin

Chardin was born May 1, 1881, at Sarcenat, in the province of Auvergne of distinguished parents with an historical legacy of service to French royalty.[1] In 1899, after four years in a Jesuit boarding school followed by a year of rest, he entered the Jesuit novitiate in Aix-en-Provence. From 1905 to 1908 he taught at a Jesuit school in Cairo. Here he was first to toy with notions of pantheism, monism, the world soul and an underlying unity evident in all that is and supporting a passion for the universe.[2,3] After the completion of his theological studies he was ordained a priest in Hastings, England, in 1911. He was then assigned to study geology at the Institut Catholique and paleontology at the Paris Museum of Natural History.[4] His studies were interrupted by the First World War. He was conscripted as a stretcher bearer and then chaplain and saw the carnage at Ypres, Artois, Flanders, and Verdun.[5] It was from this period that his first essays on the synthesis of the reality of evolution with his Christian faith took shape as did the traditionalist opposition to him.[6] Though

---

1 Mary and Ellen Lukas, *Teilhard, the Man, the Priest, the Scientist*, pp. 19-22.
2 Lukas, *Teilhard, the Man, the Priest, the Scientist*, pp. 32-33
3 R. Speaight, *Teilhard de Chardin, a Biography*, p. 35.
4 Lukas, *Teilhard, the Man, the Priest, the Scientist*, p. 38.
5 Lukas, *Teilhard, the Man, the Priest, the Scientist*, pp. 49-51.
6 Lukas, *Teilhard, the Man, The Priest, The Scientist*, pp. 52, 54-55, 57.

relatively unsophisticated these essays collected under the title,[7] contain the foundational themes that were to last throughout his life and to which he returned in the essays written closer to his death in 1955.[8] From the outset he confesses he was driven to unite to the point of coincidence the two absolutes in his life, his Christian faith and the truth of the earth sciences.[9]

After the war, in 1919, he returned to his studies in Paris toward a doctorate from the Sorbonne. In 1920 he was given the chair of geology at the Institut Catholique in Paris. In 1922 he defended his doctoral thesis at the Sorbonne on "Mammals of the French Lower Eocene and their Strata."[10] At that point, at the beginning of what appeared to be a brilliant academic future, Teilhard inadvertently took a step that was to undermine his prospects, exile him from his native France for much of his remaining life, and sentence him to die with his work on evolution and religion largely unpublished. His demise came about this way. Shortly after his doctoral defense he gave a paper on an evolutionary approach to the doctrine of original sin at a Jesuit scholasticate in Enghein, Belgium. The paper effectively denied the literal and historical existence of an original couple in a terrestrial paradise. It tentatively understood original sin as endemic to evolution framed as an uncompleted process moving toward the mutual completion of the divine and human in and through the evolutionary process itself. In 1923 Teilhard left Paris to do field research in Mongolia with a colleague who headed a Jesuit college in Tientsin, China. On his return to Paris in 1924, he was informed that his paper on original sin had come into the hands of Roman censors and that Teilhard was to sign an agreement that he would never again publish or lecture on the correlation of traditional theology with evolution. After some foot dragging on Teilhard's part the demand was repeated in 1925 with the further stipulation that he should give up his post at the Institut Catholique and leave France. Teilhard was forced to give his signature to six propositions. The most difficult stated that the Book of Genesis was to be taken literally. He signed with the dubious reservation that the signing was an external compliance but internally he continued to hold to his scientific beliefs, a dissimulation he was later to personally regret. [11,12]

---

7 Pierre Teilhard de Chardin, *Ecrits du temps de la guerre*.

8 Pierre Teilhard de Chardin, "Recherce, Travail et Adoration," in *Science et Christ*.

9 Teilhard, "Mon Univers," in *Ecrits du temps de la guerre*, p. 271.

10 Lukas, *Teilhard, the Man, the Priest, the Scientist*, pp. 67-71.

11 Lukas, *Teilhard, the Man, the Priest, the Scientist*, pp. 85-95.

12 Speaight, *Teilhard de Chardin, a Biography*, pp.136-141.

In 1926 he sailed again for China. From that point forward he was a *persona non grata* in France with both the French Jesuit establishment and French Church though never with the academic community. His exile in China effectively stretched from 1926 to 1945. It was not totally fruitless. In the world of science he was an early witness to the discovery of homo *sinanthropus* in 1929.[13] During the China exile he wrote his spiritual masterpiece,[14] and later, trapped in Beijing during the war, his summa, *The Phenomenon of Man* from 1939-1940.[15]

During this period, 1926-1945, Teilhard had returned briefly to France on a number of occasions but never with the possibility of staying. On his return after the Second World War, Europe was enjoying a short-lived liberal theological renaissance, the so-called "nouvelle theologie."[16] He hoped on this occasion that finally his work would be published. He had *The Phenomenon of Man* read by friendly theological critics, Jesuit and non-Jesuit. Revisions were asked for and made.[17] After much effort, including the revisions and a trip to Rome in 1948 to plead his cause personally, it was made evident to him that permission to publish would not be granted nor would his becoming a member of the prestigious Collège de France be allowed.[18] Shortly thereafter he willed his literary corpus to Mme. Real Mortier, his Paris secretary, who, after his death, published much of his wider corpus on evolution and Christianity.[19]

In 1950 he became a member of the French Academy of Sciences.[20] In the same year the short-lived post war liberal theology ended with the papal encyclical, *Humani Generis*. It viewed evolutionary thought with suspicion, a theory yet to be proved. It rejected polygenism, and insisted on monogenism, the doctrine that all humanity descended from a single couple, as the only theory compatible with original sin as committed by historical individuals and inherited by their universal descendants.[21]

---

13 Lukas, *Teilhard, the Man, the Priest, the Scientist*, pp. 112-114.

14 Pierre Teilhard de Chardin, Teilhard, *Le Milieu Divin*, pp. 103-106.

15 Teilhard, *Le Milieu Divin*, pp. 167-175.

16 Speaight, *Teilhard de Chardin, a Biography*. p. 277.

17 Lukas, *Teilhard, the Man, the Priest, the Scientist*, pp. 234-5.

18 Lukas, *Teilhard, the Man, the Priest, the Scientist*, pp. 263-272.

19 Lukas, *Teilhard, the Man, the Priest, the Scientist*, pp. 226-227, 290.

20 Lukas, *Teilhard, the Man, the Priest, the Scientist*, p. 283.

21 H. Denzinger, "Humani generis," 12. Aug. 1950, in *Enchiridion Symbolorum Definitionum et Declarationum de Rebus Fidei et Morum*, pp. 773, 779, 780.

Teilhard's response was to label such a position as purely theological devoid of scientific support.[22]

Teilhard spent his final years in exile in New York City where he held a position with the Wenner-Gren Foundation. It supported him in some late field work in South Africa. He died on Easter Sunday, 1955. He was then living with a single Jesuit companion in a New York hotel while his Jesuit residence attached to a large parish was under repair.[23] He was buried in a Jesuit cemetery along the Hudson River, sixty miles north of New York City.[24] Such was the end of a brilliant mind made tragic by an authority that feared the consequences of bringing its ideology into harmony with science in a culture from which it continues to grow progressively estranged.

In 1962, after Teilhard's death, the Vatican issued a "*monitum,*" a warning, against Teilhard's works which, "…abound in such ambiguities and indeed even serious errors, as to offend Catholic doctrine."[25] It was read in all Catholic institutes of theology and higher learning. In 1981 in the response to a letter appreciative of Teilhard's work published in *L'Osservatore Romano*, the Vatican reaffirmed the *monitum* of 1962. The then pope, Joseph Ratzinger, initially was rejective of Teilhard's influence on the document on the Church and World issued by the second Vatican Council but in 2009 Ratzinger praised Teilhard by name for his vision of a "cosmic liturgy where the cosmos becomes a living host."[26] In spite of this favorable bent in the evolution of Ratzinger's thought on Teilhard, the *monitum* has never been formally withdrawn nor an apology issued to its target. What was it all about?

Just as so much of Jung's later work is foreshadowed in his *Red Book* so can much of Teilhard's in his earliest essays on the topic of creation written in 1917 during his service in the First World War. The most important essays were entitled, *La Lutte contre la Multitude*, February 26, 1917, and *L'Union creatrice*, November, 1917.[27] That the fundamental themes of these essays never lost their centrality in Teilhard's mind

---

22 Pierre Teilhard de Chardin, "Monogenisme et Monophyletism, une Distinction Essentielle a Faire," in *Comment je Crois*, pp. 247-249.

23 Lukas, *Teilhard, the Man, the Priest, the Scientist*, pp. 338, 343.

24 Speaight, *Teilhard de Chardin, a Biography*, p. 332.

25 "Monitum, Concerning the Writings of Father Teilhard de Chardin," June 30, 1962, reiterated July 20, 1981.

26 "Teilhard at Vespers," the Editors, in *America*, August 17, 2009, Vol. 201, no 4.

27 Teilhard, "La Lutte contre la Multitude," in *Ecrits du temps de la guerre*, pp. 113-132. Teilhard de Chardin, "L'Union creatrice," in *Ecrits du temps de la guerre*, pp. 175-197.

is evident in their recurrence in some of his major essays in the last decade of his life, and especially in his *Comment je vois*, August 26, 1948. His earliest syntheses of his religious and scientific commitments took on the form of the reconciliation of the Christian conception of creation and fall with the truth of evolution. Looking at the empirical evidence for evolution he argued that it moves from the less complex to the more complex culminating in the human brain and stem as the most complex physical organism extant. In this process greater organic complexity always correlates with gains in consciousness. In the human the complexity of the brain enables not only consciousness but self-consciousness. These observations then become the basis of the law he saw running throughout the entire evolutionary process, the law of recurrence or of complexity/consciousness. The law simply affirms the empirical correlation between increased organic complexity in any organism and an increased consciousness in that organism.

The Extrapolations: Past and Future

It is on this basis Teilhard extrapolates both into the past and into the future. As he follows the line of evolution backwards the evidence compels him to associate lesser forms of organic complexity with diminished consciousness. Pushed to the ultimate such diminishment driven by a real force toward disintegration would vanish into a total multiplicity and so into nothing. The primeval, near mythical, scene he conjures up from this backward looking extrapolation is that of a primordial power of unification facing an near equal primordial force of disintegration moving toward non-being.[28] In this imagination of the origin, forever beyond empirical sight, the power of unification becomes a divine energy creating by reversing the power to dissolution and drawing out of such nothingness ever greater configurations of organic sophistication culminating in the human organism. This primordial battle between the power of ever greater organic unity and its possible defeat in a regression toward a pulverizing dispersion becomes the battle fought throughout the entire history of evolution. The war grants a certain preliminary victory to the power of unification evident in the organic complexity creating the soul and self-consciousness at the human level of evo-

---

28 Teilhard, "La Lutte contre la Multitude," in *Ecrits du temps de la guerre*, pp. 113-4.

lution.[29] This outcome itself then posits, as will be seen, the question of whether evolution in some sense continues through the human stratum it has presently reached toward a consciousness and community beyond the present.

Matter and Spirit

In these categories Teilhard can describe the power to dissolution as the energy of matter and the power to enhanced organic unity as the energy of spirit. These two forms of energy are never without each other. Matter always serves as the material for the greater physical organization and increased consciousness which spirit works and spirit is a product of the matter it unites in itself.[30] In this sense Teilhard will understand the deepest energy of evolution moving to spirit as it unites matter in ever greater patterns of physical complexity supporting greater consciousness and ultimately self-consciousness. Evolution becomes self-conscious in the human spirit and the human then becomes itself the matter for Teilhard's extrapolation of the future as a continuation of the process that created humanity.

He comes then to understand humanity itself and each human as currently the matter for a further unification toward a community of greater spirit, that is, of a universal human organism worked by the same power that worked the physical complexity of the human brain. This future total unity of humanity completes humanity and the divine itself as the energy bringing about this final community of total communion. This envisioned community Teilhard patterns on the image of the brain in which each individual life would act as a neuron highly differentiated in itself and yet wholly united with the total brain. Teilhard's terms this outcome "Point Omega" and that toward which evolutionary energies move. If divinity be understood as the energy empowering evolution then this final point would be the mutual culmination of both that energy and the humanity it has created and through whom it now works to complete both humanity and itself. As distinguished a respondent as Sir Julian Huxley could appreciate Teilhard's backward extrapolation and its tracing the pattern of evolution to the human level but draws back from Teilhard's extrapolation into a fu-

---

29 Teilhard, "La Lutte contre la Multitude," in *Ecrits du temps de la guerre*, pp. 114-6.
30 Teilhard, "L'Union creatrice," in *Ecrits du temps de la guerre*, pp. 177-180.

ture in which this same energy moves through the human to a final community.[31] The future remains questionable for many as does access to the energies that have lead to the present development of the brain and to Teilhard's future vision of a community of a highly differentiated but unified humanity at both the collective and personal level. For Teilhard it was never in doubt because of the impact of these energies on his person fortified by the evidence of his field work.

Individual and Collective

In this vision not only does the dichotomy between matter and spirit dissolve, so does that between individual and community. As individuals are grasped by the unifying power moving through evolution they are developed as individuals whose individuality is intensified by its relation to the totality and the final communion of individuals the underlying energy seeks. The unifying energy that runs through the depth and breadth of evolution grounds Teilhard's claim that union creates and union differentiates. Union creates because each stage of evolution is marked by greater unified organic complexity. Something new emerges as the matter seeking greater union and so higher spirit is realized. Union differentiates because to the extent the individual relates to the universal power of union the individual is made more distinct by the relationship itself rather than being dissolved in a featureless collectivity, the "isms" of Jung's critique of archetypally bonded communities of unconsciousness. Teilhard's example here is again that of the cell in the body. As a member of the most physically complex organism, the human body, the human cell is also the most developed of individual cells. On the basis of this sketch of the foundational elements of Teilhard's synthesis of the energies of evolution and religion the following six points of affinity with Jung's understanding of psychic energy emerge.

---

31 J. Huxley, "Introduction," in Teilhard de Chardin's book, *The Phenomenon of Man*, pp. 16, 19.

First: The Synthesis of Personal Integration and Universal Relatedness

Jung's description of the processes of individuation centre on two characteristics which at first sight seem to be contradictory, namely, the development of the individual as individual and an intensified relation of the individual to the totality. Development of the psychic integration of the individual correlates directly with a more positive relatedness to the totality best described as compassion. Jung can make this correlation only because he understands a universal power to be engaged in the development of the individual. This is nowhere more evident than in his understanding of the alchemical unus mundus. As the culmination of individuation, alchemically described, this state is one in which the individual attains the height of one's individuality through a conscious resonance with the ground of one's personal being which is also the "... eternal Ground of all empirical being...."[32] The union of the personal with the universal is the persistent intent and urging of the self. More, Jung's master images of individuation, namely, the mandala, the anthropos and the reality of synchronicity all assume that the culmination of individual consciousness moves toward the embrace of the totality at the insistence of the same energy that gives rise to both the mind and the totality and remains their active substrate.[33]

Teilhard's understanding of the basic energy at work in the universe works in a remarkably similar way. In a simple but incisive reflection on the evolutionary meaning of purity and charity, he understands purity to be attained in one's adherence to the personally integrating energy running through the universe and charity to be the result of such purity expressed in a heightened love of all of humanity and of all that is.[34] Thus considered purity and charity are two sides of the same evolutionary energy linked as closely as Jung's understanding of a foundational libido working to unite personal integration with extended empathy.

---

32 C.G. Jung, *Mysterium Coniunctionis*, CW 14, ¶ 760.

33 Jung, *Mysterium Coniunctionis*, CW 14, ¶¶ 662, 768.

34 Teilhard, "La Lutte contre la Multitude," in *Ecrits du temps de la guerre*, pp. 126-7.

Second: The Role of Necessity in Psychic and Religious Growth

Jung's psychology attaches a certain necessity to the development of the psyche's full potential working through the individual toward extended societal consequence. This necessity begins with the emergence of the ego from its unconscious matrix to serve as the only site in which the archetypal unconscious can become conscious. As maturation continues the ego must reenter its maternal origin in the interests of the renewal of consciousness not once but as the very rhythm of growth. Denial of either necessity, the emergence of ego or its cyclical return to its origin, impoverishes or kills psychic development.[35] Imprisonment in mind or in its origin is equally lethal. In the face of such psychic compulsion the individual must grow or die. Jung leaves no place to stand outside these options in the universal drama of maturation.

Teilhard faced strong and continued opposition for his understanding of necessity and particularly for the necessity he locates in divinity in its act of creation. The question is this: In his mythic reconstruction of creation, could the primordial power of unification facing the power of dispersal into nothingness have been anything less than necessitated in reversing this drive to non-being and in so doing creating through the evolutionary process thus initiated? Teilhard wrestled with the question throughout his life and toward its end was satisfied with the answer that where love is present there is freedom and no necessity.[36] However, one cannot escape the conclusion that had divinity as a unifying power not exercised its energy, creation would not have happened and the originating divinity would be impoverished by the absence of the completion it gains in the evolutionary process.

Not only does Teilhard seem forced by his own logic to place necessity in creation if divinity is to be completed in it, he further seems compelled to affirm the eternity of matter as that co-existing power of dispersion initially defeated in original creation and throughout ongoing evolution. A further implication of such necessity is this: Once Teilhard introduces the implication of a divine necessity to create in reversing a co-eternal force toward dispersion he also removes an arbitrary contingency and self-

---

35 Teilhard, "La Lutte contre la Multitude," in *Ecrits du temps de la guerre*, p. 425.
36 Pierre Teilhard de Chardin, "Comment je vois," in *Les Directions de l'avenir*, p. 209.

sufficiency in divinity's relation to the human.[37] Divinity must create in order to plete itself. Sin becomes resistance to this initially and continuing unifying p[...] Incarnation and redemption become the human alliance with the energy of evolution toward an eschatology envisioned as the mutual completion of the divine and the human in an eternal throbbing stability. Jung too follows Teilhard in his own way by showing each of the religious mysteries to have the more profound movements of the psyche as their basis and point of reference. Jung's eschatology also envisages the unity of all divinely based opposites in a spirit enriched by their synthesis. As Teilhard would have it, this more encompassing spirit would unite more and be itself a product of the union. The archetypal source of all opposites moves history and through history to its completion in the coincidence of its opposites in a wealth of consciousness luring humanity on though difficult if not impossible of attainment.

Third: The Mutual Completion of the Divine and Human in the Historical/Evolutionary Process

Both thinkers depart radically from a sense of divinity as self-sufficient in its transcendence over against a humanity for which it has no intrinsic need and which, in turn, is divested of an innate sense of such a distant divinity. When Teilhard would put his insight into a more poetic or mystical vein he would contend that humanity was susceptible to an immediate sense of the spirit of God working through matter. He would occasionally refer to this experience as an experience of the fire of God in the earth.[38] He was from his earliest years struck with the sense of the absolute as the imperishable which he sought even as a child in iron and stone. This radically immanent sense of God was intensified by his scientific work in the field and became the basis of his final synthetic affirmation that the energy informing evolution was itself divine and the experience of such energy was the experience of the divine.

Jung's late work on Job may be closer to the spirit of Boehme and Hegel, to whom critics have compared Teilhard, but this work is no less insistent than Teilhard that

---

37 Pierre Teilhard de Chardin, "Contingence de l'Univers et Gout Humain de Survivre," in *Comment je Crois*, pp. 268-9.

38 Pierre Teilhard de Chardin, "The Mass on the World," in *Hymn of the Universe*, pp. 23-9.

divinity seeks its completion in humanity and that humanity is latently aware of such.[39] Such unmediated archetypal suasion, currently working toward a new societal myth that will surpass the reigning monotheisms, was for Jung, the underlying truth of Anselm's ontological argument.[40] Jung understood the argument simply to rest on humanity's universal sense of the divine, a sense that his contemporary society had lost to its own great impoverishment. From the *Red Book* on, Jung sought to restore humanity's experiential connection with the depths of its own being. In his *Answer to Job* the restoration of the sense of God would move to the sense that God creates consciousness to become conscious in it and that this reciprocity was now dawning on the human as a new sense of the role of divinity and humanity in historical mutual fulfillment.

Fourth: Human Interiority as the Immediate Source of Psychic and Evolutionary Energies

Jung is explicit on the fact that the psychic energies that ground humanity's sense of God approach consciousness through human interiority. In his work on the mystic, Meister Eckhart, the intimacy Jung establishes between the divine and human makes of each a "function" of the other in historical processes of their intensifying mutual interpenetration.[41] In this same work Jung understands Eckhart's mystic regression into his interior life to culminate in an "identity" with God.[42] More, he claims that those unaware that the approach of the divine to humanity is from within humanity are unaware of the nature of religion itself.[43] Jung's understanding of the "relativization of God" expands on this notion that divinity seeks its self-consciousness and completion in human consciousness.[44] On these grounds Jung deplores the loss of a

---

39 John Dourley, "Jung on Job and the education of God in history," in *Paul Tillich, Carl Jung and the Recovery of Religion*, pp. 111-126.
40 C.G. Jung, *Psychological Types*, CW 6, ¶ 62.
41 Jung, *Psychological Types*, CW 6, ¶ 412.
42 Jung, *Psychological Types*, CW 6, ¶ 431.
43 Jung, *Psychological Types*, CW 6, ¶ 413.
44 C.G. Jung, "Answer to Job," in *Psychology and Religion: West and East*, CW 11, ¶ 595.

pantheistic sense in Christianity which in effect amounts to the removal of Christian consciousness from the "…monistic origin of all life."[45]

Teilhard too called for the recovery of a qualified pantheistic sensitivity. At times, especially in his early writing, he deplores a pantheism and monism that would be a kind of enervating regression to a world beyond form and activity, a kind of spiritual lethargy.[46] However this critique of pantheism was more generally to bow to its validity as the experience of the energy empowering evolution. This experience generates a sense of the religion of the totality, a sense embedded in the soul itself.[47] The pantheistic drive to a religion of the whole in which God and humanity are mutually completed is the basis of Teilhard's exhortation "…to bring to Christ a little fulfillment."[48] In this passage Christ is a symbol of the mutual completion of the divine and human. For those in resonance with such a pantheistic thrust he could write, "…nothing here below is profane for those who know how to see."[49]

An event in Teilhard's spiritual adventure is reminiscent of Jung's descent into the unconscious in the period after the break with Freud greatly elaborated in his *Red Book*. Teilhard refers to the event under the rubric, "The Two Hands of God." In his imagination he took lantern in hand and entered his "inmost self," the fontal abyss from which his life and activity emanate. He continues, "At each step of the descent a new person was disclosed within me of whose name I was no longer sure, and who no longer obeyed me." Finally he faced the "abyss" from which flowed, "…the current I dare to call my life." On his return to the surface he did not escape the abyss. Rather he confesses he saw it in his study of evolution toward ever greater consciousness and communion.[50] His point is that the discovery of his possession by the hand of God within was reflected in the hand of God without in the reality of evolution to whose

45 Jung, *Mysterium Coniunctionis*, CW 14, ¶ 773: C.G. Jung, "Psychological Commentary on 'The Tibetan Book of the Great Liberation,'" in *Psychology and Religion: West and East*, CW 11, ¶ 798.

46 Teilhard de Chardin, *Le Milieu Divin*, p. 116.

47 Teilhard de Chardin, "Pantheism et Christianisme," in *Comment je Crois*, pp. 81, 83-91. de Chardin, *Le Milieu Divin*, p.130.

48 de Chardin, *Le Milieu Divin*, p. 62.

49 de Chardin, *Le Milieu Divin*, p. 66.

50 de Chardin, *Le Milieu Divin*, pp. 77-8.

study he devoted his life. In this pursuit he came to identify work and worship as to sides of the same reality.[51]

Fifth: The Shared Rejection of Aristotelian/Thomistic Philosophy and Theology

Both Jung and Teilhard fought against Aristotelian philosophy and theology throughout their lives. In Jung this issue was at the heart of his fifteen year discussion with Victor White O.P. concluding with the mutual recognition that Jung's psychology was not compatible with White's Thomism.[52] The latter derived from Leo XIII's imposition of Thomism on the Church in 1879. It rested on the dualism of a supernatural over against a natural order.[53] Jung's naturalism too intimately related a divinity becoming self conscious to the development of human historical consciousness. Such intimacy could not tolerate a world of supernatural entities, one of whom was God, intervening periodically and arbitrarily in the historic flow of human maturation and the evolution of the religious instinct. Jung could not tolerate a substantialist conception of God as a divine entity and agent eternally fully determined and self-sufficient beyond the created world understood as an equally substantial or fixed entity over against Him. For Jung an experiential relation to a God within was the generative source of all religion and the basis of the projection of divinity beyond the human. As humanity currently recovered this projection its internalization contributed jointly to the advance in consciousness of the divine and the human. These same issued were at stake in Jung's earlier more vitriolic debate with Buber. In it Buber's God was revealed as the all too familiar God who dwelt in a heaven beyond humanity and beyond immediate human experience. Buber's God addressed humanity from a position beyond

---

51 Teilhard de Chardin, "Recherce, Travail et Adoration," in *Science et Christ*, pp. 283-9.

52 John Dourley, "Jung on Job and the education of God in history," in *Paul Tillich, Carl Jung and the Recovery of Religion*, pp. 95-134.

53 John Dourley, "The Jung-White Dialogue; Why It Couldn't Work and Won't Go Away," *The Journal of Analytical Psychology*, Vol. 52, No. 3, June, 2007, pp. 275-296.

it.[54] Simply capitalizing the archaic form of the second person singular could not alleviate the alienation of so wholly a transcendent God.

Teilhard's life long joust with Thomism was even more intense. He too consistently rejected from the time of his early essays the notion of a completed and self-sufficient God periodically and gratuitously intervening in human history first to create it and then to redeem it in the wake of its unfortunate and unlikely fall. Thomism ruled the church in Teilhard's day and was adamantly opposed to all that flowed from Teilhard's understanding of God as the energy at work in evolution in a process completing both God and humanity in one organic movement. As he moved through these questions Teilhard simply dispensed with a God external to the process and understood creation, fall, incarnation, and redemption as diverse moments or aspects of the one energy pulsing in all of human and pre-human nature.[55] This point is introduced and exercised because in the popular, contemporary mind of both theist and atheist the Thomistic image of a transcendent completed God continues to prevail.

Sixth: The Questionable Adequacy of Religious Orthodoxies to Foster the Future Growth of the Human Species

In one of his earliest writings Jung accused unnamed "…spokesmen of religion…" of failing to provide their time and culture with an apology for symbolic discourse and so for religion itself.[56] His target was, no doubt, Christianity. Much of Jung's later work is devoted to the development of such an apology. It went on to identify the origin of religion as the experience of the impact of archetypal forces on consciousness initially expressed in symbol because of the intensity of the impact itself. Such impact created the transcendent Gods in projection. In Jung's revision these Gods were now to be accessed primarily through the individual's personal conversation with his or her creative origin within the containment of Jung's enormous extension of the boundaries of the archetypal psyche. The conversation of the individual with the Gods operative in each life, primarily through the dream as personal revelation, then

---

54 John Dourley, "Jung, White and the End of the Pilgrimage," in *On Behalf of the Mystical Fool, Jung on the Religious Situation*, pp. 69-94.

55 Teilhard, "Reflexions sur le Peche Originel," in *Comment je Crois*, p. 224.

56 C.G. Jung, *Symbols of Transformation*, CW 5, ¶ 336.

becomes a major contributor to a now emerging societal myth in the West. Much of this myth is evident in Jung's shift to a quaternitarian perspective. In this now superseding myth all of creation would be divinized including the feminine, the demonic and the bodily. These powers are obviously present in creation but not in the Trinity as creation's alleged source. The urgency of the myth would derive from the revelatory compensation the unconscious currently affords to the religious and political mythologies controlling and now pathologizing Western societies. Jung's sense of a new emerging myth supplants the monotheisms to whose constrictive perspectives Jungian psychology cannot be reduced. His working out his apology for religion thus becomes prophetic of a new cultural religious sensitivity able to embrace all that is because it rises to consciousness from the point of humanity's native inherence in the source of all that is. The monotheistic mind cannot embrace Jung's vastly more encompassing myth without significant adjustment and the real peril of self loss.

Teilhard shares a similar sympathy with Jung intensified by his rejection by the authorities within his own tradition and by his questionable submission to them. In the end he challenged his Church to adjust to the presence of the divine in the evolutionary and psychic energies that had created the Church and in whose service it gained the only legitimacy it had. Dying rejected and unpublished, some of his later essays doubt the ability of the Church to appreciate and mediate the energies that would build the future in the face of the ongoing weight of a spiritual lethargy that would cancel it. His most incisive concluding remark is that that religion will survive and be the religion of the future which fosters the evolutionary impulse toward a universal community of communion enriched by its constitutive diversity.[57] Perhaps the most compelling question surfaced in the dialogue between Teilhard and Jung is whether there currently exists an institution, religious or political, that can take up their challenge to transcend limited ideologies toward an all inclusive embrace demanded by both evolutionary and psychological energies as the two most prominent faces of the single most rudimentary power in our universe?

---

57 Teilhard, "Contingence de l'Univers et Gout Humain de Survivre," in *Comment je Crois*, p. 272.

Bibliography

America, "Teilhard at Vespers," the Editors, in *America*, August 17, 2009, Vol. 201, no 4.

Denzinger, H. "Humani generis," 12. Aug. 1950, in *Enchiridion Symbolorum Definitionum et Declarationum de Rebus Fidei et Morum*. Rome: Herder, 1965.

Dourley, J. "The Jung-White Dialogue; Why It Couldn't Work and Won't Go Away," *The Journal of Analytical Psychology*, Vol. 52, No. 3, June, 2007.

Dourley, J. "Jung on Job and the education of God in history," in *Paul Tillich, Carl Jung and the Recovery of Religion*. Hove: Routledge, 2008.

Dourley, J. "Jung, White and the End of the Pilgrimage," in *On Behalf of the Mystical Fool, Jung on the Religious Situation*. Hove: Routledge, 2010.

Dourley, J. "Martin Buber and the Insane Asylum," in *On Behalf of the Mystical Fool, Jung on the Religious Situation*. Hove: Routledge, 2010.

Holy Office. "Monitum, Concerning the Writings of Father Teilhard de Chardin" in June 30, 1962, reiterated July 20, 1981.

Huxley, J. "Introduction," to Teilhard de Chardin's book, *The Phenomenon of Man*. New York: Harper, 1959.

Jung, C.G. "Answer to Job," in *Psychology and Religion*: *West and East*, CW 11. Princeton: Princeton University Press, 1954.

Jung, C.G. "Psychological Commentary on 'The Tibetan Book of the Great Liberation'," in *Psychology and Religion*: *West and East*, CW 11. Princeton: University Press, 1954.

Jung, C.G. *Symbols of Transformation*, CW 5. Princeton: Princeton University Press, 1966.

Jung, C.G. *Psychological Types*, CW 6. Princeton: Princeton, 1971. University Press.

Jung, C.G. *Mysterium Coniuntionis,* CW 14. Princeton: Princeton University Press, 1970.

Jung, C.G. *The Red Book*, ed. Sonu Shamdasani. London & New York: W.W. Norton and Company, 2008.

Lukas, Mary and Ellen *Teilhard, the Man, The Priest, The Scientist*. New York: Doubleday, 1997.

Speaight, R. *Teilhard de Chardin, A Biography*. London: Collins, 1967.

Teilhard de Chardin, Pierre. "La Lutte contre la Multitude," in *Ecrits du temps de la guerre (1916-1919)*. Paris: Bernard Grasset, 1917.

Teilhard de Chardin, Pierre. "L'Union creatrice," in *Ecrits du temps de la guerre (1916-1919)*. Paris: Bernard Grasset, 1917.

Teilhard de Chardin, Pierre. "Mon Univers," in *Ecrits du temps de la guerre (1916-1919)*. Paris: Bernard Grasset, 1918.

Teilhard de Chardin, Pierre. "The Mass on the World," in *Hymn of the Universe*. New York: Harper and Row, 1961.

Teilhard de Chardin, Pierre. "Pantheism et Christianisme," in *Comment je Crois*. Paris: Editions du Seuil, 1969.

Teilhard de Chardin, Pierre. *Le Milieu Divin*. New York: Harper/Fontana, 1960.

Teilhard de Chardin, Pierre. "Reflexions sur le Peche Originel," in *Comment je crois*. Paris: Editions du Seuil, 1969.

Teilhard de Chardin, Pierre. "Comment je vois," in *Les Directions de l'avenir*, Paris: Editions du Seuil. 1948.

Teilhard de Chardin, Pierre. "Monogenisme et Monophyletism, une Distinction Essentielle a Faire," in *Comment je Crois*. Paris: Editions du Seuil, 1969.

Teilhard de Chardin, Pierre. "Contingence de l'univers et Gout Humain de Survivre," in *Comment je Crois*. Paris: Editions du Seuil, 1969.

Teilhard de Chardin, Pierre. "Recherce, Travail et Adoration," in *Science et Christ*. Paris: Edition du Seuil, 1965.

Teilhard de Chardin, Pierre. *Ecrits du temps de la guerre (1916-1919)*. Paris: Bernard Grasset, 1968.

8

TEILHARD'S NOT-SO-HIDDEN GOD

Laura A. Weber, Ph.D.

"P.T." was an affectionate designation by the significant woman in his life. It stood for "Precious Teilhard,"[1] the man whose charismatic warmth and mystical insight ignited the spiritual imagination of a generation. Pierre Teilhard de Chardin, S.J. was a scientific genius credited with the discovery and interpretation of "Peking Man," a prescient visionary who found God's dynamic presence in the fiery, evolving cosmos, in the material holiness of rocks and dirt, in the stars, and in the unfolding mysteries of the universe. His ground-breaking work during the anti-Modernist crisis, blending geology, paleontology, cosmology, spirituality, and Christian mysticism marked him as a respected intellectual and spiritual pioneer in the realms of science and religion, especially his contributions to an understanding of a new Christology suitable for evolving cosmologies. Teilhard's understanding of Jesus was rooted the high Christology of the Gospel according to John, in which Christ was portrayed as the exalted, pre-existent Logos of God. Likewise, the so-called "Hymn of the Cosmic Christ" from the letter to the Colossians (1:15-20) inspired Teilhard's early Christology with its Gnostic, hierarchical cosmology, placing Christ at the apex of all creation, in whom resides the "Pleroma," or the "fullness." (Col. 1:19)

Teilhard proclaimed a knowledge and love of God in the "noosphere" – the realm of evolutionary consciousness – and his Christology, or theology of the Christ, reflected his teleology, or the study of final causes, i.e., the goal of all creation was the evolutionary culmination of divinized matter, or Christ, which he called the "Omega Point." This kind of thinking, with its specialized jargon and neo-logisms like "noosphere" and "Omega Point," got him censured, banned from pre-death publication of his most substantive works, prevented him from giving prestigious lectures, holding

---

1 Ursula King. *Spirit of Fire: The Life and Vision of Teilhard de Chardin*, p. 147.

teaching posts, and receiving appointments to distinguished chairs in the academy. Corresponding with Modernist scholar and countryman Maurice Blondel, outspoken critic of the Church's anti-Modernist attempts to clamp down on progressive thinking, Teilhard was found to be in error for his unique blend of evolutionary cosmology and Christian mysticism.[2] He was in perennial trouble with his Jesuit superiors and the Vatican, even though his Jesuit companions, like the notable Thomistic theologian, Henri de Lubac, S.J., knew he was a man ahead of his time, while remaining deeply embedded in his time. He was evolving in human consciousness, spurring on the creative development of the material universe, even though much of his life was devoted to understanding the fossils of the past. Whence did all this creative energy in Teilhard arise, and how did his natural curiosity for understanding the past converge with his intense desire to progress toward the future?

From his youthful days in the central French province of Auvergne with the volcanic remains in the forested mountains, he inherited a deep love of Mother Earth, relished her mysteries, and immersed himself in the rocks and the dirt, revealing an emerging vocation in geology and paleontology only surpassed in intensity by his spiritual fervor and theological curiosity and amazement. In a letter to long-time companion Lucile Swan, he once claimed there was no better way for rejuvenation, and even adoration, than to be "in close contact with old mother Earth." This he learned at his mother's knees. He attributed his mother's piety as the "spark" of Chris-

---

2   Henri Bergson's *Creative Evolution*, the anti-Modernist writings by Pope Pius X, and Teilhard's discovery of a fossil tooth in the chalk cliffs of Hastings, England were three occasions noted by Teilhard that had a significant impact on his thinking during his formative years as a young Jesuit. From Bergson, he adopted – and later revised – an understanding of an evolving universe, through the movement of time, an ongoing unfolding and evolving of matter. Because of Pius X's attacks on Modernism in the encyclicals "Pascendi" (1907) and "Lamentabili" (1907), which had as a practical effect the placement of Bergson's work on evolution on the Index of Forbidden Works, Teilhard responded by attempting to articulate more clearly the contributions of modern science, and the accompanying developments in philosophy, to theology and spirituality. In his association with renowned paleontologist Charles Dawson, Teilhard's discovery of a fossil tooth enflamed his enthusiasm for the study of prehistoric life, and led to his earned doctorate in the geology of the Eocene Period in 1922 at the Institut Catholique, and later to his well-known work in Tientsin, China, and the Ordos Desert west of Peking, where he was instrumental in the discovery of "Peking Man."

tian mysticism that ignited his own unique brand of spirituality.[3] If his mother's spiritual piety was the spark for his spiritual birth, it was his service as a stretcher-bearer in the Moroccan infantry in World War I that sealed his vocation. In that war he earned the medal of valor and his experience of caring for the wounded forever branded him as a compassionate servant.[4] Sharing in the suffering and death of others gave him a special affinity for the other-centered love for which he was well known. As a Jesuit scholastic, it was his studies in philosophy and theology that captured his imagination and endowed him with the notion of the "progress" or "evolution" of the universe toward an Omega Point, the "Pleroma" or "fullness," the culmination of desire, union, and fulfillment. His mother's nature-based Christian mysticism, his war-time philosophical reflections, and this theological studies formed the man some have called a "keeper of the fire." Reflecting on his spiritual journey, he said:

> The world gradually caught fire for me, burst into flames;… this happened all during my life, and as a result of my whole life, until it formed a great luminous mass, lit from within, that surrounded me. …the crimson glow of matter … the Divine radiating from the depths of blazing Matter.[5]

---

3 Pierre Teilhard de Chardin, *The Heart of Matter*, p. 4. "A spark had to fall upon me, to make the fire blaze out. And, without a doubt, it was through my mother that it came to me, sprung from the stream of Christian mysticism, to light up and kindle my childish soul. It was through that spark that 'My universe,' still but hafpersonalized, was to become amorised, and so achieve its full centration."

4 Pierre Teilhard de Chardin, *The Making of a Mind*, pp. 119-20. "I don't know what sort of monument the country will later put up on Froideterre hill to commemorate the great battle. There's only one that would be appropriate: a great figure of Christ. Only the image of the crucified can sum up, express, and relieve all the horror, and beauty, all the hope and deep mystery in such an avalanche of conflict and sorrows. As I looked at this scene of bitter toil, I felt completely overcome by the thought that I had the honour of standing at one of the two or three spots on which, at this very moment, the whole life of the universe surges and ebbs places of pain but it is there that a great future (this I believe more and more) is taking shape."

5 Teilhard, *The Heart of Matter*, p. 16.

Igniting a Fire

After his battlefield experience and intense existential questioning during the first World War, he was completely enraptured by the symbolism of fire, a transforming, fusing, purging fire, and he kept an image of the Sacred Heart of Jesus, aflame with the passion of divine love, foremost in his thoughts, devotions, and in his writings. One could merely glance at his mystical writings and still encounter Teilhard's consuming fascination and exhilaration with fire, and notice how he associated the transforming energy of fire with the Spirit's ongoing work of evolution in the universe.

"Once again the Fire has penetrated the earth." Teilhard wrote in "Mass on the World" in *The Hymn of the Universe.* He had found himself isolated in the sands of the Ordos desert without access to bread and wine, and wanted to celebrate the mass. Imagining the entire created world as God's altar and gift, and the elements of nature as sacramentals, Teilhard called down the Fire of the Holy Spirit, visible in the sunrise and the palpable energy of the universe, to consecrate the Sacred Earth and transform all matter into the Body of Christ. He exclaimed:

> Without earthquake, or thunderclap: the flame has lit up the whole world from within. All things individually and collectively are penetrated and flooded by it, from the innermost core of the tiniest atom to the mighty sweep of the most universal laws of being: so naturally has it flooded every element, every energy, every connecting-link in the unity of our cosmos; that one might suppose the cosmos to have burst spontaneously into flame.[6]

In Teilhard's case, the symbol and the signified, the poetic and the material fire were complementary aspects of one reality, never to be separated except for pedagogical demonstration. He felt consumed by the fire, and longed for the fire:

> If the Fire has come down into the heart of the world it is, in the last resort, to lay hold on me and to absorb me. Henceforth I cannot be content simply to contemplate it or, by my steadfast faith, to intensify its ardency more and more in the world around me. What I must do, when I have taken part with all my energies in the consecration which causes its flames to leap forth, is to consent to the communion which will enable it to find in me the food it has come in the last resort to seek. So, my God, I prostrate myself before your presence in the universe which has now become living

---

6 Pierre Teilhard de Chardin, *Hymn of the Universe*, p. 23.

flame: beneath the lineaments of all that I shall encounter this day, all that happens to me, all that I achieve, it is you I desire, you I await.[7]

The fire of his life was a spiritual zeal and creative dynamism he experienced both as a world-class scientist and a fervent believer. This fervor was complemented and enhanced by the profound attraction, erotic desire and creative pleasure he found in human relationship. He had remarked in a prose poem called, "The Eternal Feminine" (borrowed from Goethe's *Faust*):

> the tender compassion, the hallowed charm, that radiate from woman – so naturally that it is only in her that you look for them, and yet so mysteriously that you cannot say whence they come – are the presence of God making itself felt and setting you ablaze.[8]

Teilhard was likewise enthralled with Dante's *Divine Comedy*, especially its astounding portrayal of the feminine divine symbolized by the "holy" Beatrice. Having already adored his mother and fallen in love with his cousin, Marguerite on the eve of the First World War, Teilhard had already encountered the feminine face of the divine as a young man. Certainly, he was a man on fire for God, the not-so-hidden God who was emerging in the unfolding of creation. He also found himself enflamed by the simple beauty and infinitely complex particularity of a lovely companion named Lucile.

Dearest Lucile

Teilhard's long-standing intimate relationship with Lucile Swan, in whom he confided his deepest desires, fears, disappointments, and hopes, provides a hermeneutical key for unlocking Teilhard's interior thought processes and spiritual mysticism. Her influence is noticeable in his most influential and substantive writings, *The Divine Milieu* and *The Phenomenon of Man*. She was a talented sculptress and portrait artist from Sioux City, Iowa, who became his "dearest," a divorced Christian woman of considerable artistic skill and spiritual substance who captured his heart, and shared

---

7 Teilhard, *Hymn of the Universe*, p. 29.
8 Pierre Teilhard de Chardin, *Writings in Times of War*, p. 201.

his deepest desires. Entrusted with sculpting the bust of Peking Man that had been reconstructed from Teilhard's paleontological findings, Lucile became for Teilhard a companion and soul-friend who shared his philosophical worldview, and a fellow visionary and artist who appreciated and shared his creative artistry. In March, 1934, in reply to a "glorious letter" from Lucile, Teilhard declared:

> You have entered more deep than ever, as an active seed, the innermost of myself. You bring me what I need for carrying on the work which is before me: a tide of life. Sometimes I think I would like to vanish before you *into* some thing which would be bigger than myself, - your real self, Lucile, - your real life, *your* God. And then I should be yours, completely. What is born between us is to live forever.[9]

A humble, holy man tethered to his vow of chastity in the Society of Jesus, and unaccustomed to the obvious surprise and unscripted dance of mutual intimacy with Lucile, Teilhard put to test his understanding and resolve as a celibate Jesuit. It was in the early-going of their relationship that he penned "The Evolution of Chastity," dated February, 1934, in which he claimed that the feminine is "matter in its most virulent form."[10] Primarily his relationship with Lucile challenged his sense of the superiority of the chaste state, and of the desirability of spiritualized relationships. Since in his worldview matter was becoming divinized, and therefore spiritualized, Teilhard viewed physical relationships as a shadow only of human desires for ultimate spiritual communion with God. Being in Lucile's company, however, made him aware that she was no shadow, and he was no spirit. His old dualistic categories, inherited from the old cosmologies were, in an experiential way, collapsing. But he had neither the reconstructive categories yet, nor the interior freedom, to recast erotic human love and his experiential knowledge of the love of this woman, as anything other than a lower, less spiritual state.

---

9 Thomas M. King, S.J., and Mary Wood Gilbert, eds., *The Letters of Teilhard de Chardin and Lucile Swan*, p. 19.

10 Pierre Teilhard de Chardin, "The Evolution of Chastity" in *Toward the Future*, p. 66.

Human Love, Energy and the Desire for Union

In Building the Earth, Teilhard spoke of transforming human love into spiritual energy.

> The earth is burning uselessly. Idly. Wastefully. How much energy do you think is lost to the Spirit of the Earth in one night? Man must instead perceive the universal reality which shines spiritually through the flesh. He will then discover what has so far frustrated and perverted his power to love. Woman is put before him as the attraction and the symbol of the world. He can unite with her only by enlarging himself in turn to the scale of the world. And because the world is always larger, and always unfinished and always in advance of us, to achieve this love Man thus finds himself embarked on a limitless conquest of the Universe. In this sense, Man can reach woman only through the consummation of the universal union.[11]

Human love, he thought, was evolving in the noosphere, when

> man and woman – on whom life has laid the charge of advancing to the highest possible degree the spiritualization of the earth – will have to abandon that way of possessing one another which has hitherto been the only rule for living beings"… that "when, after harnessing the ether, the winds, the tides, and gravitation, we shall harness for God the energies of love. And, on that day, for the second time in the history of the world, human beings will have discovered fire.[12]

While the erotic tension in their relationship revealed a mutual desire for each other's presence, in an intellectual, emotional, and spiritual companionship, it was Lucile who wanted a complete, physical union between them. She lamented after some years of separation that Teilhard's evolved holiness seemed to her to render him without need for physical intimacy, although he himself repeatedly denied this. Teilhard reassured her that he was not invulnerable to his own desire for her, whom he called his "star," his "sounding board," his "spark," his "rejuvenation," the "very expression of his life." He wanted her "womanliness," as he had claimed, but he did not want her to make him the center of her being.[13] She, on the other hand, wanted to be with him completely.

---

11 Pierre Teilhard de Chardin, "Building the Earth," pp. 48-49.

12 Teilhard, "The Evolution of Chastity," p. 29.

13 King, *Spirit of Fire*, p. 153.

She lamented:

You've become more important in my life every day. Yes. The live, physical, real you, all of you. I want you so terribly and I am trying so hard to understand and incorporate into my being your philosophy, your views on life… I can't have you. Not really, so I must learn your way of having each other.[14]

His reply:

The problem, I told you, exists for me just as for you – although for some complex reasons, I believe to have to stick somewhat to an old solution. My line of answer, let me observe, does not exclude the 'physical' element, - since it is not some abstract spirit – but the 'woman' – which I discover in you.[15]

Like any long-term significant human relationship, theirs evolved over the years. The earlyperiod of intense desire was moderated later by extended periods of separation and loneliness, especially before and during the Second World War. They continued to write letters but their correspondence was less frequent and often painful and discordant.

Lucile wrote in July, 1934,

Perhaps it is because I have been trying to contemplate and write about the spirit of the world, God, and also because I have read your notebook and realize how much of you is unworldly. And I wrote you just before you left in which I spoke of the 'physical.' Please don't think I mean just sex, although that is very strong. It would make a bond between us that would add a strength that I believe *nothing* else can give. However, that is only a part. I want to be with you when you are well and when you are ill. Go see beautiful things with you and walk through the country. In other words, I want to stand beside you always, to laugh and play and pray with you. Don't you realize what a big part of life that is, and how that is what is right and normal and God-given? But I cannot.[16]

As Teilhard moved through his own physical decline and death, he still desired Lucile's companionship, but settled instead for her occasional letters and visits, and

---

14 King, *Spirit of Fire*, p. 17.
15 King, *Spirit of Fire*, p. 19.
16 King and Gilbert, *Letters*, p. 119.

for a nursemaid's solicitous care. This relationship with another woman moved Lucile to ill-temper and some notable jealousy, but he insisted,

> In the 'Chinese phase' of our life, not only you needed me – but we needed each other. – And now, apparently, we need each other (and we can help each other) in a different way.[17]

She insisted however that their relationship was seriously fragmented:

> …about 'us.' We meet and act as if nothing had ever existed between us… until just as we are parting some chance remark brings on others and the time being so short and the feeling of pressure so great, things are said that are too strong or not explicit… So we part with a feeling of frustration and ill ease.[18]

She reminded him of what he had told her repeatedly in their letters and in person, when their relationship was at its most strained: "What is born between us is to live forever."[19] Even though fragile and strained, their relationship sustained him in his hour of need, especially during that stultifying period of reaction by the Church known as "anti-Modernism," when Church traditionalists railed against progressive thinking.

During the most difficult periods of the rejection of his work by his Jesuit superiors, he turned to Lucile for solidarity and comfort, and cherished their relationship immeasurably. He longed for her companionship to strengthen his intellectual and spiritual resolve when his religious community and Church seemed to discourage and ostracize him. It was her characteristically thorough critique and exploration of his foundational philosophical and theological principles that gave him, as he claimed, his most profound insights, and the most pleasure. Of her contribution to his magnum opus, *The Phenomenon of Man,* Teilhard claimed that each completed essay was "a new result of our 'spiritual union,'" and thought of their work as a "single and common activity."[20]

It would be a great omission to speak of Teilhard's work on the evolving nature of the universe, especially during this time of intellectual repression, without including

---

17 King and Gilbert, *Letters,* p. 119.
18 King and Gilbert, *Letters,* p. 119.
19 King and Gilbert, *Letters,* p. 119.
20 King and Gilbert, *Letters,* p. 119.

Lucile. Teilhard's focus on union as the teleological grounding of human existence is further amplified if we understand how significant this very earthy, very human relationship of Teilhard and his "dearest" Lucile was to the substance of his work. Behind the man whose life work focused on the creative dynamism of the material realm, and the desire for union at its center, stood this fiery woman who loved him, challenged him, and enflamed him as only she could. She was, in a sense, a sacramental reminder for him of the sacredness of physicality, and her presence in his life was as instrumental for his understanding of "Cosmogenesis" as was the mystery of Christ.

It was not just Lucile who sustained Teilhard in his efforts, but his correspondence with Maurice Blondel, the Modernist scholar, that gave him courage in the midst of the suppression of his work on evolutionary cosmology and the Cosmic Christ. Teilhard styled himself as an "apostle of the Cosmic Christ."[21] In a letter to his friend, Leontine Zanta, Teilhard castigated the Church for tethering itself to old cosmologies, and pandering to anti-Modernist perspectives.

> …the Church will waste away so long as she does not escape from the factitious world of verbal theology, of quantitative sacramentalism, and over-refined devotions in which she is enveloped, so as to reincarnate herself in the real aspirations of mankind… Of course I can see well enough what is paradoxical in this attitude: if I need Christ and the Church I should accept Christ as he is presented by the Church, with its burden of rites, administration and theology… But now I can't get away from the evidence that the moment has come when the Christian impulse should 'save Christ' from the hands of the clerics so that the world may be saved.[22]

Teilhard believed Christianity was – or should be – concluding a natural phase of its existence, and should evolve into a new understanding of the world in relation to Christ. He saw this as quite consistent with the Cosmic Christ of the New Testament.[23] Following Blondel, Teilhard proclaimed a "pan-Christism," or as Ursula King called it, a "panchristic mysticism," a "magnificent transposition of the Ignatian theme of seeing God in all things and all things in God."[24] For Teilhard's Christocen-

---

21 Ursula King, *Christ in All Things: Exploring Spirituality with Teilhard de Chardin*, p. 75.
22 Teilhard de Chardin, *Letters to Leontine Zanta* (Intro. By Robert Garric and Henri de Lubac) London: Collins, 1969), pp. 34 ff.
23 King, *Christ in All Things*, pp. 76 ff.
24 King, *Christ in All Things*, p. 70.

tric cosmology, nothing could be outside of the "divine milieu," the "center point and sphere, a total environment in which we are all immersed if we can but perceive it."[25]

Final Union-The Omega Point

Teilhard's desire for union with the earth, with the past, with the future, even with Lucile, and with all the human energies at work in the noosphere were all connected in his desire for the fire that is God. The eternal optimist who loved the divine Spirit he saw rising in all matter, converging in the Omega Point, could even pronounce his hope for humanity after World War II, and for its final consummation. In "The Spiritual Repercussions of the Atom Bomb," he claimed:

> Exploding the atom… was also enough to ensure that the nightmare of bloody combat must vanish in the light of some form of growing unanimity. We are told, that drunk with its own power, mankind is rushing to destruction, that it will be consumed in the fire it has so rashly lit. On the contrary, I think that through the atom bomb war itself may be on the eve of being doubly and definitely destroyed.[26]

So strong was his belief that humanity was evolving in love toward ultimate union that even the temptation to domination and mutual destruction could give way to lasting peace, and eternal communion. Even the most terrible forces of death and destruction known to humanity could not dissuade him from his own brand of progressive optimism. "Everything that rises must converge" was Teilhard's motto, and this was during the rise of the nuclear age!

He died on Easter Sunday, 1955, April 10. A "wonderful visit" from Lucile late in March had produced great excitement in her: "What a wonderful talk we had." She viewed his latest theory as "the key to a real Unity which would lead to the spiritual awakening of which we dream." And then she added:

> Dearest, it makes me sad if I am partly the cause of your malaise. Don't let me be. You know I have found Peace and it is the thing I long for you more than anything else – the real Peace of God's presence.

---

25 King, *Christ in All Things*, pp. 96-97.
26 Chardin, *The Future of Man*, pp. 141-146 ff.

His reply was dated March 30:

> Yes, stupidly enough, I am still nervous – more nervous than I would – than I should be. And at the same time, I need definitely your presence, your influence, in my life. I hope (I am sure) that things will gradually settle, 'emotionally' speaking… In any case, we know, both of us, that we 'are always here' for each other.[27]

Presence and unity, two key facets of Teilhard's enduring relationship with Lucile, kept his faith intact, kept his hope alive for human love that evolves into divine love, and kept his ethereal philosophical worldview grounded in the muck of the earth. His religious mysticism, his single-hearted desire to find God's presence at the heart of matter was for him the unifying impetus for all his scientific endeavors. He engaged this quest for answers about humanity's evolution while searching among the bones set into rocks, covered by desert sands and preserved through time, and in his mystical celebration of the Eucharist, his "mass on the world," in which he called down sacred fire to consecrate the elements of matter and reveal the divinity within it. In his last essay written before his death, "Research, Work, and Adoration," Teilhard concluded that all human endeavors, whether in the life of the mind through scientific research and philosophical investigation, or through religious devotion, reflection, and acts of charity, should lead to adoration of the divine and ultimately greater unity among all. The end-goal for Teilhard was always the union, or the "com-munion" of humanity and divinity, the fiery consummation of all that is with all that might be. It was a union of potential and actualized energy.

Teilhard and Union

It is helpful to understand a bit about Teilhard's notion of the centrality of union, and how it worked with his concept of evolution. As a young Jesuit in studies, he was attracted to the high Christology of the Gospel According to John, in which the divinity of Jesus as the Logos of God was emphasized. Especially significant for Teilhard's understanding is the priestly prayer for unity in the final discourse from John 17:21, "That they may be one, Father, as you are in me and I am in you." The indwelling

---

27 Teilhard, *The Future of Man*, p. 153.

unity of Jesus in the Father, and the community of believers in Christ was for Teilhard an ultimate participation of all creation in the creative union of God. Nothing could be clearer or more concrete in how evolutionary progress works than through "Christogenesis," the evolving of all matter into the Cosmic Christ, the final unity, the Omega Point.

He also found himself immersed in the cosmic Christology of Paul's letters, and considered any theology of Christ deficient if it missed the point that all creation derives from and culminates in the mystery of the Incarnation, the definitive union of humanity and divinity. For this reason, he found the medieval christologies of the Franciscan theologian, Bonaventure, and the Franciscan philosopher, Duns Scotus most attractive, and with them was convinced that Christ was at the center of the material universe and belonged to the structure of the evolving cosmos.[28] The primacy of unity as the divine initiative and desire for all creation in fact became central for Teilhard in his reflections and writings. All thought, all desire, all relationship and all being was striving toward union, and for Teilhard, toward the Cosmic Christ, in whom resides the pleroma, all "fullness" or "completion." All evolutionary progress was leading toward the final point of consummation for all creation, the Omega Point, a process that was creative, dynamic, and had union as its ultimate goal. This was in contradistinction to the philosophical notion of "progress" he had inherited, in which progress was never-ending and multi-directional.

Creative Evolution

A formative contributor to Teilhard's intellectual history was Henri Bergson and his work, *Creative Evolution*, published in 1911. In that work, Bergson claimed that the cosmos reflected a never-ending progressive process of creation, emanating from a vital impulse and developing in divergent directions. Drawing on this idea of progress, Teilhard imagined the convergence of the cult of Matter, the cult of Life, and the cult of Energy, finding a "potential outlet and synthesis in a World which had suddenly acquired a new dimension and had thereby moved from the fragmented state of static

---

28 Ilia Delio, *Christ in Evolution,* pp. 68-69.

Cosmos to the organic state and dignity of the Cosmogenesis."[29] For Teilhard, the dynamic evolutionary process of the cosmos could only lead to union and fullness of life, i.e., the Omega Point. He spoke of "sacred evolution" a "deep-running, ontological, total Current which embraced the whole Universe in which I moved."[30] Writing as he often did upon the seas, where he spent many hours traveling from land mass to land mass, and composing his essays to the "tide of life," i.e., the unceasing rhythms and undulations of the waves, he found himself engulfed in the dynamism of organic evolution.

> This is the organic whole of which today we find ourselves to be a part, without being able to escape from it… In countless subtle ways, the concept of Evolution has been weaving its web around us.[31]

Union and evolution, the divine presence at the heart of matter pulsating vibrantly toward a final consummation, characterized the creative work of the energizing Spirit in the cosmos. In "The Phenomenon of Spirituality," Teilhard claimed that spiritual energy is the animating phenomenon of the creative dynamism in the evolving cosmos, central to its transformation into the Omega Point. The most evolved form of human spiritual energy is the unifying and synthesizing power of love, and human energy "implies faith in some final completion of *everything* around us," progressing toward the "cosmic point Omega."[32]

At this point in his intellectual and spiritual development, the love of which Teilhard spoke was as intensely physical as it was spiritual. His intellectual and mystical insight was evolving significantly from his earlier writings, catching up with his experiential knowledge. Having claimed in his analysis of fossil evidence that Peking man was capable of making tools and fire, and drawing criticism as "the Jesuit who believes man descended from the apes," Teilhard was becoming more outspoken in his reverence for the intrinsic holiness of materiality. Fire, for example, was crucial as a symbol and metaphor for spiritual energy and work in the noosphere. But fire was not only a poetic construct for Teilhard. He was as indebted to the physical necessity of fire for his long geological and paleontological excursions as he was to the notion of the "Fire"

---

29 Teilhard, *The Heart of Matter*, p. 25.
30 Teilhard, *The Heart of Matter*.
31 Teilhard, *The Future of Man*, pp. 84 ff.
32 Teilhard, *Human Energy*, pp. 137 and 139.

that ignites the universe, and that had given warmth and light to primitive people. He was also more aware and more admittedly drawn to the warmth, the spark and animation of his beloved Lucile, whom he credited with inspiring and directing his work. While writing his masterpiece, *The Phenomenon of Man*, Teilhard wrote to Lucile:

> Art and science, your friends and my friends, are so closely mixed in my last experiences, that I can hardly separate them in my feelings and my memory… More and more, I count upon you, for animating me, and directing me, ahead. Life must and will be for both of us a continual discovery – of ourselves, and of the true face of God who is the deepest bond between us.[33]

As his own consciousness was evolving about the sacredness of physicality, so his magnum opus, *The Phenomenon of Man*, reflected this awareness, and celebrated it. *The Phenomenon of Man* took two years to write, and remained unpublished until after his death. The work explores the meaning and significance of humanity in the cosmic process of evolution, in which the cosmos is ultimately transformed by the power of love and leads to union. Tracing the evolution of humanity from microorganisms to homo-sapiens, to the advent of the Christ, Teilhard takes on the basic philosophical dilemma of "the One and the many" and postulates that as diverse and multiple as organic matter appears in its various forms throughout the universe, its animating energy forms matter into a collective, complex unity.

For Teilhard, God was "not-so-hidden." God was not the abstract God of the philosophers, the disembodied "Good" or the perfectly unified "One." Nor was God the God of scholastic theologians who was imminent in Christ, but still static and hierarchical in respect to creation. For Teilhard, God was the dynamic source and destiny of all creation, involved in the intimate and ongoing creation of the universe, deeply embedded in the physicality of the earth, of humanity, and of the human heart. God was the energizing Spirit rising in the heart of matter, working with humanity to bring about its fullness. For the gentle man of science illumined by his rapturous love of God-in-all, what was central was what he had told Lucile about their "new discovery of the Fire."[34] "What is born between us is to live forever."[35] More than any other

---

33 King and Gilbert, *Letters*, p. 118.
34 King and Gilbert, *Letters*, p. 19.
35 King and Gilbert, *Letters*, p. 19.

intellectual or spiritual influence, Lucile was for Teilhard an animating fire of presence and union, a touchstone for him of the real presence of God.

Bibliography

Delio, Ilia. *Christ in Evolution*. Maryknoll, New York: Orbis, 2008.

King, Ursula, *Christ in All Things: Exploring Spirituality with Teilhard de Chardin*. Maryknoll, New York: Orbis, 1997.

King, Ursula. *Spirit of Fire: The Life and Vision of Teilhard de Chardin*. Maryknoll, NY: Orbis, 1996.

Teilhard de Chardin, Pierre. "The Evolution of Chastity" in *Toward the Future*. London: Collins, 1975.

Teilhard de Chardin, Pierre. "Building the Earth" Wilkes-Barre, PA: Dimension, 1965.

Teilhard de Chardin, Pierre. *The Future of Man*. London: Collins, 1965.

Teilhard de Chardin, Pierre. *Letters to Leontine Zanta* (Intro. by Robert Garric and Henri de Lubac). London: Collins, 1969.

Teilhard de Chardin, Pierre. *The Making of a Mind*. New York, 1965.

Teilhard de Chardin, Pierre. *The Heart of Matter*. New York and London: William Collins Sons & Co. Ltd and Harcourt Brace Jovanovich, Inc, 1978.

Teilhard de Chardin, Pierre. *Human Energy*. London: Collins, 1969.

Teilhard de Chardin, Pierre. *Hymn of the Universe*. New York: Harper & Row, 1961.

Teilhard de Chardin, Pierre. *Writings in Times of War*. London: Collins, 1968.

Thomas, M. King, S.J., and Gilbert, Mary Wood, eds., *The Letters of Teilhard de Chardin and Lucile Swan*. Washington, D.C.: Georgetown U. Press, 1993.

9

THE HORSEWOMEN

Women in the Life of Carl Gustav Jung

Jane A. Kelley, LCSW

The horse also plays the part of a psychopomp who leads the way to the other world – souls of the dead are fetched by horsewomen, the Valkyries.[1] –C.G. Jung

Strong-Unmarried-Professional-Wealthy-Intelligent-Cultured

If you Google these characteristics, what do you imagine you would find? Well, I did and it was quite fascinating. Of the first two pages of the search, two of the sites were for IQ testing, presumably keying in on the characteristic of "intelligence." The majority of the rest was online dating sites geared toward helping men enhance these particular traits to get their "desired woman" or mate.

This list of qualities is impressive. It belongs to the common characteristics of the loyal group of women who surrounded Swiss psychiatrist, Dr. Carl Gustav Jung. They weren't just "groupies," they also supported him financially, collaborated with him professionally, and loved him dearly for most of their adult lives.

In my search, I deliberately left out one other important character trait every woman possessed: *troubled/neurotic*. When I included it on the list, almost all of the sites directed me to psychological resources, of one sort or another, especially tailored for women.

---

1 C.G. Jung, *Symbols of Transformation*, CW 5, ¶ 427.

After I calmed down my initial irritation at the apparent lack of sufficient progress in the world regarding the value of women, many questions began to surface for me with this experiment. Who were these women that not only followed Jung but were integral in getting his theories out into the world? Did they influence his thinking and formulations about his psychology? If so, what kind of woman would do this for him in today's world? If Jung were alive and vibrant today, who would his thought partners be?

The "Valkyries"

This group of women was referred to by various names from the students who attended Jung's lectures and other events. Jungfrauen was a favorite. Noted Jungian psychotherapist, scholar and author, Maggy Anthony called them the Valkyries.[2] She admits others before her also used that term to describe the group. In Norse mythology, the Valkyries are female horsewomen who act as guides from the underworld. Their job is to visit battlefields and decide which fallen soldiers souls will live or die. The ones chosen to live are then swooped up by the galloping women and accompany the men to Valhalla where they are delivered, as heroes, to the god Odin. To stay with the myth that found its way to not only these women but to Jung as well, it suggests Jung was in need of them.

Viewed symbolically, the mythical Valkyries are psychopomps who assist psychic "travelers" between conscious and unconscious realms. They will present in dreams or fantasy images and can be utilized in active imagination processes to help clarify and deepen one's understanding of his/her unconscious contents. Jung, however, was fortunate enough to have these women materialize in his external world as actual living, breathing women he could communicate with on the outer level. As such, they each had great impact on one another.

These women all came to Dr. Jung initially because they had a psychological problem. Most were seeking analysis due to a neurosis. The one exception to this is his wife, Emma. They did not learn of one another, nor engage their relationship, on the basis of any need for Jung's professional services. Jung's Valkyries came from wealth

---

2 Maggy Anthony, *Jung's Circle of Women.*

and had ample time and opportunity to travel. Most were unmarried. Some were presumed to be lesbians. A few were married with much time on their hands to pursue their intellectual desires. All were considered to be quite intelligent by Jung who was the analyst of each and every one. Most went on to become practicing analysts in their own right.

What is remarkable to me is how Jung took the time with each of these women to see them for who they were as individuals. Even though a product of his time with long-standing patriarchal customs, it did not matter that they were women...or did it? He wanted to learn their unique story, find the secret they were keeping that activated their neurosis, and work to unlock the door to their inner freedom. He used his model, analytical psychology, as the technique.

Naturally, this was mutually beneficial. He had a caseload of women who were open to learning his methods, practicing them and then giving him immediate and direct feedback. This practical application had to have been priceless to Jung who felt certain the established Freudian model was so dogmatic and limiting that he had to cut ties with it and him. This decision had great ramifications for Jung in the psychoanalytic community as Freud was its "father."

Barbara Hannah points out in her biographical memoir of Jung that he had to answer to himself, particularly to his inner "daimon" or creative spirit. She reminds the reader of Jung's struggle with the end of the friendship with Freud,

> When people no longer understood him – as Freud was unable to understand the facts and ideas in *Symbols of Transformation* – Jung still had to move on. He wrote that he often felt as if he were on a battlefield, saying: "Now you have fallen, my good comrade, but I must go on...I am fond of you, indeed I love you, but I cannot stay." That was just it; he was fond of Freud, he even loved him, and it tore his heart to leave him, yet he *could not* stay. He had to follow his creative daimon and somehow make his own place with the new ideas that were crowding in on him....[3]

The battlefield image is poignant. In his mind, there is a battle and he risks his own "life" if he stays and supports Freud and his theories. At the same time, how can he make it alone? Without Freud's endorsement will he and his own theories survive? His image suggests there is still a war...still an enemy.

---

3 Barbara Hannah, *Jung: His Life and Work*, p. 91.

Here Come the Horsewomen

This is the point where Jung's plunge into a "state of disorientation" begins. In his autobiography, he calls it his "confrontation with the unconscious" and it lasts for seven years. Much of this period of time has been documented, included in the long-awaited *Red Book* that chronicles his encounters with his unconscious elements and processes. It is far beyond the reach of this discussion to examine his experience. Suffice to say that, symbolically, Jung went to the Underworld.

Author and British statesman, Sir Lauren van der Post, says in an interview,

> Jung had an instinct of what was wrong with life…what made life tear apart…made it incomplete was because the feminine was rejected, driven insane, driven mad, by a world of men rejected by a masculine dominated world. And that time when he let himself go, and when he landed deep down in what he came to call the collective unconscious…all this rejected feminine in himself confronted him.[4]

During this period, he was regressing…flooded with images to translate and emotions to manage, and countless pairs of opposites to contain. It was indeed a battle.

The following words from Jung are descriptive of his understanding of the deeper psyche and his view of it as feminine.

> The "mother," as the first incarnation of the anima archetype, personifies, in fact, the whole unconscious. Hence the regression leads back only apparently to the mother; in reality she is the gateway into the unconscious, into the "realm of the Mothers." Whoever sets foot in this realm submits his conscious ego-personality to the controlling influence of the unconscious…For regression, if left undisturbed, does not stop short at the "mother" but goes back beyond her to the prenatal realm of the "Eternal Feminine," to the immemorial world of archetypal possibilities where, "thronged rounds with images of all creation," slumbers the "divine child," patiently awaiting his conscious realization. This son is the germ of wholeness, and he is characterized as such by his specific symbols.[5]

---

4 G. Wagner, (Producer), S. Wagner, (Writer) and M. Whitney, (Director), "Matter of Heart" (motion picture), 1985.

5 Jung, *Symbols of Transformation*, CW 5, ¶ 508.

And, I propose, that without this coterie of women surrounding him, he and Analytical Psychology, would not be anything close to what it is today. Apparently, Jung knew this. In the 1985 documentary, "Matter of Heart," one of the notable analysts in the group, Lillian Frey-Rohn, states that Jung often said, "Without you women, I could not have developed my psychology."

The women around him can be seen as the positive aspect of the Valkyries, the *Horsewomen*, who came to Jung to be healed themselves and ended up assisting the healer through understanding, augmenting, researching and furthering his work. In essence, they carried Jung from the battlefield, where he left Freud, to the Other World…via the Underworld…to his own world. He wasn't just one voice, he became many voices with the work they produced and the clients they reached through their analytic work. Today, almost a century later, people continue to buy books written by these early pioneer women.

It is necessary to name and credit some of the women who contributed to our ability to benefit from Jung's work. For the sake of ease, I have categorized them into three groups: the Lovers, the Donors, and the Producers. These groups are distinct; however, some women belong in more than one category. It must be noted that, indeed, Emma Jung belongs, and is firmly rooted, in all three.

The Lovers

There are three women that are known to have been intimately involved with Jung, whether sexually, emotionally, or both. They are: Emma, his wife; Sabina Spielrein, his first patient; and Toni Wolff, his "other or soul wife." Sabina and Toni carried Jung's anima projection. However, the relationship with Sabina had ended before the split with Freud and onset of Jung's dark night of the soul.

Toni Wolff was particularly important to Jung as he fell into the treacherous waters of the collective unconscious. She was his soul guide. Even though their relationship began with him as her analyst, she eventually analyzed him keeping him able to function. Emma was the "good mother" he never had which kept his external world grounded in reality. She was safe, dependable, trustworthy and practical. She also was able, in time, to work out a solution regarding the "soul wife" where her love for him outweighed her jealousy. She eventually accepted Toni with the understanding that she was giving Jung important aspects he needed that Emma herself could not. Both women stayed with Jung for the remainder of their lives. Toni died two years before Emma after 42 years as his "soul wife." Emma and Carl Jung were married 52 years.

The Donors

There were many women who came from considerable wealth that subsidized Jungian ventures. For example, the American-born, Edith Rockefeller McCormick, gave large sums of money. She also bought the property to establish and house the Zurich Psychological Club in 1916. Other generous donors included Drs. Esther Harding, Katherine Mann, and Eleanor Bertine who together founded the New York Analytical Psychology Club as well as set up the first Bailey Island Conference in 1937.

The Producers

Everyone fits into this category since they all contributed their own unique gifts to the development of Analytical Psychology in one way or another. For instance, the literary scholars provided dissertations on Jungian thought that enhanced the dialogue in the local and international communities. Marie-Louise von Franz is credited with being the most prolific writer of the bunch and an expert in the areas of fairy tales, typology, and alchemy. Others not only wrote, but gave through acts of service, i.e. Jolande Jacobi, who was tenacious about seeing that the operations were running smoothly. As has been stated, almost every woman became an analyst allowing Jung's psychological method to be reachable to increasing numbers of people.

There is no doubt in my mind that Jung was deeply inspired by the Horsewomen. These were women who were having trouble with finding their own voice in the world of men. He honored the strength, intellect and curiosity he saw in them through their analyses with him and encouraged them to channel it according to their individuated path. They were eternally grateful to Jung and felt he saved their lives. Jung was able to get his work out to the public through the combination of the women around him and what each individual person provided. As a collective, it appears they save each other.

Today, I believe Jung would be inspired by those scientists, doctors, clinicians, religious leaders, etc. who are looking at the field of integrative medicine. In *Memories, Dreams, Reflections,* he writes about the healing power of science, image, and listening,

> In many cases in psychiatry, the patient who comes to us has a story that is not told, and which as a rule no one knows of. To my mind, therapy only really begins after the investigation of that wholly personal story. It is the patient's secret, the rock against which he is shattered. If I know his secret story, I have a key to the treatment. The doctor's task is to find out how to gain that knowledge. In most cases exploration of the conscious material is insufficient. Sometimes an association test can open the way; so can the interpretation of dreams, or long and patient human contact with the individual. In therapy the problem is always the whole person, never the symptom alone. We must ask questions which challenge the whole personality.[6]

These were his words in 1961… timelessly true and profound. Yet, he may be enlightened to know of the current thinking of contemporary healers who carry a commitment to finding the connection to wholeness through the integration of mind, body, emotions, and spirit. In the words of Jungian analyst, Ashok Bedi, M.D.:

> The new psychology of the Healing Zone connects the past, present, and future of medicine and emerging healing paradigms into a quantum reality of fundamental transformation. Contemporary physicians, therapists, and healers must transcend the mind/body/soul/Spirit/nature split and think of individuals in their present state of health as the current readout of the program of existence. In other words, what we see today in any individual is merely the present page in the book of his or her life, not the whole book. When you become curious about the rest of your own book – your own life story – you can access the potential of deep healing and the purposeful alignment of the present page and chapter with the rest of the story.[7]

Jung was a healer who was interested in every page, in every book of the lives of these women who gave him access to their souls. An everlasting impact was made by their mutual relationship.

---

6 C.G. Jung, *MDR*, p. 117.
7 Ashok Bedi, *Crossing the Healing Zone*, p. 209.

Bibliography

Anthony, M., *Jung's Circle of Women*. York Beach, ME: Nicolas Hays. 1999.

Bedi, Ashok. *Crossing the Healing Zone*. Lake Worth, Florida: Ibis Press, 2013.

Clark-Stern, E. *Out of the Shadows: A Story of Toni Wolff and Emma Jung,* Carmel, CA: Genoa House, 2010.

Hannah, Barbara. *Jung: His Life and Work*. Wilmette, Illinois: Chiron, 1997.

Jung, C.G. *Memories, Dreams, Reflections*. N.Y., New York: Vintage Books, 1963.

Jung, C.G. *Symbols of Transformation*, CW 5. Princeton, N.J.: Princeton University Press, 1966.

Jung, Emma. *Animus and Anima*. Woodstock, Connecticut: Spring, 1957.

Wagner, G. (Produce), Wagner, S. (Writer) and Whitney, M. (Director). Matter of Heart" (motion picture), 1985.

Wikipedia. "Valkyrie." Found September 13, 2013. http://en.wikipedia.org/wiki/valk

10

EMBRACE OF THE FEMININE

Impressions of Pierre Teilhard de Chardin

Robert Henderson, D.Min.

From the critical moment when I rejected many of the old molds in which my family life and my religion had formed me, I have experienced no form of self-development without some feminine eye turned on me, some feminine influence at work.[1]

I had heard of Father Pierre Teilhard de Chardin but did not know much about him when my close friend Fred Gustafson asked me to write this chapter. I was hesitant as I generally associate dullness with Catholic priests and what I had read of Teilhard had always been quite difficult to read. I have spent my life being inspired by C.G. Jung and I would have rather written about him. But Fred convinced me that this could be a growth exercise for me.

I have known many Catholic priests throughout my years in the ministry. I have had many priests as students in my role as a supervisor in clinical pastoral education. In the past few years, I have also been an adjunct faculty at a nearby Catholic seminary. I have heard stories about the formation process of becoming a Catholic priest from men who have become Catholic priests. I have had several Catholic priests as friends and colleagues and have gotten to see what their daily lives are like. So, I decided to immerse myself in reading about Teilhard and see what kind of man and how

---

1 Pierre Teilhard de Chardin, *The Heart of Matter*, p. 59.

he compared with what I had learned about Catholic priests. I wondered if he would eventually inspire me as I have been by Jung.

Embracing the Feminine

As I have gotten to know Catholic priests, I have had a difficult time understanding the need for them to have vows of chastity and celibacy. As a Jungian psychotherapist my view is that many men discover the feminine through their relationships with women. Men need a connection with the feminine if they are to discover their Soul and the deeper parts of themselves.

As I have spoken with Catholic priests, I have wondered what happens developmentally to men when the natural instincts for relating to woman are disrupted.

I have known many Catholic priests who have secret women friends, some with religious sisters, some with single mothers, and some with young girls. I have often felt such priests to be responding to the deep need within themselves to find the feminine. It is sad that often these priests feel shame in having such relationships as it counters the vows they have made, and that shame often clouds their relationship with the feminine.

I have known other priests who felt they have maintained their vows by staying away from women and diverting their sexuality toward young boys.

I have known other priests who have not had close relationships with women and maintained a long and loyal commitment to their vows, sacrificing any sexual interest or desire to be with a woman. The men I have known like this have had an absence of the feminine in their lives. Such an absence has resulted in a lifeless daily life, giving homilies that are not grounded in human life to which few people listen.

Building a relationship with the feminine is important for a man if he is to find his creativity, discover his passion and calling in life, and learn the meaning of love. Working through a relationship with an actual woman often provides a man with these opportunities.

In my study of Teilhard, I became curious how he handled himself as a Catholic priest. How a man learns to relate to the feminine will determine what kind of man he becomes. What I discovered was a remarkable man. Ursula King devotes an entire chapter to Teilhard's relationships with women in her book *Spirit of Fire: The Life and Vision of Teilhard de Chardin*.[2]

Teilhard had close relationships with women beginning with his mother. He credits his mother for his appreciation for people, art, and religion. He stated: "At the age when other children, I imagine, experience their first 'feeling' for a person, or for art, or for religion, I was affectionate, good, even pious: by that I mean that under the influence of my mother, I was devoted to the Child Jesus."

A close relationship with a woman helps men leave their Mothers. When a young man begins priest formation and is guided to not have intimate relationships, often their relationship with feminine is wounded. Often such young men remain devoted sons to their mothers and their development as a man is stunted. I have known many Catholic priests who are older and still feel like a teenager. When this happens, often the relationship with the feminine does not develop and a man has difficulty in finding their creativity, passion, and love.

Teilhard's close relationship with his mother led to a significant relationship with his cousin and eventually to meeting Lucille Swan, a sculptor and portrait artist from Iowa, with whom he was to have a lifetime relationship. She was an artist and had worked on the reconstruction of the skull of the Peking man, a project in which Teilhard was the geologist.

They maintained a very close relationship during most of Teilhard's professional life. I think they had fallen in love with each other and with such relationships there are questions as whether they had been involved sexually. No one will ever know for sure if they did but, if they did, it would undoubtedly have been a soulful sexual experience. They spent considerable time in person sharing with one another and also maintaining a long and rich correspondence. He shared many of his ideas with Lucille. No doubt she was an important part of the "feminine eye," which Teilhard felt was important in his life. Teilhard's relationship with Lucille reminds me of C.G. Jung's relationship with Toni Wolff, and Francis of Assisi's relationship with Saint Clara.

Some people call the kind of relationship they had an *anima* relationship, which means it is intense, powerful, and probably filled with projections. Only they know

---

2 All of the quotes by Chardin in this article were taken from Ursula King's incredible book on Teilhard de Chardin, *Spirit of Fire: The Life and Vision of Teilhard de Chardin*.

whether it was lived out sexually. I have a feeling it could have been if they chose. It was a relationship which kept them both on their toes and alive.

Through working out a relationship with a woman, a man is slowly embracing something within himself, the feminine. The feminine is the life giving depth of a man, which enables him through his work, and words to bring aliveness and substance. This quality of a man is apparent to others around him and to the world. Along with the woman friend, a man who accomplishes this has saved the relationship from being a sexual affair. Such a relationship becomes a place of soul for both the man and the woman.

He also had significant relationships with other women. His cousin Marguerite, who edited many of his letters, was his first love. Others were Leontine Zanta, an early feminist, Ida Treat, Jeanne Mortier, who arranged for the publication of his works after his death, and Rhoda de Terra.

A Man of Fire

Embracing the feminine leaves a man in touch with his passion. I think this is what Teilhard meant by fire. He was alive to his passion in science and ministry. His passion made his life into an adventure that kept him thinking and occupied night and day. He stated: "Someday, after mastering the winds, the waves, the tides and gravity, we shall harness for God the energies of love, and then, for a second time in the history of the world, man will have discovered fire."

A Man of Creativity

Embracing the feminine leaves a man in touch with his unique creativity. Father Pierre was a voluminous writer of science, theology, and the soul. He was a paleontologist who did significant research in China and participated at the excavations of the d other sites in Europe. Again he said: "Our duty, as men and women, s if limits to our ability did not exist. We are collaborators in creation." here is almost a sensual longing for communion with others who have a large vision. The immense fulfillment of the friendship between those engaged in furthering the evolution of consciousness has a quality impossible to describe."

A Man of Love

Embracing the feminine leaves a man to know love as something known only to the heart. Steeped in tremendous intellectual powers from a rigorous Jesuit education, Teilhard might have known love only as a theory. Being in love with a woman opened him to his heart and he was led to find how love and his work with the earth connected. He expressed so many times this issue of love:

"Driven by the forces of love, the fragments of the world seek each other so that the world may come into being"

"Love is the most powerful and still most unknown energy in the world."

"Love alone is capable of uniting living beings in such a way as to complete and fulfill them, for it alone takes them and joins them by what is deepest in themselves."

"Love is a sacred reserve of energy; it is like the blood of spiritual evolution."

"Love is the affinity which links and draws together the elements of the world... Love, in fact, is the agent of universal synthesis."

"Driven by the forces of love, the fragments of the world seek each other so that the world may come to being."

"The most telling and profound way of describing the evolution of the universe would undoubtedly be to trace the evolution of love."

A Man of the Earth

Embracing the feminine leaves a man to know the sacredness of all of creation. Once when Father Pierre was on a scientific adventure, he found himself one day alone in the Ordos desert. He did not have the usual elements for saying the Mass so he improvised saying, "I have neither bread, nor wine, nor altar. I will raise myself beyond these symbols, up to the pure majesty of the real itself; I, your priest, will make the whole earth my altar and on it will offer you all the labors and sufferings of the world." If you, the reader, have not read Father Chardin's *Hymn of the Universe*, I strongly recommend it.

A Man of Courage and Integrity

Embracing the feminine allows a man to stay true to himself. Maintaining intimate relationships with women and even allowing oneself to fall in love with a woman is walking on the edge as a Catholic priest which Father Pierre did with courage and integrity. Many of his ideas and writings were condemned by the Vatican and were removed from the public. Fortunately, Father Pierre continued to circulate his ideas privately in mimeographs.

A Man of Soul and Death

Embracing the Feminine allows a man to know his soul and face his death. When a man discovers his soul he starts to live his mystical side. People in ministry do not necessarily know their soul, though that is often projected onto them. Father Pierre wanted to die on Easter, which he did on April 10, 1955 at 73 years of age. His life journey could be summed up in his words: "We are not human beings having a spiritual experience. We are spiritual beings having a human experience" and again, "God is not remote from us. He is at the point of my pen, my (pick) shovel, my paint brush, my (sewing) needle - and my heart and thoughts."

In closing, it has indeed been a growth experience to write this chapter. Pierre Teilhard de Chardin lived a full life and I have thought that he and Jung would have enjoyed each other. They spoke a similar language and their contributions have made the world a fuller place to live.

Bibliography

For many of the observations and impressions in this essay, I am indebted to conversations with many Catholic Priests and candidates for ordination into the Catholic Priesthood which I encountered in my work as a Supervisor in Clinical Pastoral Education and as an adjunct instructor at Holy Apostles Catholic Seminary in Cromwell, Connecticut. I am greatly indebted to Ursula King and her incredible book on Teilhard de Chardin, *Spirit of Fire: The Life and Vision of Teilhard de Chardin*. Maryknoll, New York: Orbis Books, 1996. All of the quotes by Chardin were taken from her book.

11

WHAT JUNG AND TEILHARD CAN TELL US ABOUT COMING TOGETHER AS A PEOPLE

Peter T. Dunlap

How many of you are afraid about the future? Certainly, the future for each of us is uncertain, except for the assurance that we will grow old and die. But, how many of you are afraid for the future of your children and their children, the future for our culture, for humankind? I think we are experiencing a convergence of tragedy, collectively, as a people. Our ills are numerous: environmental degradation, economic turmoil, political-religious warfare, the abuse of institutional power, and the chronic lack of belonging that too many of us experience. We live in a frightening time. What Carl Jung wrote during the Cold War in 1957 seems even more applicable today.

> We are living in what the Greeks called the *kairos*—the right moment—for a "metamorphosis of the gods," of the fundamental principles and symbols [we live by]... Coming generations will have to take account of this momentous transformation if humanity is not to destroy itself through the might of its own technology and science.[1]

Pierre Teilhard de Chardin adds "sociology" to Jung's list above when he writes about the need of our time to respond to the "explosive development of science, technology, and sociology."[2] Here we see Teilhard viewing modernity with a complexity that accounts for the place that the social sciences have in supporting cultural transformation; something Jung would likely recognize but may not have focused on sufficiently. As holistic as Jung clearly intends to be, Teilhard's vision of humanity is more so, which gives his writing an optimism missing in Jung. Not only do we need

---

1 C.G. Jung, "The Undiscovered Self," in *Civilization in Transition*, CW 10, ¶ 585.
2 Pierre Teilhard de Chardin, *Activation of Energy*, p. 253.

to manage science and its technologies, but many of those technologies, including sociology, are exploding with *answers*. While Jung uses social science to realistically assess the human condition—the threat to humanity of both mass-mindedness and the individual's shadow—he does not seem to discuss the possibility of an institutional response, a science of human transformation: Teilhard offers this essential balance.

Teilhard believes that we live in a time of a rising self-awareness asserting that the pressures of modern life are forcing us to deal with one another and either succumb to the entropy of depleted resources or rise to the occasion and cultivate a vitalizing connection to one another that would enable us to collaborate across our differences. Teilhard's hope is significant as he views all of our sciences as providing opportunities for a convergence of thought that imagines the human species as a single community. And, he does so without foolish hope for he recognizes the threat of failure:

> …we see that the great problem for man is coming to be to find how to control in himself the inevitable but supremely dangerous work of the forces of unification… For one form of synthesis that brings freedom there are hundreds of others that lead only to the vilest forms of bondage.[3]

If we are to imagine that we could control "the forces of unification" in order to form a single human community we will need to recognize that we are a people. Such recognition will require that we find a way of focusing our attention together, in a manner that converges on resolving our troubles. In order to do this we will need to attend to and hold together the profound divergence of thought that has typified human inquiry, dividing science and religion, natural from social science, and even subdividing the social sciences and humanities into narrow beams of inquiry. Only through such concentration of our effort will we be able to activate the "generational attention" needed by our time.[4] The desire to collaborate across all of these divides requires some guiding vision. While there may be multiple sources for such a vision I find Jung's realism and Teilhard's optimism to hold the key for my own faith in the

---

3 Teilhard, *Activation of Energy*, p. 47.

4 Peter T. Dunlap, *Awakening Our Faith in the Future: The Advent of Psychological Liberalism*, p. 13. Peter T. Dunlap, "Generational attention: Remembering how to be a people." *Jungian Society for Scholarly Studies,* Vol. 8, 2012.

future.[5] Secondarily, I also draw on the vision of John Dewey whose philosophy adds a needed sociopolitical flavor to Jung's psycho-spiritual and Teilhard's bio-religious broth.

Jung, Teilhard, and Dewey were 20th century thinkers who worked to maintain the integrity of human inquiry despite the radical divergence that challenges that veracity. They set out to integrate the emerging research and mythos about human evolution within their own fields of inquiry and surrounding disciplines. They succeeded in generating a range of images, thoughts, and research that supported the notion that human beings can resolve their problems by *focusing on their own development*. In theorizing about that development, they attempted to bridge biological, psychological, sociopolitical, religious, moral, and historical dimensions of human experience.

Their faith in and understanding of human development emphasized the reciprocal relationship between the individual and human culture. They identify the way in which individualism, for all its risks, represents an emerging human consciousness that enables the species' developmental process to emerge from being passively experienced to being actively pursued. As individuals attend to their own emerging identity they activate the capacity needed by her culture, which, simply put, is the capacity to influence human destiny: to participate in the larger patterns of cultural transformation. Also, an implicit dimension of Teilhard and Dewey's vision is understanding that the movement from passive to active not only takes place within the individual but also within emerging institutions that are increasingly able to take up the cry for freedom through development.

Jung's, Teilhard's, and Dewey's work did not culminate in the systematic research needed to advance such a holistic vision of human development. More specifically, their theorizing has not been sufficiently differentiated to the point where it could be tested, that is, founding the practices that would simultaneously activate individual development and cultural transformation. And, unfortunately, a gulf between the involved disciplines has arisen that restricts such confluence. The accomplishments of scientific and humanistic learning have been limited by the necessary but problematic

---

5 Pierre Teilhard de Chardin, *The Future of Man*, 1964. Opening epigram reads: "The whole future of the Earth, as of religion, seems to me to depend on the awakening of our faith in the future."

need for inquiry to follow every fracture line in the human community brought about by stresses of modernity as well as the pressures to professionalize these disciplines.[6]

Fortunately, there are opportunities to synthesize the vision of these men by establishing research projects that support the coalescence of thought needed to address the ills of our time and to formulate a more definitive theory and approach to human development. In order to advance this work it is necessary to clearly identify the individual identities and institutional forms that have historically activated human freedom.

The idea of 'progress' has too readily fallen into disrepute. Teilhard attributes this to the "habitual illusion" that we always think that what we imagine could be achieved quite readily, "within the space of a generation."[7] Unfortunately the reality is much different and too many professionals have backed away from using their disciplines to complete research about the exploration of the history of our development. When viewed with sufficient distance, a bird's-eye view over time and space, we can follow the likes of Jung, Teilhard, and Dewey to account for the rise in human freedom over the course of modernity. In particular, what we will see is the function that individual consciousness plays in creating institutional forms that accelerate our movement toward freedom.

For more than six hundred years we have witnessed the emergence of unprecedented waves of individual and cultural freedom. If we go back to the Renaissance, Reformation, and Enlightenment we might think of these cultural forms as waves of aesthetic, religious, and philosophical liberty. Looking closer to the present we can identify the way that these liberalizing forces were extended into politics as the implications of aesthetic and religious freedom took hold of Western culture. This emerging freedom extended into our politics through Laisse-faire liberalism, giving rise to new efforts to change the social order. By the late 18th and 19th centuries, this desire was expressed through revolution, woman's suffrage, the abolition of slavery, and the labor and farm movements. All of these political activities are based in the egalitarian values championed by cultural leaders interested in the fundaments of individual freedom and what that freedom could bring to society. While for many the very notion of 'liberalism' starts and stops with the political, the root word is *liberty*, that which supports our freedom. Accordingly, I speak of each cultural and institutional

---

6 Robert Bellah, *Habits of the Heart*, p. 299.
7 Teilhard, *Activation of Energy*, p. 174.

movement toward human freedom as a *form of liberalism*, with political liberalism not being the last. There has been at least one more call for liberty that appeared during the 19th century to add its voice to the chorus demanding that we increase our self-awareness and care.

I think of the new institutional form of organized liberty as "psychological liberalism," by which I mean the effort to help us *understand* and *treat* human suffering, starting with the individual.[8] Psychological liberalism begins as an attitude that focuses attention on how the past influences the present and how the present is governed by dynamics that can be understood and consciously engaged.[9] This voice may have first sounded in literature, philosophy, and numerous spiritualist movements of the 19th century; however, by the early 20th century much of its energy had been harnessed within the burgeoning fields of psychology: clinical and developmental. While myopically focused on the individual, the advent of psychological liberalism marks a turn from passive to active, as the developmental process of the species was becoming a more significant focus of attention individually and institutionally.

Liberalism (aesthetic, religious, philosophical, political, and now psychological) is a response to human suffering; each voice and each institution pursuing its agenda, speaking its own language of change, to create a more beneficent human community. Each form of liberalism responds to the modern condition in which the individual rises out of historical confines but, losing footing, searches for a new way to belong to and re-form the human community.

Between the horrors of modernity and the cries for liberty in response to this suffering, we live in a time of profound dichotomies. Jung describes the way in which modernity has given birth to an individual cut off from instinct, isolated from a human community susceptible to being submerged in mass-mindedness; yet, Jung's individual is also capable of creativity and moral discernment through the unique unfolding of an individuated identity. While Jung theorizes that such an individual can become a moral leader, his own introversion and the pressures to professionalize psychology restricted efforts on his part to develop the psycho-cultural practices that would activate that function. As a result, his relationship to psychological liberalism was restricted.

---

8 Dunlap, *Awakening our Faith in the Future.*
9 Joseph Henderson, *Cultural Attitudes in Psychological Perspective*, p.72.

Like Jung, Dewey also identifies the way we form individuals as a distinct advance in human evolution, he notes, "the recognition of 'subjects' as centers of experience together with the development of 'subjectivism' marks a great advance."[10] Yet, despite Dewey's focus on the individual, much of his attention went to the difficulty of forming humane institutions, which he championed through his own focus on political liberalism. Both Jung and Dewey stand near the apex of unique institutional forms, yet speak different languages reflecting our current difficulty in bringing political and psychological liberalism together.

Teilhard does not offer a clear means for bringing our institutions together, though he holds that it is necessary. He adds his voice to this emerging reprise, looking for a way for the individual to participate in cultural transformation. He speaks of the *granularity* of human consciousness or the process of "hominization" by which he is commenting on the rise of an individual identity capable of becoming aware of its own development and of larger processes of cultural transformation.[11] During this stage the 'individual' is emerging as a unique center of consciousness, capable of responding to human suffering, her own and that of others, in ways that catalyze the transformation of the collective. Yet Teilhard recognizes that individualism does not automatically lead to that transformation. Teilhard is concerned that our hyper-individualism has led to a *loss* of experience of ourselves as a species. He writes, "The individual…finds that he obtained a richness of life which, increasing almost without limit his own incommunicable values, makes him stand alone amongst his own kind, gives him an 'absolute' quality and makes him autonomous."[12] In response to the risks of this distinctness, Teilhard speaks of the need for the individual to identify with the species, that is, "there must be a never-failing concern to stimulate, within the personalized living mass…a generalized sense of man," which he also refers to as a "new sense of the species."[13]

What an odd, intense juxtaposition: we awake to recognize the severity of our circumstance and have the chance to become agents in the transformation of that suffering but lack the language, the means, to do so. The dilemma of individual agency is expressed by Matthew Arnold when he writes, "wandering between two worlds, one

---

10 John Dewey, *Experience and Nature*, p. 13.
11 Teilhard, *Activation of energy*, p. 34.
12 Teilhard, *Activation of Energy*, p. 200.
13 Teilhard, *Activation of Energy*, pp. 202-3

dead, the other powerless to be born."[14] On the one hand modernity has led to an extreme individualism that has distorted human values, overemphasizing shortsighted, materialistic, individual gain; on the other hand, our freedom has unleashed a level of human creativity that is remaking our personal and cultural identities, giving rise to a post-conventional moral vision of humanity.

Based on the vision of moving from passive to active, we can learn to harness our splinter-like individuality and guide it in an increasingly humane direction, which will enable us to fulfill the individual's creative and moral destiny while renewing our collective values and identity. This goal is clearly identified by Jung when he writes:

> It is obvious that a social group consisting of stunted individuals cannot be a healthy and viable institution; only a society that can preserve its internal cohesion and collective values, while at the same time granting the individual to greatest possible freedom, has any prospect of enduring vitality.[15]

The troubles and opportunities identified by Jung, Teilhard, and Dewey are a result of a crisis of identity that has been at least hundreds of years in the making. Can we find an image of the individual's brilliance while learning how to see ourselves as a people? Dewey recognizes this challenge when he writes, "The problem of constructing a new individuality consonant with the objective conditions under which we live is the deepest problem of our time."[16]

If we are to form a new individuality, one based on the individual's increased conscious involvement in cultural transformation, we would need to establish the way in which each one of us is uniquely connected to the future of the species; we would each be, in our own distinct way, a *responder* to the multiple crises of our time. Such uniqueness would also have to be patterned, otherwise dissociation results, for where there is no pattern there can be no connection, which sometimes is celebrated such as in the troubled vision of post-modernism. We need our originality to crystallize into cultural forms that enable us to sit together, to form into the groups, organizations, and the institutions needed to respond to our circumstances.

In the following pages I will tell the tale of my effort to find such a pattern in my own life, connect that story to my readings of Jung and Teilhard, as well as to my own

---

14 Bellah, *Habits of the Heart*, p. 277.

15 C.G. Jung, *Psychological Types*, CW 6, ¶ 758.

16 John Dewey, *Individualism Old and New*, p. 32.

institutional identifications with liberal politics and psychology. Based on this story I will draw out what I see to be the opportunities to bring political and psychological liberalism together, which I attend to in my own work as a clinical and political psychologist.

If I, as a human being, could become a unique responder to my time, focused on my own individual development but also on the transformation of culture, then how could I identify my role, the place where I belong to contribute to my community? Working out this question supports Teilhard's agenda of helping the individual find a sense of the species. It also supports Jung's agenda of finding the right harmonic between individual and collective experience. This is my agenda, to find out where I belong. Such agendas are also supported by the work of Erik Erikson who combines historical and psychoanalytic analyses for the sake of showing the way in which individual character and history are co-emergent. Taking such historical figures as Thomas Jefferson, Martin Luther, and Mahatma Gandhi, Erikson identifies the way in which these men form identities that support the psycho-cultural development of their times. Through a process of internalizing conflict, these leaders are forced to "mobilize capacities to see and say, to dream and plan, to design and construct, in new ways." The results of the activation of these capacities is the creation of "something potentially new: a new person; and with this new person a new generation, and with that, a new era."[17] This sentiment is expressed before Erikson when James Joyce's main character in *A Portrait of an Artist as a Young Man*, Stephen Daedalus, exclaims at the end of the book "within the smithy of my soul I create the uncreated future of my race"[18] and by Rilke when he writes about Michelangelo:

> He was the kind of man who turns
>
> to bring forth the meaning of an age that wants to end.
>
> He lifts its whole weight
>
> and heaves it into the chasm of his heart.
>
> The anguish and yearning of all those before him
>
> become in his hand raw matter

---

17 Erik Erikson, *Young Man Luther*, pp. 14-15, 20.
18 James Joyce, *A Portrait of the Artist as a Young Man*, p. 237.

for him to compress into one great work [19]

While Erikson focus on the way great men bring into themselves and transmute the troubles of their time, Jungian political psychologist Andrew Samuels believes we each are capable of such responsiveness as we learn to attend to our private and *public* lives, which can activate our "political energy."[20] In his workshops he has people tell the story of their "political history" to show the way in which their identities are created by their times and can be intimately connected to that of their neighbors, colleagues, family, and friends in a shared story of community.[21] By sharing our political histories we can come to see the way in which we are all involved in the evolution of our communities.

Following both Erikson and Samuels, while staying closely connected to Teilhard and Jung, I will set out to tell my own story about how I discovered and cultivated my own unique contribution to the development of my community, which represents the activation of my own destiny. I believe that in this manner I can talk *about* the importance of Teilhard and Jung's work and also *show* the way in which it has influenced my life as I set about making the contribution I can make to a world in crisis. In the sense, I'm offering myself as evidence that supports the thesis of this paper: 1) human problems can be resolved by focusing on human development; 2) there is a reciprocal or co-emergent relationship between individual and cultural transformation; 3) through the activation of individuals as centers of consciousness human development is going from being passively experienced to actively pursued; 4) there is a need to bring the diverse institutional forms of liberalism together to forge a single language and practice of human development.

I grew up in rural Napa County California in the mid-and late 20th century. My mother was a loving, funny, and intense woman who grew up with some fear of going to hell if she had thoughts that weren't 'Christian,' which limited what I could do with my own religiosity in my childhood. She met my father on a train during World War II, married him and moved from Pennsylvania to the Napa Valley, where my father's family could be traced back to my great-great-grandfather Nathan Coombs who founded the town of Napa. Beginning with Nathan and ending with my father, the Dunlap/Coombs clan participated in the leadership of the Napa Valley including

---

19 Anita Barrows and Joanna Macy, *Rilke's Book of Hours*, p. 91.
20 Andrew Samuels, *The Political Psyche*, p. 57.
21 Andrew Samuels *Politics on the Couch*, p. 28.

representing it in the California state Senate for four generations. While traditionally conservative, my father helped bring into the family the egalitarian values of political liberalism. However, there was little room for the psychological liberty a family needs for its own self-care especially in times of cultural transformation.

In my family my mother's psychological sensitivity had no voice, for the notion of *psychological need* had not worked its way into our life as yet, but would become central to my mother's life's work, which included studying psychology and reading Jung (my first copy of the *portable Jung* had her name handwritten on the inside cover). The fact that my father's political sensitivity could manifest in our family's culture ahead of my mother's psychological sensitivity reflected the relative status of the two liberalisms in our culture: political liberalism appears first, only to be eventually followed by psychological liberalism. As a result of the disparity between my mother's emerging psychological vision and my father's own sense of familial direction, she and my father regularly engaged in high-energy conflict. In effect, the conflict and possible collaboration between the languages and culture of political and psychological liberalism played out in my household, with no clear resolution ever found, and thus became part of my inheritance. The conflict between my father's politics and my mother psychology left little room for any other source of freedom. My own child-like religiosity brought me moments of joy but—there is no speaking about this in my family. Only later, as I will report, was I able to capitalize on this part of my nature.

In 1966, when I was nine years old, my father was elected to the California legislature. It was a wild ride that included eating as many donuts and drinking as much chocolate milk as I wanted at the back of the legislative chamber, as well as riding in parades and other 'glorious' events with my father. While I was not naturally cut out to be the extroverted community leader that he was, the excitement of his life became engraved on my identity. Also, I did not find another path to pursue. While I tried acting in school, I derive so much of my identity from being my father's son that I could only imagine following him and the family's lineage into politics. No one helped me find my own calling. All of this led to my efforts in college to study political science and economics falling flat, as I had no psychological backbone to use to wrestle with my demons.

In the mid-1970s I had the benefit of being part of a time of fluid change, which led me toward experimenting with altered states of consciousness. These experiences initially helped me to have psychological insight, which led me to a vision of my unique potential. Part of this new self-awareness included the realization that my body was not just mine, not just Peter Dunlap's, rather, it was a human body having its own history that preceded my life experience by hundreds and thousands of years. In effect my imagination opened up the experience of my body extending down into human history. I did not know what I should call such experiences; were they 'visions' or 'fantasies,' were they objective, delusional, or neither? What did they mean and could I trust them?

At times, this imaging even went further, connecting my humanity to my identity as a mammal, as a divine form of life on earth, woven into the fabric of the universe in which I *did* belong. These altered experiences seem to be *sensory*, that is, it was as if I were *seeing* something as true as looking at my feet and knowing that I could trust them to carrying me in a direction of my choosing. Yet nothing in my upbringing—not family, school, or community—had prepared me to understand what was happening to me. Later I found this comment by Teilhard that helped me understand my prior state of restricted awareness.

> We should be... stifled if we had to accept the narrow boundaries into which our ancestors, right up to the 19th century, squeezed the ages of the universe, without discomfort. The perspectives of unbounded time with which we fill our lungs have become so natural that we forget how recently and at what cost they were conquered.[22]

Teilhard's idea of "unbound time" fit well with my experiences of my body's history, which was even further clarified by Jung's idea of "intuition." From Jung I learned that there was more to my consciousness than my sensory, emotional, and cognitive experience. From his book, *Analytical Psychology: Its Theory and Practice,* I learned that, "sensation tells us that a thing *is*. Thinking tells us *what* that thing is, feeling tells us what it is *worth* to us."[23] Finally, I learned that a fourth function of consciousness, namely "intuition" tells us something about "time," that is, about the past and possible future of a thing. Jung's understanding of intuition and his own exploration of the historicity of the human psyche helped me understand the imagery I had experienced. This led to a great sense of optimism as Jung's own vision suggested significant opportunities for human development, despite the tragedies of what we have actually

---

22 Pierre Teilhard de Chardin, *Human Energy*, p. 168.

23 C.G. Jung, *Analytical Psychology: Its Theory and Practice* from the Tavistock Lectures. p. 13.

done with our powers of consciousness. These images and the hopes they evoked remained central to my life's pursuits.

Following my chosen path led me to begin awkwardly to speak a psychological language poorly connected to the dialect of political liberalism spoken in my family. While these languages are siblings, born of the same liberalizing currents of modern culture, their distinctive focus makes communication between *older brother politics* and *younger sister psychology* almost impossible. While my own sensitivities and training in psychotherapy were helping me to follow the psychological path initiated by my mother, I still wanted more than anything to be a community leader like my father. I would not give up trying to bridge the gap between political and psychological liberalism—this has turned out to be my life's work. However, neither of these liberalisms was sufficient to fully account for my intuition. I needed the breadth of vision offered by Teilhard to fully understand my experience.

From Teilhard I learned to view human experience quite broadly, not allowing it to be reduced to either the narrow confines of political or psychological liberalism. Rather, he conceives of humanity as a whole, within which we are gaining conscious awareness of the processes that lead to our evolution. According to Teilhard, this perspective represents an "awakening of our minds to the perception of a world that is in a state *of operating an organic shift upon itself.*"[24] While such language is extremely obtuse, or at least esoteric, this statement echoed the visions I had had of human history and within my body. I 'experienced,' or—following what I learned from Jung—"intuited" this "shift" as it was taking place within my own consciousness.

Implied by Teilhard's way of speaking is the notion that events taking place in the sociopolitical realm of human experience are continuous with—going down—our biological evolution, and—going up—the individual's unique experience of self as well as religious states of consciousness. While he speaks complexly, too much of the time making up his own vocabulary, Teilhard was successfully describing what I had experienced. Here he emphatically states the continuity between these levels of emergent phenomena:

> The ontogenesis of the microcosm (which each one of us represents) has no physically possible significance or context unless it is restored to its correct place not only in the phylogenesis of some zoological branch but in the very cosmogenesis of the entire

---

24 Teilhard, *Activation of Energy,* p. 253.

universe; and that it is in the perception of this fundamental dynamic unity that we find the essence of the great modern advance represented in the idea of evolution.[25]

Teilhard argues that humankind is being "compressed." The growth of the "noosphere," a "thinking envelope," i.e., the advances of telecommunications, expansion of industry, population, the emergence of the age of information, etc., leads to an intensification of a process of "hominization" which brings individuals, communities, and nations continually closer together, forcing them to either learn to rebuild their individual identities to compassionately include the *other* in some new level of organic organization or to be destroyed by the pressure. According to Teilhard this pressure leads humanity to be:

> …biologically confronted with the following dilemma…of either remaining psychologically in…[a] state of disordered agitation: and of being crushed…or of developing with in itself a faith in the future precise enough and ardent enough, through the very excess of compression upon itself, for it to emerge from the ordeal mentally and effectively made one.[26]

In these lines Teilhard helped me to understand my own intuitions about the continuities between biological, cultural, religious, and psychological evolution and, thus, my own place in the equation. Based on my intuitions and Teilhard's thinking, I began building a fuller understanding of my own development. My intuitions presented me simultaneously with images of my own individual work and with more general images of what human beings would be like at higher levels of consciousness. And my extensive exploration of science fiction also helps me imagine the possible futures of the species.

Teilhard's optimistic vision of activating a Christ-like consciousness within the species inspired me. Teilhard describes this consciousness as an apex or "Omega point" a point of "convergence," for the human species.[27] In these statements Omega is realized through the development of individual centers of experience, in a new relationship with one another that activates a larger self-awareness as a collective identity echoing the Christian image of god. In fact, Teilhard's god might be thought of as a combination of every individual on earth into a single organism whose dimensions

---

25 Teilhard, *Activation of Energy,* p. 256.

26 Teilhard, *Activation of Energy,* p. 346.

27 Teilhard, *Activation of Energy,* pp. 49, 345.

are not clearly imagined. The image of this new being shares little resemblance with more traditional conceptions of god, as Teilhard is attempting to integrate the bio-cultural and individual with an image of a supreme being. Such imagery echoed my own intuitions about the possibility of a great awakening of collective intelligence and compassion.

Between my unusual experiences of consciousness and Teilhard's writings I experienced a small budding of my largely neglected religiosity. I became determined to cultivate this; however, my own introversion kept me from joining any traditional or new-age religious/spiritual group. Instead, I just wanted to study. I wanted to find out how much of Teilhard's vision, his descriptions of the depth of religiosity that human beings could share, could be achieved. Was it possible for the human species to awaken to itself, to its own process of development and transformation? This question drove me. However, I could not find a community interested in such exploration. The institutional divides between psychology, politics, and religion seemed too daunting for me to bridge (though this might have been due to my own insufficient efforts).

Many of those I could find to talk to spoke about spiritual transformations in a way that didn't seem realistic to me. I was driven by the conviction that we were not on the edge of a new-age transcendence. My direct experience of political work precluded such nonsense. Instead, I was certain that the transformation ahead would require the cultivation of a political backbone capable of addressing the social ills of our time. Such thinking sobered any fantasies of imminent bliss.

As I made the turn toward clinical psychology I had the good fortune to do my doctoral studies at Meridian University where students were not only trained to be effective clinicians but also psychologically-minded "cultural leaders."[28] Much of the research I pursued at Meridian focused on pulling forward my past understanding of Jung with several current trends in post-Jungian thought as well as in political psychology and other related fields. From the research I had completed in my 20s and early 30s I was able to maintain my connection to a vision of humanity as an evolving living organism. While Teilhard's imagery was most beneficial in this territory, Jung too imagined such possibilities such as when he wrote:

---

28 Aftab Omer, "The Spacious Center: Leadership and the Creative Transformation of Culture" from *Shift: At the Frontiers of Consciousness* 6, 2005, pp. 30–33.

If it were possible to personify the unconscious, we might think of it as a collective human being combining the characteristics of both sexes, transcending youth and age, birth and death, and, from having at its command a human experience of one or two million years, practically immortal. If such a being existed, it would be exalted above all temporal change; the present would mean neither more nor less to it than any year in the hundredth millennium before Christ; it would be a dreamer of age-old dreams and, owing to its limitless experience, an incomparable prognosticator. It would have lived countless times over again the life of the individual, the family, the tribe, and the nation, and it would possess a living sense of the rhythm of growth, flowering and decay.[29]

Teilhard frequently evokes the imagery of a collective, self-aware humanity. Jung was also interested in the possibility of such a collective being; however, this citation is one of the rare times I have found that he spoke of such a prospect. While Teilhard is tapping into the intuition's capacity to discern future possibilities, Jung is actually looking for the psychology that could support the realization of such an advanced consciousness. Somehow, I found this image of Jung's to be more substantial, it, almost, seemed more real, as if there would be a way of getting from here to there. However, try as he might Jung did not find a way of taking such images and linking them pragmatically to his own research. Instead, he *infrequently* seems to take up the question about whether the unconscious could have some self-aware center, paralleling the ego in individual consciousness. And, he concluded that such hope may be unfounded, that such a center was at best "asleep" or "dormant."[30] I suspect his inability to connect the exploration of such a group consciousness to his science of the individual, as much as anything else, was part of his misery and his lifelong ambivalence about groups of people that too easily become mobs joining a mass-mindedness that leads to the worst horrors of modern history. Nevertheless, Jung did try to work from the individual toward some idea of cultural transformation, which opens a path to move toward the species-level collective consciousness he had imagined and searched for.

Jung offers imagery about the way in which the individual actually does contribute to cultural transformation. He begins with ways that individuals are sensitive to and

---

29 Jung, "*The Structure and Dynamics of the Psyche,* CW 8, ¶ 673.

30 C.G. Jung, "Conscious, Unconscious, and Individuation" in *The Archetype and the Collective Unconscious,* CW 9i, ¶ 509.

capable of being responsive to the unique suffering of their time. This is evident when he writes:

> Social, political, and religious conditions affect the collective unconscious in the sense that all those factors which are suppressed by the prevailing views or attitudes in the life of a society gradually accumulate in the collective unconscious and activate its contents. Certain individuals gifted with particularly strong intuition then become aware of the changes going on in it and translate these changes into communicable ideas. The new ideas spread rapidly because parallel changes have been taking place in the unconscious of other people.[31]

Implied by the citation is the idea that there is a psychological dimension to cultural transformation, a specific role for the individual to play in the process. While this may not seem new, Jung's angle on this also implies that there is a role for the *Institution of psychology* to cultivate the individual's capacity to bring about such transformation consciously.[32] My earlier citation of Erikson parallels this thinking in that Erikson thought that the individual could "mobilize capacities," in such a way that leads to a "new person; and with this new person a new generation, and with that, a new era." John Dewey also brought a psychological dimension to cultural transformation when he views the goal of our time to be to form a "new psychological and moral type."[33]

What psychology generally and Jung's psychology in particular make available at this time in history is an institutional form that focuses on the activation of the individual's capacities, the way we are each a responder to our times. Unfortunately, as a result of historical necessities such as the pressure to professionalize, psychology has myopically focused on the private lives of the individual, not their lives as citizens. This has limited the effectiveness of psychology to create the technologies Teilhard clearly asks for to set out to implement the species' developmental and transformational process. Jung, himself, seems to barely keep his focus on the psycho-cultural implications of his work.

---

31 Jung, *The Structure and Dynamics of the Psyche* CW 8, ¶ 594.

32 Peter Dunlap, "A Transformative Political Psychology Begins with Jung," *Jung Journal: Culture and Psyche*, 5:1 Winter 2011, pp. 47-64.

33 Dewey, *Individualism Old and New*, p. 83.

Over the course of my mid-thirties through current times, my mid-fifties, I have maintained my own hold on Teilhard's image of the transformational possibilities of the species. However, having let go of Teilhard's language and finding some leverage within Jung's analytical psychology, I've attempted to explicate the theory of their understanding of human development. For a long time I approached this as a matter of our "political development," which successfully ties together many dimensions of human experience.

The concept of political development as used within political science primarily account for democratic institution building;[34] however, it has also been used to refer to the cultivation of an effective citizenry.[35] More recently Samuels speaks of the political development of the individual.[36] Similarly, political scientist Stephen Chilton identifies political development of having both individual (micro) and cultural (macro) dimensions.[37] In my own research I draw heavily on the idea of political development to identify primary dimensions of what I'm coming to think of as the broader construct of our "psycho-cultural" development.[38]

To date, I'm simply following my mother's path to try to reconnect to my father's liberal political ambitions, that is, to create more just social structures. In the context of this hybrid calling I'm stumbling into, I use traditional and newly emerging psychotherapy techniques to support community leaders and activists to be as interested in changing themselves, to become the type of people needed in their communities, as they are interested in helping with *other* people's problems. This is the bridge between political and psychological liberalism I'm cobbling. Fortunately, there are many social scientists pursuing similar agendas. This is evident in Bill Moyer's writing when he says:

> Social movements have primarily focused on changing social systems and institutions to achieve their goals of a more peaceful, democratic, just, and sustainable world.

---

34 Francis Fukuyama, *The Origins of Political Order*.

35 Lucian Pye, *Aspects of Political Development*, pp. 38-9.

36 Samuels, *The Political Psyche*, p. 53.

37 Stephen Chilton, *Grounding Political Development*.

38 A tentative definition of "psycho-cultural" development includes the following domains of human experience: biological, psychological, sociopolitical, group-oriented, moral, religious, and historical. See my chapter "Jung's Relationship to Science and His Concept of Psycho-cultural," in Raya Jones (Ed.), *Jung and the Question of Science*.

However, there are many reasons why these goals cannot be achieved without equal attention to creating personal and cultural transformation—starting with activists ourselves.[39]

In the groups that I work with I'm cultivating the attitude identified here by Moyer, toward a synthesis of political and psychological liberalism. There will always be political activists who don't have much interest in psychology or who simply want to use psychology to understand and engage others. Similarly, there will always be psychologists that are not overly concerned with the political, they are incline to use politics to protect and advance their profession. However, I see no future without the cultivation of an institutional form, and practitioners who are developing that form, that brings these two together. I am working out ways of gathering people together for the sake of learning how to support each other's psychological healing and development while keeping a primary interest in each person finding their own level of community engagement.

This is my story about how the wisdom of early 20th century evolutionary thinkers can be engaged in ways that draws from their vision of human growth. Each of us have some unique contribution to make as a *responder* to the ills of our time. And as we collaborate across our differences, as we explore the depths of our own unique experience, as well as our emotional connection to one another, we become capable of collaborative efforts that are simultaneously political and psychological, that is, they are psycho-cultural.

This is also the story of my own redemption, my efforts to bring the wisdom of my family to life in a new way in my generation. It doesn't look likely that I will realize my dream of following in my father's footsteps; however, I have found a way that my mother's path, that of the citizen therapists naturally turns back toward the world and toward community. This began in the natural tension between my parents that I passively experienced, found its way into my intuition, and then it arose actively in my psyche as I fortunately turned with great gratitude toward the wisdom of Teilhard and Jung. These men both imagined that we are capable of becoming self-aware individuals who can create and join self-aware groups, which I take literally to mean that small groups, and then bigger ones, can learn to attend to their own development while focusing on the larger needs of their communities. Where this image leads, we will find out.

---

39 Bill Moyer, *Doing Democracy*, p. 197.

Bibliography

Barrows, A., Macy, J. *Rilke's Book of Hours*. New York: Riverhead Books, 1996.

Bellah, R., Madsen, R., Sullivan, W., Swidler, A., & Tipton, S. *Habits of the Heart*. Berkeley: University of California Press, 1985.

Chilton, S. *Grounding Political Development*. London: Lynne Rienner Publishers, 1991.

Dewey, J. *Experience and Nature*. New York: Dover Publishing, 1929.

Dewey, J. *Individualism Old and New*. New York: Capricorn Books, 1930.

Dunlap, P.T. *Awakening Our Faith in the Future: The Advent of Psychological Liberalism*. London: Routledge Press, 2008.

Dunlap, P. T. "A Transformative Political Psychology Begins with Jung." *Jung Journal: Culture and Psyche*, 5:1, 2011.

Dunlap, P. T. Generational Attention: Remembering How to be a People. *Jungian Society for Scholarly Studies*. V 8, 2012. Available online

Dunlap, P. T. The Unifying Function of Affect: Founding a Theory of Psycho-cultural Development in the Epistemology of John Dewey and Carl Jung in Inna Semetsky (Ed.) *Jung and Educational Theory*. Oxford: Wiley-Blackwell, 2012.

Dunlap, P. T. Jung's Relationship to Science and His Concept of Psycho-cultural Development in Raya Jones (Ed.). *Jung and the Question of Science*. London: Routledge.

Erikson, E. *Young Man Luther: A Study in Psychoanalysis and History*. New York: W.W. Norton, 1958.

Fukuyama, F. *The Origins of Political Order*. New York: Farrar, Straus and Giroux, 2011.

Henderson, J. *Cultural Attitudes in Psychological Perspective*, Toronto: Inner City Books, 1984.

Joyce, J. *A Portrait of the Artist as a Young Man*. New York: Colonial Press, 1916.

Jung, C.G. "The Psychological Foundations of Beliefs in Spirits." In *The Structure and Dynamics of the Psyche,* CW 8. Princeton: University Press, 1969.

Jung, C.G. *Psychological Types,* CW 6. Princeton: University Press, 1921.

Jung, C.G. "Basic Postulates of Analytical Psychology" *The Structure and Dynamics of the Psyche,* CW 8. Princeton: University Press, 1969.

Jung, C.G. "Conscious, Unconscious, and Individuation." *The Archetype and the Collective Unconscious,* CW 9i. Princeton: Princeton University Press, 1968.

Jung, C.G. "The Undiscovered Self." *Civilization in Transition,* CW 10. Princeton: Princeton University Press, 1957.

Jung, C.G. *Analytical Psychology: Its Theory and Practice.* New York: Vintage Books, 1968.

Moyer, B. *Doing Democracy.* Canada: New Society Publishers, 2001.

Omer, A. "The Spacious Center: Leadership and the Creative Transformation of Culture." *Shift: At the Frontiers of Consciousness* 6, 2005.

Pye, L. *Aspects of Political Development.* Boston/Toronto: Little, Brown & Co., 1966.

Samuels, A. *The Political Psyche.* London: Routledge, 1933.

Samuels, A. *Politics on the couch.* London: Profile Books, 2001.

Teilhard de Chardin P. *Human energy.* New York: Harcourt Brace Jovanovich, 1962.

Teilhard de Chardin P. *The future of man* New York: Harper and Row, 1964.

Teilhard de Chardin P. *Activation of energy.* New York: Harcourt Brace Jovanovich, 1970.

12

STORY OF TRANSFORMATION

Francisco (Paco) Martorell

What you are about to read is my personal story, deeply touched by the vision and life of Pierre Teilhard de Chardin. I have tried to enrich it with Carl Jung's reflections on the human psyche. It is the story of my transformation as a singular human currently immersed in the majestic hominization of the universe. This is the term that Teilhard uses to define how the development of humans is both the product of fourteen billion years of creative evolution as well as the crucial agent that will impact the present and future of all. How are the efforts of all women and men, individually and collectively, advancing evolution? How am I advancing it? How are you advancing it? Because I am convinced that I have a role in the evolution of all, this writing is not a private story. Neither is yours. This is why I have dared to apply Teilhard's magnificent vision of the human phenomenon and Jung's immersion into the human psyche to my personal story.

In writing about my personal life I am encompassing the story of the whole universe. Let me illustrate this. I just saw the movie *The Flight of the Butterflies*. There is a protagonist butterfly named Dana who, as a singular butterfly, explains and personalizes the phenomenon of millions of migrating Monarchs. Last year, visiting the sanctuary of the Monarchs in my home state of Michoacán, México, I felt in my warm hand the dying of a single butterfly. I saw the movement of the flapping wings become inert oranges and blacks. The stiff antennae and legs no longer were detectors of scent and solar radiation. Reluctantly, I let it fall to the ground where it joined many other dead butterflies. Dana and the other dead butterflies would become soil and nourishment for the fir trees that compose the sanctuary of the Monarchs. The butterfly Dana, the human Paco from Michoacán, you the reader—we all will die. I lifted my eyes and I saw millions of butterflies fluttering around, vibrant masterpieces of color, grace, and agility. We were there all together, the migrating living and dead butterflies, Mother Earth, the forest, the skies, and also a migrating human being consciously reflecting on the communion of all. What ultimately has prevailed—now, in the past, and will in the future—is the communion of all, the mysterious transcending reality of the universe: its harmonious creative wholeness. I found myself contemplating this mystery while activating my own will in deciding to protect, to share, and to re-create the generous reality of creation.

My story will focus on three aspects or perspectives: harmony, co-creativity, and communion. Like threads, I will weave them into the vision of Teilhard and Jung. Teilhard will have preeminence because he has affected me at key stages of my life. My formative years will correspond to the search for harmony. Building a family and working in my profession will relate to co-creativity. My current and future experience will be about communion. My story is organic. It is restless, evolutionary, and transformative, in constant ascension toward the more. The three perspectives of harmony, co-creativity and communion permeate all my chronological and geographical life stages. Increasingly conscious and able to make my own decisions, I have been creating my own *camino,* as the poet says: *Caminante, no hay camino, se hace camino al andar.* Migrant, there is no path, one creates it while walking.[1] This is the way of the universe.

Harmony, My Formatives Years

It was a year in the late sixties in Mexico City. I had finished the equivalent of a Bachelor's degree in Philosophy plus two more years of fieldwork teaching middle and high school seminarians. I was a third-year theologian in the Congregation of the Misioneros del Espíritu Santo. Father Superior was rendering his weekly "formation" session to our community of about 80 scholastics. It was a solemn, sacred atmosphere. Inside of me there was anguish, uncertainty, and longing. I was shy and terrified of speaking in public. Nevertheless I raised my sweaty hand and stood up. I was about to break fifteen years of silence. "Padre, I am close to being ordained and I have never received any formation about dealing with women." Out of breath, I could not elaborate any

---

1 Antonio Machado, "Caminante no hay Camino." *Proverbios y Cantares.*

more. "Hermano Martorell, what you are asking is about the natural world. Here, we are dealing with the supernatural." Total silence followed. No more explanations. No more questions. I was paralyzed.

I was born in Michoacán, (México) near where the Monarch butterflies migrate to their winter sanctuary. My mother, Doña Aurorita, was from Toluca, the highest city in the country, near the high mountain Xinantencatl ("volcano with lake craters" in the Nahuatl language). She inspired in me a profound sense of the sacred within the Catholic tradition. She was a "home mystic." My father, Don Paco, was born into a Spanish Catalan and Galician migrant family. He grew up on the Caribbean island of Cuba. He gave me the joy of life, adventure, sports, and openness for friendship. He migrated to México at age 16. Being near the ocean or in the mountains have always been my favorite places to live. Now I realize why.

A vibrant young Catholic priest, a mountain climber, Fernando de la Mora, embodied my young aspirations. I followed his invitation to a great adventure of life, to become a priest. I was eleven. Not an appropriate age to choose a life style. I was unaware of all the implications. Little did I know that mountain climbing and De la Mora's tragic death were going to be significant in my story.

So, I grew up as an adolescent, teenager, and young adult in the seminary. I was an avid learner, excelling in academics. I enjoyed daily sports, friends, hiking, and classical music. I experienced daily intense religious/spiritual practices celebrating daily Mass. The Sunday majestic liturgical celebrations, perfumed with incense and Gregorian chant fascinated me. In its secluded and protective ways, the seminary offered me an enriching atmosphere. At the same time I lacked family life. Significantly, the feminine was not only absent, it was forbidden.

My most profound alienation was how I experienced God. I was encouraged to imitate the suffering of Jesus who was God incarnated as human to expiate the sins of humanity. In this way he gained the forgiveness of God the Father and, at the same time, he demonstrated how compassionate God was. The more suffering, the more love, the more cleansing of sins. Jesus offered himself to save us. He was both the sacrificial victim and the offering priest. Renouncing the world I became a suffering imitator of Jesus, continuing his redemptive mission. My relationship with Christ and God would evolve in later years.

I experienced a drastic duality of nature and spirit that hindered my personal identity and growth, my relationships, particularly with respect to women, my studies of philosophy and theology, my perception of the universe, and ultimately my relationship to the Transcendent. My milieu was suffocating and frustrating. I was living in an exclusivist institutional religion that emphasized clerical male exceptionality, doctrine versus experience, and the blatant exclusion of women. It was not a harmonious world for me. Those words I heard "what you are asking is about the natural world; here, we are dealing with the supernatural," kept resonating in my heart both as a curse and as a challenge. I was thirsty and hungry for existential harmony.

In the last years of my theological studies I experienced three tipping points that transformed my life. The atmosphere of the sixties was the electrifying catalyst. The first was the Vatican II Council convened by the Catholic Church. It uncovered the promise of the Catholic Church becoming a true communal "church" where Catholicism would share the ways of "salvation," or the fullness of life, with other religions. The Council also proclaimed that clerical life was not the exceptional life style, that the Church governance was collegial, that the Bible was embedded in history and human expression, and that liturgy was the celebration of common life. Nothing on women yet. Married priests was not an option.

The second tipping point was my intentionally seeking friendships with women, well aware that I was deciding against many years of my formation since I was eleven. This was a big time duality in my moral conscience, a totally uncharted and fascinating decision. One of these women became my "unofficial" spiritual director. How grateful I am to this woman. For the first time in my life I was experiencing an incipient integral human life, albeit under the shadow of an existential duality.

Like an abundant rain soaking an arid soil, Pierre Teilhard de Chardin "found" me at this time of my life. This was the third tipping point. I had experienced the separation from my family. Alien to the mutually fulfilling relationship with women imposed by mandatory celibacy, I had renounced the co-creation of a family of my own. Mass was the expiatory sacrifice offered for the sins of the world. For so many years, every single day, I had participated in the liturgical mass that sacramentalized these dualities. And here was this Jesuit priest, celebrating the same Mass but with a universal vision, offering the whole universe in the Cosmic Christ in thanksgiving, harmonizing all that exists with his Christian faith, with the fire of his poetic imagination, with the knowledge of his science, and with the fullness of his heart.

At times we sat on the shores of Valle de Bravo Lake when the evening sun placidly painted skies and waters with reds and yellows and purples. At times we were immersed in the sacred forests near the sanctuary of the Monarch butterflies. At times we climbed high rocks that kept the memory of eons of evolution. At times, we gathered in our cluttered and untidy *celdas* (personal rooms) in *el Altillo,* our seminary in Mexico City during long lingering nights. My friends, Fernando Jiménez the philosopher, and Rosendo García the poet, and me, the mystic, spent hours and hours reading aloud and absorbing the little book, *The Hymn of the Universe*, by this unique Jesuit: a scientist, a poet, and a mystic. We felt harmony all around us but not in our compartmentalized life. Teilhard was transporting us to the universe as a home. We were inflamed by his own fire.

> Since, Lord, ...in the steppes of Asia, I have neither bread, nor wine, nor altar, I will raise myself beyond these symbols, up to the pure majesty of the real itself; I your priest, will make the whole earth my altar and on it will offer you all the labors and sufferings of the world...[2]

We had discovered a new, harmonious, and fulfilling liturgy, the liturgy of all in the universe. This was a different kind of a priest. A priest of the universe, of the real itself.

Teilhard was not defining God or explaining a doctrine. He was describing his mystical personal experience, fruit of a life-long search for the "consistent," the unifying of all. Suffering, labor, and death were part of this total experience. Everything was sacred. He had grown in the consciousness of that union. Would this be possible for me too?

> Because of the ultimate objective, the totality to which nature is attuned has been manifest to me, the powers of my being begin spontaneously to vibrate in accord with a single note of incredible richness wherein I can distinguish the most discordant tendencies effortlessly resolved: the excitement of action and the delight of passivity: the joy of possessing and the thrill of reaching out beyond what one possesses; the pride of growing and the happiness of being lost in what is greater than self.[3]

Again, was this achievable for me too?

---

2 Pierre Teilhard de Chardin, *Hymn of the Universe*, p. 19.
3 Teilhard, *Hymn of the Universe*, p. 27.

Teilhard's experience of Christ and Christianity was beyond the constraints of doctrine, far away from the expiatory perspective of suffering. It was the life of his own being; it was the life-evolution of the entire universe.

Was I able to be congruent and achieve a harmonious life that embraced the Universe within the clerical life style? Fernando and Rosendo did not think they could and left the community. I felt an immense loneliness, the loneliness humans experience when facing life decisions. So I went to a Carmelite monastery (called "deserts") to decide. I spent one entire night in the terrifying pitch-dark chapel of the monastery, literally arguing, fighting with God who for many years had called me to be a priest. I had been told that only those that remained in the congregation would have assurance of "eternal salvation." I was angry, resentful, and fearful. How could I fight against the all-powerful, distant up above me, almighty God? Crushed, I lost the battle. I had to stay…I felt forced. I really had not made a decision.

Co-Creativity, Family, and Professional Life

I was in my third year as ordained priest. I had been a living ambiguity and after my first year I had engaged in an intense discernment including professional psychotherapy. I was making a retreat in Valle de Bravo, along with 30 other priests including those in the top governance of the congregation. I could not stand being undecided any more. This was it. An American Jesuit, Harold Cohen, formed in the same spirituality that had inspired Teilhard, was directing the weeklong retreat. On the first day, in a five-minute exchange, I shared my predicament with him. He asked me to look for two signs that would manifest: one, that God had forgiven all my sins, and two, that he loved me tenderly. These were Harold Cohen's own words. To the consternation and bewilderment of all around me, I cried all day every day. But unlike my experience in the Carmelite monastery where I was before an overpowering God, here God was quiet, waiting compassionately inside my being, letting me reflect and decide, letting me be fully human. I was in pain but it was my own, it was not inflicted. Seven days passed. No decision. My whole body was a single nerve. We were celebrating the last Mass of the retreat. The gospel reading was the story of a paralytic who was brought by friends to Jesus through the roof of his own house where he was teaching.[4] Immediately I thought, "I am this paralyzed guy." Without any questioning, without complaining to the friends for damaging his house, moved by their act of friendship and their intense desire for the healing of the friend, Jesus said to the paralytic: "Your sins are forgiven." Here was the first sign. Righteous people thought this was too much. But Jesus went even farther telling the paralytic: "Stand up, pick up your mat, and go home." At that moment I decided to leave the life style of a priest, go home, and build a family. Was that the second sign of the "tender love"? Before we left the retreat everyone shared the highlights of the retreat experience. The priest who spoke before my turn shared that he had had an affair with a woman but the retreat had been a healing experience and he was going to continue a fresh new priestly ministry. Then I shared: "I have decided to leave the priestly ministry because the clerical life is not for me and because I have decided to build a family." A friend said to me at that time, and I quote him: "Paco, when I gave you the sign of peace during the mass, I felt a tender love for you." This was, indeed, the second sign.

To be forgiven of my sins meant taking ownership of my decisions and their implications in the past, then, and in the future. To "go home" meant walking on my own and acting out my decision: leave the clerical life and build a family. I had decided to re-create myself. The whole universe had evolved fourteen billion years to reach to this point in me. Now, I needed to "walk" beyond consciousness and journey through the rocky path of decision-making, the exciting life of creativity. I had to "re-create" my own personal life. And, since I had decided to build a family, not the endeavor of a single individual, the full reality of my decision was not to be done solely on my own: I had to co-create.

When I decided to leave the ministry I was cut off (this is the Latin meaning of *decidere*) from financial resources. I did not receive *ni un centavo* (not even a cent) from the congregation I belonged to. I knew that my decision was going to hurt people, particularly my mother. She did not speak to me for five years. I lost the aura of clerical prestige. This was my gain. So what did I do? I migrated to *El Norte* (the North). I felt impelled to recreate my life completely anew, in a new place. The Jesuit priest involved in my deciding experience at Valle de Bravo had offered to help me. He was part of Loyola University in New Orleans and there I went. My only possessions were a VW beetle loaded with books and the equivalent of hundred dollars for food and gasoline in Mexican money. I slept in the car. Creativity became my life, like the life of

---

4 Mark, 2, 1-12.

all immigrants according to my own will (*por mi propia voluntad*). I was about to gain a new culture, a new language but, at the same time, determined not to relinquish my own. Was this going to be possible? I lived in the exuberance of New Orleans for almost two years working in a community center that addressed the social and religious needs of Latinos from the Caribbean, Central and South America.

I met Elizabeth, my wife, at the end of the sixties in Mexico City. Her deep spirituality, thoughtfulness, and feminine affection were a balm for the insanity of my life in the seminary. Three years after leaving the ministry I married her. Like all that exists in the universe it was impossible for me to imagine what marriage and family life would become. The seminary certainly had not prepared me for this.

We have raised four children, wonderful children, a girl and three boys. They became the focus of our marriage. Elizabeth and I have joined hearts, minds, and hands to give them the best. They are now hardworking adults, compassionate, committed to the common good around them. That was a profoundly co-creating experience. I am still in awe when I reflect on bringing our children into being and nurturing their evolving lives.

What about the two of us? Again, the seminary certainly had not prepared me for marriage. I did not distinguish between becoming myself, "creating" my individuality, and being married. Remember that I said that I was not going to relinquish my culture (my values, language, history, relationships—more than typical traditions). This was painful. At times I felt a profound sense of not belonging. I felt isolated and lonely. Worst of all, not in touch with my psychological and relational dynamics, I did not always communicate and found myself brooding inside. Immersing myself in my work became an outlet but not a solution for my individuation.

In the middle of my marriage-family-work adjustments, Teilhard came to my rescue for the second time. May of 1994. It was a gift from Elizabeth. She made it possible for me to spend a week in the wilderness of the Rocky Mountains. I brought only one book with me, *El Medio Divino* (The Divine Milieu). The same beat-up book I had read surreptitiously in Mexico City in 1968. Why this book only? I don't know. What I know is that I had a true mystical experience. As such, bear with me. This is difficult to express. There is no English word that translates the rich meaning of the French word *milieu* or the Spanish *medio*. The term perfectly describes Teilhard's entire vision: the divine is actively present at the center, the core, the heart, as well as surrounding all that exists. The divine milieu is present as a source of existence, as energy that attracts, connects, generates, and unites. What Teilhard described in his book was what I experienced, a mystical experience (*una vivencia mística*). Every morning I climbed the mountains around me from five until noon. In the afternoons I meditated on *El Medio Divino*. Becoming alive in the birthing of the new day, I sensed in myself the dawn as the passage from the dark womb to the slowly increasing luminous day. While eagerly climbing, I filled my chest with the fresh breath of the morning. One day I experienced an electrical storm at a high altitude. The deep voice of thunder-singing drama echoed inside me and throughout the surrounding mountain peaks and ravines. I felt infinitely vulnerable, sensing the proximity of death. In this overwhelming immensity I felt my smallness. During those days I felt the tight embrace of Mother Nature, bathing in luminous harmony and magnificent beauty that reverberated in my heart, in my bones, at the center of my entire being. I felt her protecting me, warning me, telling me that I am contingent, that I will endure death that I belong to All. I felt, in me and outside of me, a perfect union with all, a powerful peaceful energy, fully at home with the transcending and unifying *Medio Divino*.

> *It is precisely* because he is so infinitely profound and punctiform that God is infinitely near and dispersed everywhere. *It is precisely* because he is the Center that he fills the whole sphere…In the divine milieu all the elements of the universe *touch each other* by that which is most inward and ultimate in them. There they concentrate, little by little, all that is purest and most attractive in them without loss and without danger of subsequent corruption.[5]

Yes, there was a river of powerful peaceful energy in me. Reflecting now, I realized how dynamic, creative, and unitive my vivencia in that *Medio Divino* was.

> There (in the Divine Milieu) we shall discover, with the confluence of all beauties, the ultra-vital, the ultra sensitive, the ultra-active point of the universe. And, at the same time, we shall feel the plenitude of our powers of action and adoration effortlessly ordered within our deepest selves.[6]

Energy to create, to co-create, is for Teilhard the essence of *The Divine Milieu*. In his book he clearly maps out the path expressing how that happens in practice. His whole life was indeed the tireless ascension of that path. In summary he is telling us

---

5 Pierre Teilhard de Chardin, *The Divine Milieu*, pp. 91-2.
6 Teilhard, *The Divine Milieu*, p. 93.

that all that we experience as our own actions, all that we endured as not coming from our own will, all that enriches us, all that diminishes us including suffering, evil, and death—all these human experiences are the path to harmony, growth, creativity, and the communion of all in the plenitude of the Divine Milieu. This milieu is the source, the path, and the end. It is the evolutionary journey that every existing being has taken in the universe. In our human species we merge our minds in the divine milieu and enlighten this path by increased consciousness. Energized by the same divine milieu, our wills and hearts are empowered to decide. As co-creative agents, then, we advance the evolution of universe. However, can suffering be creative in the path to growth? Can the evil we inflict in others generate good? How can we humans create communion when we actually observe so much greed, violence, and exclusion? More significantly for my story, how could I let the Divine Milieu enter the center of my being and energize me to co-create in my own family, in my professional life, in my living on this mother planet? How could I move toward communion with all?

Communion Today and the Future

I returned home from the mountains energized by the clarity and depth of the vision of the Divine Milieu. That was also when I entered into the most "productive" time of my professional work. I engaged in a massive collaborative enterprise between the Milwaukee Public School System and community resources of Milwaukee. But productivity trumped interiority. My relationship with Elizabeth did not deepen. I did not keep the presence of the Divine Milieu alive in me. Its light and energy did not abandon me, though, and the universe was ready to put me back on track using several rounds of suffering, detachments, and global insights. First, I had open-heart surgery. The surgeon literally took my heart out of my body while he worked (modern Aztec ritual?). Contingency and death became real. Second, after retiring I offered to volunteer for life, full-time in an organization. But then I was dismissed for moving too fast on my own. Didn't the governing body of the organization realize that I had given up my life for the organization? I painfully recognized that I was working on my own ideal, holding the ownership of my own individual life separate from the other people in the organization. Third, my relationship with Elizabeth became more difficult. Hadn't I chosen building a family with her to be the purpose of my life? Yes,

I had committed to the children but I had taken her for granted. Suffering in all its forms engulfed and permeated my being at that time.

Teilhard came to me at this crossroads of my life for the third time. It was through Elizabeth again, and through our intentional small community, the Ramos Ignatian Associates. In 2002 a group of Associates had a retreat conducted by John Surette, a Jesuit. He talked about the "new cosmology" and it transformed them. Elizabeth was so inspired by their enthusiasm that for a year she insisted that I learn about it. It sounded esoteric to me. She pressed on and, at last, I began reading Brian Swimme. Soon I "discovered" that he sounded like my old Jesuit friend, Pierre Teilhard. In fact, Brian had been profoundly influenced by Teilhard after Thomas Berry had asked him to read *The Phenomenon of Man.*[7] Ursula King's biography of Teilhard, *Spirit of Fire,* was a revelation for me.[8] At this crucial and profoundly painful time of my life I was in contact with the very life of the man that had changed the course of my life at a young age. This was the man who had described my own mystical experience in the Rocky Mountains through the book that he had identified with himself, *Le Milieu Divin*. He was the flesh and bones man whose heart was inflamed in the heart of the Cosmic Christ. My encounter with him this time opened the floodgates of the "new cosmology" and I got immersed in the exuberant river of the "evolutionary movement." The universe had prepared me for this moment.

This last part of my life has been the steepest stage of my life that, like climbing a mountain, will take me to the summit of my death. Mountain climbing became a powerful archetype in climbing the summit of life. With increasing consciousness and decisive willingness, I have been facing the sufferings that have surrounded me as well as the limitations of my aging. I sense the attraction of the summit and the anticipation of the fullness of communion—step by step, ascending, sweating, surrounded more and more by emerging harmony and beauty. What is happening? What is energizing me? What is clearing my vision? What type of communion am I talking about?

To experience the total satisfaction of mountain climbing requires being in "good shape." I call this being in healthy communion with myself. This includes knowing my physical strength, having full awareness of the route and possible risks, intentionally focusing on the beauty and harmony of the surroundings, and exercising a deter-

---

7 Pierre Teilhard de Chardin, *The Phenomenon of Man.* (*"The Human Phenomenon"* is the title of an improved recent translation of the original *"Le Phénomèn Humain"*).
8 Ursula King, *Spirit of Fire: The Life and Vision of Teilhard de Chardin.*

mination to endure the efforts I need to reach the summit. Full satisfaction is at each step. Reaching the summit would be the confirmation of the satisfaction that is built up in each step of ascension.

As expected, my most arduous effort has been deepening my relationship with Elizabeth. So I tried hard, very hard, to change her. Wrong. I realized, after experiencing a great deal of pain, that the first and the only way to begin the climbing was to look at my own integrity, my own individuation. Echoing Jung's words, I realized that there is no birth of consciousness without pain. I have had to question and redirect all my expectations and assumptions. There were so many shadows, so many unconscious masks, so much dark matter that I needed to embrace to integrate their energy in me. I needed to enrich the fabric of my psyche in my effort to re-encounter her. I could hear Carl Jung screaming at me while I was digesting his words in *The Undiscovered Self*:

> His (the individual) environment cannot give him as a gift that which he can win for himself only with effort and suffering. On the contrary, a favorable environment merely strengthens the dangerous tendency to expect everything to originate from outside – even that metamorphosis which external reality cannot provide, namely, a deep-seated change of the inner man… This is hardly possible except through a process of self-nourishment.[9]

Even though Jung wrote this book in the context of the Cold War, vehemently valuing the individual over communism, I applied his message to my relationship with Elizabeth. The very first step had to be my own personal transformation. The most urgent and significant communion I needed to build was, therefore, within myself. How difficult has been what Jung unfolded throughout all his work on the human psyche: discovering my unconscious, embracing my shadows and integrating all their potential energy in me, and in my relationships, particularly, of course, with Elizabeth. I have realized that it is only when I integrate all my given capacities: body, senses, emotions, consciousness, unconsciousness, will, and spirit (capacity to transcend), that I can grow in my full individuation. I have produced my own pain when I have disconnected my personal unity (communion). This has occurred when I have regarded myself as the center of the universe, deciding and acting without thinking, thinking without being in touch with my emotions, feeling without observing, and

---

9 C.G. Jung, "The Undiscovered Self" in *Civilization in Transition,* CW 10, ¶ 537.

the most evident, not listening to my body, which never lies. In fact, I needed to have my heart taken out of my own body so that it could tell me directly looking at my face: "You need to change, body, I am not kidding you."

I like Jung's expression: "process of self-nourishment." This has happened when I meditate; when I open to the Divine Milieu and let it permeate my life. I do it at no specific time. I value the life energy that germinates in me from all my capacities and experiences. This has helped me to regain the communion within myself.

But full integration with my self was just one of the energizing aspects in the ascension to the mountain of my life. The next risky step was to face my relationship with the "other," point in case, with Elizabeth. Enamored with my own individuation, it has been difficult for me to let it go. Suffering reappears and lingers when I do not open my circle. My energy, then, is invested in defense, attack, or escape—all well known responses. This has been the source of my own pain and the harm I have inflicted on myself, on Elizabeth, and others. The only way to redeem and transform my suffering and evil was to experience a change of heart, taking the risk of entering into a co-creative communion. How would I pursue that and make it a reality? Simple! Just looking at how the universe has evolved in a magnanimous ascension of co-creativity. Here is my anthropomorphic reflection on one example. Hydrogen and oxygen attract each other; they "mold" their beings recognizing their own capacities in themselves and in the other. They risk losing their individuality, dying to themselves and dive into each other. They connect. The emerging creative surprise is water. They become co-creators of one of the most magnificent beings on earth, the one that makes up 70% of our own human body, indispensable for life. The evolution of the universe is really not that simple after all. In fact, the "hominization" of this universal co-creativity implies consciousness and willingness. Complexity is constantly increasing as the whole vision of Teilhard's points out. I call it enriching. "Adding" consciousness and willingness is immensely enriching, fully creative: it is, indeed, the hominization of evolution. It implies, however, more effort, integration of body and psycho-spiritual functioning, teamwork, the sharing of energy and purpose, seeking and co-creating communion, common-union. Once and for all let me call this the hard and fulfilling path of love. So, how am I experiencing this creative role in my communion with Elizabeth? Twofold. First, opening to her, letting her know that I am contingent, imperfect, that I am appealing to her own individual richness.

Recognition of the shadow leads to the modesty we need in order to acknowledge imperfection. And it is this conscious recognition and consideration that we are needed whenever a human relationship is to be established. A human relationship is not based on differentiation and perfection, for these only emphasize the differences or call forth the exact opposite. It is based, rather, on imperfection, on what is weak, helpless and in need of support - the very ground and motive of dependence.[10]

Second and most significant, I am trying to affirm her as she is. Consciously I decide to let her be. Basically, using all my faculties and energies, I move unconditionally to seek what she thinks is the best for her. I connect center to center with her. I am "dying" to my individuality in isolation. I do not annihilate it. I open my fullness to the other.

It is the same risk that every single thing in the universe takes to advance evolution, to co-create and enrich the whole. Is this possible? Jung called the effort to connect opposing perspectives, such as life and death or the merging of two individuals, "the transcendent function." It can become the source of new creative energy in our deepest being. It is my ascension toward death. This is real. This is profoundly harsh. Painful. However, I believe that my death transcends all and becomes the summary of all my creativity: the paradoxical and absolute surrendering into the Divine Milieu. Teilhard would call it the total attraction to the Omega Point, the fullness of communion.

Now, it is Teilhard talking to me:

To become fully ourselves we must advance toward a convergence with all other beings, toward a union with what is other than ourselves. The perfection of our own being, the full achievement of what is unique in each one of us, lies not in our individuality but in our person; and according to the evolutionary structure of the world, the only way we can find our person is by uniting with one another. From top to bottom the law is forever the same. There can be no spirit without synthesis; and this same law holds good everywhere in created reality, from top to bottom. The true self grows in inverse proportion to the growth of egotism. In the image of the Omega Point that attracts it, the element becomes personal only by becoming universal.[11]

---

10 Jung, "The Undiscovered Self" in *Civilization in Transition,* CW 10, ¶ 579.

11   Pierre Teilhard de Chardin, *The Human Phenomenon*, p. 187. Teilhard used the term "person" throughout his writings to indicate an individual who has transcended him or herself and become spiritualized in direction toward the Omega Point.

My complementarity with Elizabeth and the "other" was the same as everything in the universe: co-creative. Just imagine the millions and millions of interactions that have made it possible for me to use this computer and write what I am writing. In Teilhard's vision all the efforts of the universe have the same purpose and same direction: through co-creativity, unfold the universal communion in the Divine Milieu toward the Omega Point.

Being in communion with my self and my spouse is the "preparation" for the ascending communion with the larger world.

Fernando de la Mora, the mountain climber priest that guided me to the seminary, comes now to my memory. He died in the Aconcagua, the highest mountain in the Americas. He was descending from the summit when his team encountered a German team that was ascending toward the summit, only 800 feet from the top. He offered to guide them while his two teammates waited for him. A snowstorm engulfed them after they reached the summit. He died just 50 feet away from the shelter where his friends were waiting for him. Morita, as we called him, was in good shape, in full communion with himself. He was a wonderful selfless team member as I experienced it climbing with him the three highest mountains in Mexico. He reached death when he cared for the German team.

So, as an individual, what is my current awareness, attitude, and will toward the other team, toward other nations, toward earth, our communal others? I realized that we humans have engaged in two World Wars and continue creating new ones, that we have changed the climatic atmosphere and radically affected life in oceans and in forests, and that we have tinkered with DNA. We humans are destroying our home earth and are causing the extinction of our own species. Jung and Teilhard were in the middle of the two World Wars. How did they react? Jung looked at the psyche of the individual and urged us all to get in touch with our conscious and our unconscious and use those energies for the good of all. After Teilhard bloodied his hands bearing injured men in a stretcher for four years in WWI and after being exiled by his Jesuit superiors, he wrote the most optimistic and hopeful writings of his life: *Le Milieu Divin* and the *Le Phénomèn Humain*. He has been criticized for not expanding on suffering, evil, and death. More than writing about them, he deeply experienced them. He addressed them by integrating them as part of the creative energy of evolution and as part of the path of the direction signaled by hominization, the fullness of communion.

Humanity, the spirit of the Earth, the synthesis of the individual and the peoples, the paradoxical reconciliation of the element and the whole, of unity and multitude – for all these things, said to be utopian, yet which are so biologically necessary, to actually take shape in the world, is not all we need to do, to imagine our power of loving develops until it embraces the totality of men and women and of the earth?[12]

For the last 20 years of my life I have directly worked promoting collaboration among organizations and institutions first in the Milwaukee Public School System and lately in the Milwaukee Inner-city Congregations Allied for Hope (MICAH). It has been both a discouraging and hopeful experience. Milwaukee is a segregated city. Unemployment of African-American males is above fifty percent. Immigrants live in the shadows. I want to bring a message of hope. I want to promote a culture of collaboration, erasing one of competition, superiority, and exclusion, in order to be congruent with the third type of communion I need to experience in my life.

Among many movements I want to promote, there are two that attract me in particular.

The Pachamama Alliance that spreads its message through the *Awakening the Dreamer* symposium that "inspires and educates participants around the world to bring forth an environmentally sustainable, socially just, and spiritually fulfilling world."

The other movement is the one experienced and articulated by Parker J. Palmer in one of his latest books: *Healing the Heart of Democracy*. His five "habits of the heart" constitute a practical road map to live the Jungian inner vision and the Teilhardian cosmic vision:[13]

- An understanding that we are all in this together.

- An appreciation of the values of "otherness."

- The ability to hold tension in life-giving ways.

- A sense of personal voice and agency.

- A greater capacity to create communion.

---

12 Teilhard, *The Human Phenomenon*, p. 189.
13 Palmer Parker, *Healing the Heart of Democracy,* p. 172

Cosmic Christ

In a time of intimate sharing, Elizabeth asked me: "How do you pray? How do you pray for people?" She caught me off guard, so my response was spontaneous: I try to center, leaving out any mental function. I try to "empty" myself, or detach myself from my own activity to become totally receptive. I experience the presence of a "milieu" that transcends me and permeates me. I let it soak into my being, like blood circulating in my arteries, like the air that I breathe. This is the Divine Milieu. After a while, people, events, emotions, ideas, desires come to my mind, on their own, like significant visitors. I welcome all. Gently, one at a time I connect them with each other at the light or fabric of the Divine Milieu…

Then, Elizabeth remembered my experience in the Rocky Mountains and she asked me: "Do you know the meaning of "keystone," the name of the place where you stayed in the mountains? It is the stone that locks the others in place."

Teilhard's last writing, one month before his death, was an essay that he called "The Christic." He describes as a mystical experience the synthesis of his entire life, at the summit of his life: He identifies the Cosmic Christ as the transcending fullness of the universe. The archetype keystone that holds all together tangibly (Christ is the fullness of what is human, in total harmony), expansively (universal influence, total creativity), assimilative (integrating all, total communion), is the Cosmic Christ.[14]

> I saw how the joint coming of age of Revelation and Science had suddenly opened a door for twentieth century Man into a sort of ultra-dimension of Things, in which all differences between Action and Passion (in the sense of being acted upon) and Communion vanish – not by being neutralized but by reaching an explosive climax: and this at the high temperatures of the Centre and on the scale of the Whole. I saw the universe becoming amorized[15] and personalized in the very dynamism of its own evolution.[16]

I dare to apply Teilhard's vision to the evolution of my own life in its three stages of communion: with myself, with my spouse, and with earth. The agency of the three types of communion is realized only through love: creating goodness and harmony

---

14 Pierre Teilhard de Chardin, "The Christic" in *The Heart of Matter*, p. 89.
15 The term "amorized" is derived from "*amor*," love, in Latin.
16 Teilhard, "The Christic" in *The Heart of Matter*. p. 83.

in and with the other, consciously and willingly. Love the other as you love yourself. Love even your enemy because the love of God is cosmic. This was the essence of the gospel of Jesus as his followers experienced him—a man who proclaimed and lived a universal love. As such he became the Christ. In Teilhard's vision, this love is the attraction, energy, and the unifying keystone of evolution. My experience of Christ is to live the fullness of my humanity in the majestic, restless process of evolution, which implies dying to my individuality by consciously and willingly integrating it into the communion of all. How does this relate to my daily life experience?

While I was writing this final paragraph I received the sad news that members of my community of Ignatian Associates had lost their only son, age twenty. He drowned in a lake. I remembered the butterfly that died in my hand. At his wake I heard many young people telling story after story of the amazing love this young man had for all, of his exuberant joy for life. Excruciating pain in a milieu of love. His individuality had been resurrected in the tangible, expanded, and communal experience of all who remember his love. This is my experience of the Cosmic Christ. All humans along with the whole universe move in the direction toward the full communion in the Omega Point.

Conclusion

I relate my story with a profound gratitude. I have a growing awareness that all that I am, all that I have lived and achieved, all that I will experience has been and will be possible because of the capacities that I have received. The most significant of all has been the gift of "will," mi voluntad: the capacity to become a decisive agent to grow, to interconnect, to love, to co-create, and to transcend.

My death is the ultimate source of my gratitude. It tells me that my greatest given reality is not my own private contingent life but its progressive integration into the communion of all. My story reveals a transformative journey impossible to achieve on my own. Everything in the past has contributed to the present experience. My gratitude is a *gracias* to the ineffable source, to the sustaining and directing energy, and to the glorious end that immerses me in the fullness of communion. Many humans express these realities by the word God. Teilhard calls them Divine Milieu and Omega Point. In my gratitude to God, I also make explicit my gratitude to include the primordial elements, the stars, our sun, our home Earth, all living creatures, all the reflecting decision-making humans of all times. I think of my parents, Elizabeth, and all those who have touched my life. The universe has carved my existence. As a gift, I am a part of the All and for that I am humbly grateful.

Like light surrounding everything, so is my story permeated with love. It is the same love that exploded in the initial flaring-forth when the universe was born; the same love that has energized the heart of all matter, the same love that infused life in the womb of the oceans; the same love that has inhabited the hearts of humans in their restless journey toward full communion. It is the very same love that many humans have encountered and universalized in the Jewish man of Nazareth, Jesus, the Christ, who Teilhard experienced as the Cosmic Christ.

I share my story with you with a sense of urgency. Our "role" is crucial. I sense it when I realize that we humans, for the very first time in fourteen billion years, are the only species that has the capacity to decide whether to advance or hinder evolution. We have contributed with immense advances in all areas but at the same time we have made terrifying destructive decisions particularly when we have not been motivated by a universal common good but by selfish individualistic or nationalistic interests. My story is a challenge. It is not a sentimental voice but a loud scream from the depths of my heart, that shouts: see! decide! act! It is a call to share and coalesce so that we can move and transform our activities into a harmonious, creative, and communal universe, now.

In telling my story I try to convey a passionate hope. It is the luminous unlimited hope that scientists, artists, and mystics have enkindled throughout the existence of humanity. The very same hope that Pierre Teilhard embodied all his life and that Carl Jung uncovered in the complex human psyche. It is the hope that embraces both growth and healing for continuous transformation. It is the hope that has impelled me to constantly seek beauty and goodness, emerging newness and creativity. It is also the hope that has kept me fully alive in times of pain and in facing the harm that I have inflicted on others. My hope is vibrant and unlimited when I realize everything in the universe has the inner capacity to complement, to innovate, to regenerate, and to transform. Science attests that this magnanimous creative journey has been going on for 14 billion years and will continue until the unknown. My story is a microcosm of the universal evolution. So is yours.

Bibliography

Jung, C.G. "The Undiscovered Self" in *Civilization in Transition,* CW 10. New York: Bollingen Foundation, 1964.

King, Ursula. *Spirit of Fire: The Life and Vision of Teilhard de Chardin*. Maryknoll, New York: Orbis Books, 1996.

Machado, Antonio. "Caminante no hay Camino." *Proverbios y Cantares*. Madrid: Movimiento Cultural Cristiano, 2006.

Parker, Palmer. *Healing the Heart of Democracy*. San Francisco, CA: Jossey-Bass, 2011.

Teilhard de Chardin, Pierre. *The Divine Milieu*. New York: Harper & Row, 1960.

Teilhard de Chardin, Pierre. *Hymn of the Universe*. New York: Harper & Row, 1965.

Teilhard de Chardin, Pierre. *The Human Phenomenon*. Portland, Ore: Sussex Academic Press, 1999/2003.

Teilhard de Chardin, Pierre. *The Phenomenon of Man*. New York: Harper & Row, 1960.

13

TEILHARD, JUNG, AND THE
ENVIRONMENTAL CRISIS

Dennis L. Merritt

Carl Sagan, co-chair of A Joint Appeal by Science and Religion for the Environment, presented a petition in 1992 stating:

> The environmental problem has religious as well as scientific dimensions…As scientists, many of us have had a profound experience of awe and reverence before the universe. We understand that what is regarded as sacred is more likely to be treated with care and respect. Our planetary home should be so regarded. Efforts to safeguard and cherish the environment need to be infused with a vision of the sacred. At the same time, a much wider and deeper understanding of science and technology is needed. If we do not understand the problem it is unlikely we will be able to fix it. Thus there is a vital role for both science and religion.[1]

An international team of climate experts recently reported they were 95% confident that climate change is a result of human activity. Dick Cheney advocated an Iraq war if there was a 1% probability Saddam Hussein had weapons of mass destruction. Americans went to war in the Middle East, but there is little action on climate change. Why? What can be done to meet Sagan's challenge?

An examination of "that vision thing" mentioned by George H. W. Bush is necessary, plus an in-depth analysis of environmental problems suggested by deep ecologists. Two remarkable men of the 20th century, the French Jesuit scientist and mystic Teilhard de Chardin and pioneer Swiss psychoanalyst Carl Jung provide guidance. They walked the earth at about the same time, Teilhard from 1881 to 1955 and Jung from 1875 to 1961. Both formed deep connections with their childhood environ-

---

1 Carl Sagan, "To Avert a Common Danger," *Parade Magazine,* March 1992, pp. 10-12.

ments, which profoundly affected their visions and concepts. Teilhard, a consummate paleontologist and geologist, was involved in the discovery of Peking man and had beautiful visions of the Spirit of the Earth. Jung developed an ecological concept of the psyche and a psychology to analyze environmental problems at their deepest levels—the myths that drive cultures. These two men complement each other in responding to Sagan's challenge. Their work can be encompassed within ecopsychology, a new field that examines how our attitudes, values, perceptions and behaviors impact the environment. It calls for a reformulation of our political, cultural, economic, and educational systems to enable us to live sustainably. Like deep ecology, it maintains that humans are capable of a far deeper connection to nature, serving as a natural basis for protecting the environment.

The Omega Point

Teilhard's envisioned a universe evolving since its inception, the Big Bang, towards an Omega Point, the climax of creation and evolution.[2] This will be a conscious experience of a Cosmic Christ—the universe as the transfigured body of Christ.[3] Teilhard noted the cosmos has always demonstrated a remarkable ability to generate new, more complex and symbiotically integrated forms via a synthesis of existing elements.[4] This extends from the creation of large atoms from smaller ones that are generated by forces in the collapse of certain types of stars to the emergence of complex, interdependent elements of an ecosystem. Teilhard, like Jung, maintained that everything has a material and spiritual dimension. These spiritual/psychic dimensions increase in complexity as matter generates more complex forms.[5] Teilhard associates God with the generative forces of the universe, evolutionary processes, and an increasing synthesis that eventually produced humans. He anthropocentrically considers humans to be the epitome of evolution as only humans are reflective and conscious of their spiritual nature, conscious of God. Jung put it differently: God is largely unconscious

---

2 Pierre Teilhard de Chardin, *The Human Phenomenon*, pp. 183-185, 209-215.

3 Pierre Teilhard de Chardin, *Hymn of the Universe*, pp. 19-55.

4 A. Fabel and D. St. John, eds., *Teilhard in the 21ˢᵗ Century: The Emerging Spirit of Earth*, p. 3.

5 Teilhard, *The Human Phenomenon,* p. 217.

as demonstrated by being unaware of his split-off side, the Devil.[6] Teilhard's views are Eurocentric and Christian with a belief that Christianity and the West are the leading edge of an ongoing positive evolution.

Evolution is divergent, producing 5-10 million species of living organisms, until humans arrived on the scene only 200,000 years ago. With humanity as the summit of evolution, according to de Chardin, evolution of individuals and societies must now be convergent. The natural process of complexification leads to "a confluence of thought, the convergence of people at a higher collective level, the growth of a super-consciousness, and ultimately the appearance of some 'ultra human,' which [Teilhard] calls the 'Omega Point'."[7] If this evolution does not occur, we may self-destruct, but the thrust of evolution towards increasing synthesis hopefully will save us.

The Power of Love

Love is the prime mover towards the Omega Point. Human love is the ultimate evolution into the most complex and nuanced form of Eros/relationships/connectedness, which began with the simple attraction between atoms.[8] It is essential to realize humans are all basically alike and have the same basic needs, Jung's concept of the archetypes, with love as the most foundational and transformative human experience. This beautiful, sustaining energy is also a significant unifying force as both Jung and Teilhard emphasized. Teilhard described the sublimation and transcendence of the personal experience of love and attraction between a man and a woman as one of the strongest human experiences of the cosmic process of union and synthesis. It can lead to the highest form of spiritualization of the earth, and an avenue to experiencing God as love. At its deepest level, Jung described the anima and animus (a man's inner feminine and a woman's inner masculine) as a mediator and guide to the Self (personal image of God): they energize, fascinate and entice a person into relationship with the other expressed in highest value concepts: what one would climb the highest mountain for and swim the deepest ocean.

---

6 C.G. Jung, *Psychology and Religion: West and East*, CW 11, ¶¶ 560, 591, 594.

7 Ursula King, *Spirit of Fire: The Life and Vision of Teilhard de Chardin*, pp, 175-6.

8 Teilhard, *The Human Phenomenon*, p. 188. King, *Spirit of Fire: The Life and Vision of Teilhard de Chardin*, p. 72.

We are most alive, creative, and uniquely expressive as an individual when we are in love—fascinated by another. This illustrates what de Chardin meant by unity increasing individuality. The paradox is that the most intimate relationship is where each member feels most autonomous, individuated in Jungian terms, which allows their partner to be fully autonomous as well. Co-dependency and subtly forcing the partner into your soul image (anima and animus) are absent.

The Mystery of Matter

For Teilhard, God is to be found through the transpersonal dimension of human love and by fully immersing oneself in matter, including our bodies. Fascination with the universe draws us out of ourselves to transcend our ego boundaries. This engages us with Other in its myriad forms, processes, and levels of interrelationships—"a communion with God through earth."[9] To be deeply drawn into an object is to penetrate to its essence, ultimately a mystery, as indeed we are to ourselves.

Science becomes a revelatory process for Teilhard by exploring the mysteries of the cosmos. Increasing scientific knowledge moves us closer to God as God is imminent in the universe: the universe is the extraverted space-time side of God. Christianity presented two paths to knowing God: through divine revelation and by studying what God created and how it operates. "The light of nature" was the alchemists' focus with their god Hermes as the "green spirit" in nature.[10]

The forces of the universe did not have an impersonal sense of awe and capriciousness for Teilhard as they did with Jung's "personality number two."[11] This sense, experienced strongly through Jung's adolescence, was conditioned by his wounded Eros experience as a child.[12] Number two became the basis for Jung's concept of the collective unconscious. Universal forces and forms become divine and personal for de Chardin through his vision of the whole universe being offered up to Christ and transmuted into his living body and blood, just as the host is believed to be trans-

---

9 King, *Spirit of Fire: The Life and Vision of Teilhard de Chardin,* p. 55.

10 C.G Jung, *Alchemical Studies,* CW 13, ¶ 229.

11 C.G. Jung, *MDR,* pp. 44-45, 66-68, 72, 74-75, 77-78, 210-11, 313.

12 Dennis Merritt, *The Cry of Merlin: Jung, the Prototypical Ecopsychologist: The Dairy Farmer's Guide to the Universe,* Vol. 2, pp. 159-165.

muted during Roman Catholic mass. Christ is the ultimate unification, the Center of centers, as the universe synthetically coalesces into the body of a Cosmic Christ.[13] Transcendence of the personal experience of sex and love (they have physiological dimensions) becomes the ultimate human experience of the penetration of the Divine Fire into every atom of existence. This pushes every element to its maximum individual existence; every individual from atom, to ant, to human is a display of as an aspect of the Divine.

To immerse oneself in matter/psyche is to cast oneself into development, continual change, and synthesis, for Teilhard saw change and evolution are constants in the universe. Such immersion requires faith, hope, love, courage, and a vision of bringing all creation to the unifying Center of centers. Only this approach is strong enough to transcend petty egotisms, jealousies, racism, nationalism, and religious hatred. Today de Chardin would say that a vision of this strength is necessary for everyone to work together to address the catastrophic dimensions of climate change and environmental degradation.

Spirit of the Earth

Most impressive is Teilhard's relationship to matter and the world. For him, the Divine will only be revealed by exerting oneself to the utmost in touching God in the world of matter. Teilhard states he "received from [God] an overwhelming sympathy for all that stirs within the dark mass of matter; because I know myself to be irremediably less a child of heaven than a son of the earth."[14] The universe is like our flesh in that "it attracts us by the charm which lies in the mystery of its curves and folds and in the depth of its eyes."[15]

Teilhard's clearest statement of the Spirit of the Earth is described in an imaginal encounter of a man with the essence of matter. It had "an immeasurable pervasive subtlety." A whirlwind engulfed the man and he felt possessed by,

---

13 Teilhard, *Hymn of the Universe*, pp. 41-55.
14 Teilhard, *Hymn of the Universe*, p. 21.
15 Teilhard, *Hymn of the Universe*, p. 24.

an irresistible rapture...as though all the sap of all living things, flowing at one and the same moment into the too narrow confines of his heart...And at the same time the anguish of some superhuman peril oppressed him, a confused feeling that the force which had swept down upon him was equivocal, turbid, the combined essence of all evil and all goodness...The tempest of life, [was] infinitely gentle, infinitely brutal.[16]

Matter, entire and untamed, says "You had need of me in order to grow; and I was waiting for you in order to be made me holy." Its spirit is found in "untouched wilderness" beyond a world "grown weary of abstractions... [and] the wordiness of social life." "Because in my violence," Matter proclaimed, "I sometimes slay my lovers; because he who touches me never knows what power he is unleashing, wise men fear me and curse me." "Son of man, bathe yourself in the ocean of matter; plunge into it where it is deepest and most violent; struggle in its currents and drink of its waters. For it cradled you long ago in your preconscious existence; and it is that ocean that will raise you up to God."[17]

Teilhard perceived matter as the "'matrix of spirit': that *in* which life emerges and is supported, not the active principle *from* which it takes its rise." Since creation is an evolutionary process, "then existence of matter is the necessary precondition for the appearance on earth of spirit." Matter is acclaimed "as the divine *milieu*, charged with creative power."[18]

Complexity Theory

Many of de Chardin's revolutionary concepts have been described by chaos and complexity theories, which began to emerge in the 1960s. Complexity theory, which incorporates chaos theory, has been put on a par with relativity theory and quantum mechanics in terms of its significance. It concerns the genesis of complex systems and the interactions and interconnectedness which emerge by increasing energy input into even relatively simple systems.

---

16 Teilhard, *Hymn of the Universe*, p. 60.
17 Teilhard, *Hymn of the Universe*, pp. 60-65.
18 Teilhard, *Hymn of the Universe*, p. 70.

Complex arrangements emerge when two opposing forces act simultaneously on a system, such as one force seeking homeostasis and another force acting to destabilize the system. When energy is increased beyond a certain point, the system goes into a chaotic state and graphed data reveal the emergence of bifurcations—new possibilities and choice points—the origin of our sense of freedom of choice. The most astonishing discovery is that systems self-organize into new patterns and arrangements as they pass through a transitional phase and then settle into a new stable state. This is the unifying and synthesizing activity in the universe described by Teilhard.

With complexity theory, the future is open and evolving, as Teilhard proclaimed, and individual variables cannot be isolated in the classic scientific research procedure. Teilhard fully embraced the evolutionary paradigm and extended it to all human systems—historical, economic, and even religious.

Consciousness as the interiority of complex arrangements of matter is highly developed in humans. The human brain is the most complex structure in the known universe and operates on complexity theory principles. This makes it capable of imagining and experiencing many dimensions, including a spiritual sense of a unity of all things.

Teilhard believed God works within the natural processes of the universe as he lures humans forward with the vision of an Omega Point. Jung associated numbers with spirit, powerful ordering factors, and described numbers as the purest form of archetypes.[19] He noted the uncanny link between them and physical phenomena. Jung thought the process of evolution that eventually produced humans was too chaotic and random with too many redundancies and dead ends to have been guided. Rather, it is more like humans were stumbled upon during the evolutionary process. Jung saw humans as the conscious part of God's creation, the conscious part of God. He articulated the myth for modern man as completing God's creation by "becoming conscious of *all we can* (cf. Teilhard) and thus to give [creation] 'objective existence.'"[20]

Both Teilhard and Jung described humans as having acquired many of God's powers (Jung would add the powers of the gods) so humans are now co-creators of the universe as we experience it on planet earth. This arises through our intelligence, generalist human form, and our abilities to manipulate and alter the environment with

---

19 C.G. Jung, *The Structure and Dynamics of the Psyche,* CW 8, ¶¶ 870-871.
20 Barbara Hannah, *Jung: His Life and Work,* p. 185.

hands and head; through powers of observation and ability to accumulate and pass on knowledge; and through the use of rigorous scientific techniques.

The Self

Teilhard's Cosmic Christ can be placed in an archetypal context using Jung's concept of the Self. The Self is described as the center and a centering force in the psyche which unites all aspects through the center. Especially important is the way Jung described an individual's deep experience of the Self. Its phenomenology includes a holistic, all-encompassing, emotional, intellectual and numinous experience that first appears in an individual. It feels like an eternal truth that has been revealed which answers all questions. That spirit can generate a band of followers. A religious movement may develop, which as time passes tends to become dogmatic and rigid, losing its original wholeness. Religions, like everything else, can age and decay unless the mythic base continues to evolve.

Jung stated that it was irrelevant whether the message comes through, or out of, the psyche: the phenomenology is the same. The divine message bears the stamp of the particular historical and cultural context from which it emerges. The fractal Self, at the cultural level, has appeared as Jesus, Mohammed, Buddha, and *Wakantanka* (Lakota Sioux) along with many other forms. It is impossible to know how close the Self images are to the essence, how good the map is. Given the number of absolute truths clearly at odds with each other, it helps to think of portrayals of the Self as coming from blind men describing the various parts of an elephant they are touching, the elephant being a metaphor for the Self.

Alchemy

Jung realized that a symbolic understanding of alchemy provided the historical context for understanding his heroic "confrontation with the unconscious" after the split with Freud in 1913. Alchemical imagery provides a guide for following the deep, symbolic, transformative processes of turning the lead in our lives, our complexes, into gold. Western alchemy traces its roots to the early centuries AD, peaking in the 17th century with the rise of chemistry and science. Alchemists were looking for spirit in matter using their dreams and visions to explain what was eventually discovered to be basic chemical processes.[21] They felt Christ had saved the microcosm, the soul, but they were working with God to save the macrocosm, to re-sanctify matter—the world. Jung regarded them as the first depth psychologists, projecting a post-Christian unconscious into matter. Alchemists evolved the Christian myth and attempted to heal the split between spirit and matter in the process of trying to unify opposites. They dealt with excluded elements of Christianity: the body, matter, the feminine, sexuality, and the natural world.

Jung's personal image of the goal occurred in 1939 when he awoke to a beautiful vision of a greenish-gold Christ, bathed in bright light, at the foot of his bed. Jung realized an analogy was being made between Christ and the "green spirit" of the alchemists, the life-spirit that animates the entire universe—man, nature, and the inorganic realm:

> My vision was thus a union of the Christ-image with his analogue in matter, the *filius macrocosmi* [son of the macrocosm]… [It was an] undisguised alchemical conception of Christ as a union of spiritually alive and physically dead matter.[22]

The Age of Aquarius

Jung approached the concept of God incarnate in matter, the spirit in matter, from a very different perspective from de Chardin. He analyzed the Judeo-Christian myth and claimed that Christianity was not a monotheistic religion due to its dualistic God/Self image: the Devil has power equal to God on Earth. God projects his dark split-off side, about which he is unconscious, onto humans. Jung emphasized the importance in Western culture of realizing that God wants to incarnate in the sinful human, fully entering space-time and matter via the human body. (Humans must rid themselves of as much darkness as possible to enable them to take in this tremendous

---

21 Marie-Louise von Franz, *C.G. Jung: His Myth in Our Time*, pp. 204-5.
22 Jung, *MDR*, p. 211.

infusion of energy. We suffer the split in the God image when we get close to God. The hope is that by an act of grace a unifying image will emerge through the action of the transcendent function in the psyche.

Jung predicted a paradigm shift in Western culture, now spread worldwide, when he coined the terms "New Age" and "Age of Aquarius." He associated the birth of Christ synchronistically with the beginning of the 2000 year Age of Pisces represented by two fish swimming in opposite directions. Jung interpreted the first thousand years of this Age with the building up of the bright side of God; the second thousand years revealed the dark side of God represented by the second fish. Signs of the dark side for Jung were two World Wars, the atom bomb, Communism and Fascism, the population explosion, and the increasing rate of environmental destruction. Jung found hope in a scene in the *Book of Revelation* when a very "pagan" mother began to descend from heaven with a newborn male. God withdrew the baby into heaven and sent the woman into the wilderness after they were confronted by a seven-headed dragon. Jung interpreted the baby to represent a consciousness Christianity was not ready for 2000 years ago. This consciousness will begin to emerge in the Age of Aquarius that Jung thought began its 2000 year eon in 1940. Aquarius, the water bearer, is pouring water from his jug, the vessel of consciousness, into the mouth of the Southern Fish, symbolizing a bringing of conscious energy to the instincts and the collective unconscious. It will lead to a new rising of spiritual energy, a special role for the feminine, and a new fullness and greater completeness of the God image. Jungian analyst Marie-Louise von Franz stated that the task of the Aquarian Age could be "to become conscious of his larger inner presence, the Anthropos, and to give the utmost care to the unconscious and to nature instead of exploiting it."[23] The Anthropos is the god-man as universe and union of all opposites, including spirit and matter. Teilhard's Cosmic Christ is an excellent example of this archetype.

---

23 von Franz, *C.G. Jung: His Myth in Our Time*, pp. 135-136.

Dreams and an Ecology of the Psyche

Jung's ecological concept of the psyche is best illustrated by thinking of a dream that we are in along with several other people. Our dream ego is closest to our conscious ego state. Who are those other people? They are, and are more than, parts of ourselves.

The challenge is to be in good relationships with these people for how we relate to them is how we relate to others in our waking state and to the environment. They emerge out of the wholeness of nature as we humans experience the energies of the universe, the tide of life in our animal aspects, and the accumulated history of personal, family, national, and cultural identities. As Jung described it, "The psychic depths are nature, and nature is creative life."[24]

Psychotherapy, Big Dreams, and Complexity Theory

Psychotherapy, when used well, is an important aspect of ecopsychology. Most significant in the psychotherapeutic process are the occasional Big Dreams—numinous (inner light) dreams, sacred dreams. These are personal images of the archetype of the Self, one's personal image of God. It can appear as a landscape, an animal or plant, a crystal (precisely ordered arrangement in the mineral realm), or unlimited other forms.

The Self can be framed as an organism as described by complexity theory and related to Teilhard's concepts.[25] It can be thought of as the source of dreams. In a dream, no part can be separated from another; every part qualifies every other and dream story lines are presented with gestalts of images inseparable from feelings.

Jungian analyst George Hogenson and others present the concept that humans inhabit a symbolic universe, more discovered than invented.[26] The primary evolution since 3.3 million year-old Lucy has been in the evolution of our symbolic systems.

---

24 C.G. Jung, *Modern Man in Search of a Soul*, p. 215.

25 Dennis Merritt, *Hermes, Ecopsychology, and Complexity Theory: The Dairy Farmer's Guide to the Universe*, Vol. 3, pp. 190-195.

26 George Hogenson, *"The Self, the Symbolic and Synchronicity: Virtual Realities and the Emergence of the Psyche"* in *Journal of Analytical Psychology*, 2005, p. 280.

The most basic symbolic stories, the big attractors in the psyche, are the myths. Myths set the foundation of our perceptions, behavior, values, and attitudes and myths are *other* people's religions. A type of Darwinian process selects those myths that give meaning to individuals in a culture in particular historical periods and help cultures survive in their particular environment.[27] Western culture is currently in the dangerous position of being without a myth. We have little that gives meaning to individuals and societies, and most alarmingly, we have no myth to help us live in a sustainable manner on our home, planet Earth.

Individuation

Individuation is the goal in Jungian work and the best antidote to consumerism. It is the process of becoming a whole person with fully developed potentials and living a meaningful life. Jung said, "Man cannot stand a meaningless life."[28] The process of individuation is dependent on developing a good Ego-Self axis, best illustrated by the Chinese ideogram for the Sage—"The ear listening to the Inner King," the Inner King or Queen being the Self. For Teilhard a person realizes their unique essence after being penetrated and expanded by the Divine Fire. These approaches require a certain degree of living the simple life. There is a pre-occupation with one's inner journey, a valuing of reflection, time out and time away from it all, removal of clutter, and moving at a slower pace so one can be in a good "listening" position. Jung commented on how difficult it is to live the simple life and railed against an increasingly noisy world, time-saving gadgets that increase the pace of life, and "keeping up with the Jones."

---

27 George Hogenson, *"What are Symbols Symbols of? Situated Action, Mythological Bootstrapping and the Emergence of the Self"* in *Journal of Analytical Psychology,* 2004, pp. 74-75.
28 W. McGuire and R.F.C. Hull, eds., *C.G. Jung Speaking: Interviews and Encounters,* p. 439.

Meeting Sagan's Challenge

Jung and Teilhard have strengths and weaknesses in helping us meet Carl Sagan's challenge. Teilhard has a mystical, powerful sense of unity and spiritual completion with his vision of a Cosmic Christ. This may work for many Christians, especially Catholics, but is a problem for many non-Christians and biologists. Biologists view all living forms as being equally successful. Many see humans as a cancer on the planet increasingly out of the control of the self-regulating and integrating forces in nature, actively consuming Earth's resources and destroying the web of relationships.

A vision of wholeness shared with both these men comes from Black Elk, a Lakota Sioux Holy Man. Part of Black Elk's vision in 1874, when only nine years old, included the sacred hoops/circles of all the tribes, including white men, forming a giant circle around a huge flowering tree.[29] Plains Indian families sat in a circle within their circular teepees, adding to this vision of centers within centers, selves within selves, nested organisms. The flowering tree resonates with Jung's Self image in a dream of a flowering magnolia tree bathed in its own light at the center of Liverpool. The tree was on an island in a round pool in the center of the city square. Streets radiated out from the corners of the square to city quarters, each containing a replica of the city center.[30] In Black Elk's vision each nation, its peoples and religions, retain their unique identities while being linked in a sacred organic unity as implied by the flowering tree at the center. The flowering tree is a more "natural" and non-anthropomorphic Center of centers than a Christian Cosmic Christ associated with its Divine Light.

Establishing a deep attachment to non-humans can begin with Jung's suggestion that we extend the concept of loving our neighbors to include the animal world and the animal in us. Plants, animals, and all elements of the natural world would then be related to as subjects, not objects for our use. When the Lakota say, "We are all related," they include all peoples of the natural world—the four-leggeds, standing brothers (trees), etc.

---

29 John Neihardt, *Black Elk Speaks: Being the Life Story of a Holy Man of the Oglala Sioux as Told to John G. Neihardt*, p. 43.

30 Jung, *MDR*, pp. 197-99.

Science and Education

All elements on earth are linked through the evolutionary history of our planet, a planet where matter has evolved to the point of being self-conscious. We need more science as Teilhard emphasized, science that reveals these mysteries and increases our understanding and appreciation of the natural environment. It would study the human psyche and ways to support a more holistic development of individuals and societies. Jung was more pessimistic about science and technology, noting how its overly rational approach destroys a vital mythic spirit and sense of connection between living things. It feeds our addiction to progress and releases powers we are unable to use wisely. Teilhard would see this wisdom arising as we move closer to the Omega Point.

Thomas Berry, a renowned Catholic eco-theologian and great admirer of Teilhard, was inspired by him to develop the Universe Story as a myth for modern men and women. Berry pointed out that de Chardin was rather blind to the negative aspects of scientific endeavors, too enamored with progress and its thrust to conquer nature, and he ignored damage being done to the environment. However, environmental problems certainly were not as apparent in 1955 when Teilhard died.

Both Teilhard and Jung saw great value in the development of integrated knowledge and in a good education. Teilhard believed this would increase our sense of interconnectedness, lead to societies beyond nations, and a convergence of spiritual beliefs. Jung said there can be no holistic systems without including a sense of the numinous, the sacred. This could be done in education by establishing and maintaining a mythological base throughout the system by studying myths, fairy tales and film. Greek myths and images about Hermes suggest an ideal focus to develop a symbolic and mythological venue to discuss sexuality, relationships, nature, advertising and consumerism, business, transitions including adolescent initiations, etc. Hermes as the personification of significant aspects of complexity theory can be used to integrate math and science with mythology and symbolism. Teenage love songs and films present many examples of the anima and animus as functions of the Self. Both Jung and de Chardin experienced and praised this aspect of the anima. Studying the guiding myths and religions of various cultures would lead to a sense of the uniqueness offered by unity.

It is imperative that our educational systems make us conscious and wise in our relationship to nature and focus on living sustainably. We must be educated about our cultural evolution, the evolution of our religious forms, and the archetypal dynamics of the God-image within. Jung said we need more psychology, and famously added, "We are the source of all coming evil."[31] Education at all levels, including adults, can be used to connect us to the land in multiple ways. A holistic education will use science, myths, the arts, stories, and symbols to develop an appreciation of nature. Native American stories associated with particular environments are especially useful.

The Ecology of Psychology, the Psychology of Ecology

The concept and conduct of psychotherapy needs revamping along eco-psychological lines. Hillman stated it well in his book: We've Had a Hundred Years of Psychotherapy— And the World's Getting Worse. His claim is that psychotherapy has contributed to environmental problems by focusing on intra-psychic and interpersonal phenomena to the exclusion of the environment people live in. Hillman's proposal to consider Aphrodite as the Soul of the world is a means of moving therapy beyond the confines of the therapist's office and re-establishing a sense of the soul of the world. This is a neo-pagan compliment to de Chardin's Cosmic Christ.

Jung's concept of the layers of the collective unconscious help place the individual within a historical and evolutionary construct, transcending the narrow range of interpersonal interactions. Teilhard offered a good development of the primal human layer, Jung's "two million-year-old man within." Jung thought of archetypes as emerging from these deep layers of the psyche and strongly expressing the natural world within a symbolic language. Dream images and stories are a link to our bodies, the evolutionary history of our species, and nature. To meet Jung's challenge to unite our cultured side with "the two million-year-old man within" means we would relate to nature in a symbolic and emotional manner, conducting ourselves in a reciprocal, sustainable way. Dreams can facilitate this process. Big dreams of animals, plants, and natural elements like rocks, wind and thunder, and landscapes should be treated like spiritual elements just as an indigenous person would. They are personal spirit guides to connect with through artistic expression, studying their biology or geology, and

---

31 McGuire and Hull, eds., *C.G. Jung Speaking: Interviews and Encounters*, p. 436.

most importantly by immersing oneself in the habitat of that plant or animal. This enables the environment to work directly on the individual.

A Big Change Has Gotta' Come

Our species needs a paradigm shift to face and address the frightful realities of current and future environmental situations. We will have to confront our collective guilt for the damage we continue to do to the planet and to the poor and disenfranchised who will suffer the most from climate change. We must acknowledge the demonic role we will play in the coming extinctions of millions of species. What is not brought to consciousness comes to us as fate Jung said.[32] We can either consciously adopt an ecological perspective or let fate, as ecological disasters, force such a perspective upon us. This perspective will permeate all levels of human consciousness and behavior. To quote Jung, "We are beset by an all-to-human fear that consciousness—our Promethean conquest—may in the end not be able to serve us as well as nature."[33]

There are no actions big and bold enough to address the gestalt of conditions that are producing climate change and contaminating the environment in a myriad of ways. Bold actions are needed at all levels: personal, cultural, social, political, economic, educational, and spiritual. We may have already exceeded the amount of carbon dioxide in the atmosphere that will push us over the tipping point leading to irreversible destruction. There is precious little time to usher in a necessary paradigm shift, Jung's New Age or the dimensions of Teilhard's Omega Point. Both men have much to offer in an attempt to meet Carl Sagan's challenge. The stakes are high. We must not lose. It is an exciting time.

---

32 C.G. Jung, *Aion*, CW 9ii, ¶ 126.

33 Jung, *The Structure and Dynamics of the Psyche*, CW 8, ¶ 750. Prometheus was the Greek Titan who stole fire from the gods for human use, enabling progress and civilization. His punishment was to be chained to a rock and have his liver pecked out by an eagle, the emblem of Zeus. The liver grew back by the next day and again eaten, a scenario eternally repeated.

Bibliography

Fabel, A. and St. John, D., eds. 2003. *Teilhard in the 21st Century: The Emerging Spirit of Earth*. Maryknoll, NY: Orbis Books, 2003.

Hannah, B. *Jung: His Life and Work*. Boston: Shambala, 1991.

Hillman, J. 1989. "Cosmology for Soul: from Universe to Cosmos" *Sphinx* 2: 17-33, 1989.

Hillman, J. *The Thought of the Heart and the Soul of the World*. Woodstock, Conn.: Spring Publications, 1992.

Hillman, J. and Ventura, M. *We've Had a Hundred Years of Psychotherapy—And the World's Getting Worse*. New York: HarperCollins, 1992.

Hogenson, G. 2004. "What are Symbols Symbols of? Situated Action, Mythological Bootstrapping and the Emergence of the Self." *Journal of Analytical Psychology* 49 (1): 67-81.

Hogenson, G. "The Self, the Symbolic and Synchronicity: Virtual Realities and the Emergence of the Psyche." *Journal of Analytical Psychology* 50: 271-285, 2005.

Jung, C.G. *The Structure and Dynamics of the Psyche*, CW 8. New York, N.Y.: Pantheon Books, Inc., 1960.

Jung, C.G. *Aion*, CW 9 ii. New York, NY: Pantheon Books, Inc., 1959.

Jung, C.G. *Psychology and Religion: West and East*, CW 11. Princeton, N.J.: Princeton University Press, 1958.

Jung, C.G. *Alchemical Studies*, CW 13. Princeton, N.J.: Princeton University Press, 1967.

Jung, C.G. *Modern Man in Search of a Soul*. New York, NY: Harcourt Brace and World, 1933.

Jung, C.G. *Memories, Dreams, Reflections*. Aniela Jaffe, ed., New York: Vintage, 1965.

Jung, C.G. *Man and His Symbols*. Garden City, N.Y.: Doubleday & Company, Inc., 1964.

King, U. *Spirit of Fire: The Life and Vision of Teilhard de Chardin*. Maryknoll, NY: Orbis Books, 1966.

McGuire, W. and Hull, R.F.C., eds. *C.G. Jung Speaking: Interviews and Encounters*. Princeton: Princeton University Press, 1977.

Merritt, D.L. *Jung and Ecopsychology: The Dairy Farmer's Guide to the Universe:* Vol. 1. Carmel, CA: Fisher King Press, 2012.

_____ *The Cry of Merlin: Jung, the Prototypical Ecopsychologist: The Dairy Farmer's Guide to the Universe*, Vol. 2. Carmel, CA: Fisher King Press, 2012.

_____ *Hermes, Ecopsychology, and Complexity Theory: The Dairy Farmer's Guide to the Universe*, Vol. 3. Carmel, CA: Fisher King Press, 2012.

_____ *Land, Weather, Seasons, Insects: An Archetypal View: The Dairy Farmer's Guide to the Universe*, Vol. 4. Carmel, CA: Fisher King Press, 2013.

Neihardt. J. *Black Elk Speaks: Being the Life Story of a Holy Man of the Oglala Sioux as told to John G. Neihardt.* Lincoln: University of Nebraska Press, 1972.

Ryley, N. *The Forsaken Garden: Four Conversations of the Deep Meaning of Environmental Illness.* Wheaton, IL: Quest Books, 1998.

Sagan, C. "To Avert a Common Danger," *Parade Magazine,* March 1992.

Teilhard de Chardin, P. *Hymn of the Universe.* New York, NY: Harper & Row, 1965.

Teilhard de Chardin, P. *The Human Phenomenon*, Sarah-Appleton-Weber, trans. Portland, OR and Sussex: Academic Press, 1999.

Von Franz, M.L. *C.G. Jung: His Myth in Our Time.* London: Hodder and Stoughton, 1975.

14

THE FRENCH PRIEST AND
THE SWISS PSYCHOLOGIST

An Enterview with Fred Gustafson about Pierre Teilhard de Chardin
and Carl Gustav Jung by Dr. Robert Henderson

RH: I know Pierre Teilhard de Chardin has been important to you for several years.
What does he mean to you?

FG: I first heard the name of Chardin from one of my seminary professors back in
the late 60s. I do not even know the context in which he mentioned him but the
name stuck with me. Over the years, and more so lately, I realize how important
he has become for me and for the world we live in today. It is important to know
that Chardin was a priest and had with it a deep-in religious life in the best sense
of what we can imagine that to be today. He was also a scientist in paleontology,
a geologist, and a student of physics. He studied the earth and the evolutionary
roots of not only the human species but of the entire universe. He is important
first of all because he really brought together these two historically opposing ways
of looking at life, namely, science and religion. His scientific studies brought him
ever greater clarity to his religious beliefs, which were for him obviously Christian. That leads to the second and even greater reason I find him important. He
brought the idea that all life has a "within of things" as he would say. This is not
dissimilar to what physicists might say in that all things are in motion. For him
God was not just operative in history as we might think in an Old and New Testament manner; God was operative from the beginning in every particle of life.
He said the "Christ seed" was in every bit of matter. He did not say the "Jesus
seed." As the word, Christ, means, everything is an "appointed one." Everything
carries the divine spark. So, any understanding of incarnation has to be extended
to all of life not to just Jesus 2000 years ago. The old idea that matter is dead is

very much a part of our modern theology still today. Because he said matter is very much alive and plays a vital part in the evolution of all things, especially the human psyche, Rome silenced him from publishing any of his books of a religious nature. So, in short: "Why is he important to me?"—because he is saying and has shown that all of matter down to the tiniest particle is vibrant with life. That has a lot to say as to how we treat the earth, our own body, and one another.

RH: Your response led me to think of shamanism. Do you see Pierre as Shaman?

FG: Bob, I never thought of Chardin as a shaman but the question is intriguing. Shamans throughout the world were people who communicated with the spirit world and were then able to help a person find their soul again that maybe a spirit had taken or brought a spirit back to the spirit world that inhabited a person. Today we use different language like neurosis or psychosis. We say "What got into that person" or "I don't know who I am anymore, I feel empty." In many ways, psychotherapists, psychoanalysts, and clergy have shamanism as their spiritual lineage in terms of helping people with soul issues. In that sense Chardin was a shaman in the best sense. As priest and basic human man, he was able to put people at ease. He was described as a kind, generous, and socially present person that made people relax in his company. Maybe in this small way they felt more of themselves around him and thus more in touch with their own soul. But what really makes me put him in the category of shaman was his ability as scientist and priest to recover the soul of the earth, or matter itself and, because of this, pave the way for those of us today to find a deeper understanding of our own soul individually and collectively that has for so long been disconnected from matter as living and soulful. This has been poetically described in his beautiful book *Hymn of the Universe* in the chapter titled "The Spiritual Power of Matter." It is here he sees Matter coming toward him as a woman bidding him to do battle with her. She had been the scorned and rejected one. She says to him, "You had need of me in order to grow; and I was waiting for you in order to be made holy." And again later she says, "Never say, then as some say: Matter is accursed, matter is evil...Life shall spring forth out of death and then finally, the words which spell my definitive liberation, 'This is my body'."[1] In so far as Chardin challenges us to know and experience the soul of the world, of matter and the matter of our own bodies, he

---

1 Pierre Teilhard de Chardin, *Hymn of the Universe*, pp. 60, 64.

is undoubtedly the shaman reminding us there is no sense of real soul or spirituality disconnected from the earth or, for that matter from the entire cosmic story.

RH: With all of matter being so alive to Chardin, I wonder how the earth felt about his ministry to it especially given how we modern people often are hurtful and insensitive toward it.

FG: The word "felt" or "feel" is a word we associate humans having. We are not in the mind of thinking the rest of creation has feelings. Yet, anyone that has ever had an animal pet certainly knows animals have feelings. But when we apply this to the earth itself the leap may seem too big to make. The earth having feelings!! Nonsense, we would say. Well, perhaps not as we might but then again how do we even know how the word applies to the earth itself. Yet, I am confident to surmise that every indigenous group in the world still existing today along with the indigenous nature of every human being if ever unconscious knows that the earth is personal often referred to as "Mother" or "Grandmother." So, does She have feelings? Let us suppose She does. If so, what is that feeling? Again I surmise it is anger and sadness both the result of how humankind in its indifference, ignorance, arrogance, and short-sightedness is causing unbelievable damage to the worldwide environment. I know there have been natural devastations throughout the history of our planet, but the increase and severity of the ones in the last ten years are by the facts of science around the world influenced by man-made damage to the environment. In Her anger, we are and will continue to pay a serious price until we, on a worldwide basis turn the environmental crisis around. This is what Chardin foresaw in the sad treatment of matter and what Jung saw in the psychological problems of people.

RH: Father Teilhard died an interesting death in 1955. I understand that he hoped to die on Easter and he did. Apparently he died from a heart attack during a heavy discussion at a friend's in New York City. Do you have any reflections on that?

FG: As for Chardin's death on Easter which he had mentioned long before his death had hoped for, I can only accept as remarkable. This seems to fit well into Jung's understanding of synchronicity which is based on a-causal connections that unite inner and outer phenomenon. Would this not be a testimony to Chardin's deep faith belief that was so profound that it could constellate the apex moment of

Christian theology, namely, Easter as the symbolic and expressive culmination of his life and career? It makes sense both religiously and scientifically and one with which, I am sure, Jung would agree. Chardin might say, "I have completed my small part in the evolution of the cosmic story" while Jung might say, "Chardin achieved the successful completion of his individuation and made his contribution to humanity."

RH: What would have the relationship between Father Teilhard and Jung been like, so you suspect?

FG: I have little doubt that both of these men would have gotten along famously. The reasons are many. Both were deep thinkers in their respective fields and pushed the boundaries of their calling. In some ways both were seen by the traditional thinkers of their times as having gone too far in their researches and being "heretical" to their fields. Yet, both plunged the depths of their professions: Jung in psychology had opened up the world of the collective unconscious and archetypes and Chardin in the world of paleontology and geology had freed the existing notion of evolution of the survival of the fittest to seeing the first moment of life as the beginning that leads to evolution's fulfillment in the unfolding of consciousness in the human being. Both started from different professions but wound up in the same place, namely, consciousness in its ancient depth and future possibilities. Neither of them, however, were naïve enough to believe that just because consciousness continues to evolve means the human race will make the right decisions ethically.

This brings me to the second thing that they would find agreement on and that is the religious foundation of the human psyche. It is true that they both come from different religious backgrounds and practices but both would be comfortable in each others psycho/spiritual views. I do know that Jung and Victor White had their falling out but I don't think that would have happened with Jung and Chardin. They both could tolerate differences of viewpoint. The accounts I have heard of Chardin was how accepting and affable he was of people of differing backgrounds. I believe the same was true of Jung. Though there are other connectors that would have made good conversations between these two men, what they both shared was a good sense of humor and I am sure a good glass of wine.

RH: How would you compare and contrast Jung's and Chardin's notion of God?

FG: Without question, both Jung and Chardin had a notion of God. As a young boy, Jung raised questions about religious issues with his Swiss Reform minister father. It was the beginning for him of frustration with traditional institutional religious dogma. Yet, the issue of the notion of God never left him. It followed him into his career, can be seen in his writings most recently witnessed in *The Red Book*, again powerfully in his struggle to deal with the dark side of God in *Answer to Job* and culminated in the famous interview with John Freeman of BBC who asked him if he believed God exists to which he answered, "I do not believe God exists; I know God exists." That statement has been tossed around in the Jungian world wondering if he really meant that so categorically or, was he just being symbolic. We know he said the Self is like what theologians called the image of God in that it contains both wholeness and totality. Is that what he meant; he stating God exists really was meant to say the Self exists. For myself, I am content to believe he meant just what he said—God exists whether manifesting in the notion of the Self or cosmic/transcended Self humankind has come to call God.

As for Chardin, it is easier to understand where he was coming from. He was raised in an accepting Christian environment and trained as a Jesuit. In spite of tremendous odds against him from the religious powers that silenced and exiled him from his own country, he did not give up his vows or his belief in God. What is important especially here is how that notion of God he carried all his life was deepened into the very fabric of matter itself because of his paleontological and geological studies of not just the beginning of life but where, he was convince, it was headed. Christ was just not a title given to Jesus 2000 years ago but was reflected and embedded in all aspects of life. His reference to what he called "the Christ seed" seems to say it all. God is not just up in the heavens somewhere but permeates all of life. I have a small ceramic plaque at home with a stylized picture of the earth on it with the words: "This is my Body; this is my Blood." I doubt Jung nor Chardin would use the same language to describe such things. But, I am convinced they would truly know what each other was saying and would have little conflict with the deeper meanings each was trying to convey.

Other Fisher King Press Titles

Re-Imagining Mary: A Journey Through Art to the Feminine Self
by Mariann Burke, 1st Ed., Trade Paperback, 180pp, Index, Biblio., 2009
— ISBN 978-0-9810344-1-6

Advent and Psychic Birth
by Mariann Burke, Reprint, Trade Paperback, 170pp, 2014
— ISBN 978-1-926715-99-5

Sea Glass: A Jungian Analyst's Exploration of Suffering and Individuation
by Gilda Frantz, 1st Ed., Trade Paperback, 240pp, 2014
— ISBN 978-1-77169-020-1

Transforming Body and Soul
by Steven Galipeau, Rev. Ed., Trade Paperback, 180pp, Index, Biblio., 2011
— ISBN 978-1-926715-62-9

Lifting the Veil: Revealing the Other Side by Fred Gustafson & Jane Kamerling,
1st Ed, Trade Paperback, 170pp, Biblio., 2012
— ISBN 978-1-926715-75-9

Resurrecting the Unicorn: Masculinity in the 21st Century
by Bud Harris, Rev. Ed., Trade Paperback, 300pp, Index, Biblio., 2009
— ISBN 978-0-9810344-0-9

The Father Quest: Rediscovering an Elemental Force
by Bud Harris, Reprint, Trade Paperback, 180pp, Index, Biblio., 2009
— ISBN 978-0-9810344-9-2

Like Gold Through Fire: The Transforming Power of Suffering
by Massimilla & Bud Harris, Reprint, Trade Paperback, 150pp, Index, Biblio., 2009
— ISBN 978-0-9810344-5-4

The Art of Love: The Craft of Relationship by Massimilla and Bud Harris,
1st Ed. Trade Paperback, 150pp, 2010
— ISBN 978-1-926715-02-5

The Water of Life: Spiritual Renewal in the Fairy Tale
by David L. Hart, Rev. Ed., Trade Paperback, 160pp, 2013
— ISBN 978-1-926715-98-8

Divine Madness: Archetypes of Romantic Love by John R. Haule, Rev. Ed.,
Trade Paperback, 282pp, Index, Biblio., 2010
— ISBN 978-1-926715-04-9

Tantra and Erotic Trance in 2 volumes by John R. Haule
  Volume 1 - Outer Work, 1st Ed. Trade Paperback, 215pp, Index, Bibliograpy, 2012
  — ISBN 978-0-9776076-8-6
  Volume 2 - Inner Work, 1st Ed. Trade Paperback, 215pp, Index, Bibliograpy, 2012
  — ISBN 978-0-9776076-9-3

Eros and the Shattering Gaze: Transcending Narcissism
by Ken Kimmel, 1st Ed., Trade Paperback, 310pp, Index, Biblio., 2011
— ISBN 978-1-926715-49-0

A Jungian Life: A Memoir
by Thomas B. Kirsch, 1st Ed., Trade Paperback, 224pp, 2014
— ISBN 978-1-77169-024-9

The Sister From Below: When the Muse Gets Her Way
by Naomi Ruth Lowinsky, 1st Ed., Trade Paperback, 248pp, Index, Biblio., 2009
— ISBN 978-0-9810344-2-3

The Motherline: Every Woman's Journey to find her Female Roots
by Naomi Ruth Lowinsky, Reprint, Trade Paperback, 252pp, Index, Biblio., 2009
— ISBN 978-0-9810344-6-1

The Dairy Farmer's Guide to the Universe in 4 volumes
by Dennis L. Merritt:

    Volume 1 - Jung and Ecopsychology, 1st Ed., Trade Paperback, 242pp, Index, Biblio., 2011 — ISBN 978-1-926715-42-1

    Volume 2 - The Cry of Merlin: Jung the Prototypical Ecopsychologist, 1st Ed., Trade Paperback, 204pp, Index, Biblio., 2012
    — ISBN 978-1-926715-43-8

    Volume 3 - Hermes, Ecopsychology, and Complexity Theory,
    1st Ed., Trade Paperback, 228pp, Index, Biblio., 2012
    — ISBN 978-1-926715-44-5

    Volume 4 - Land, Weather, Seasons, Insects: An Archetypal View,
    1st Ed., Trade Paperback, 134pp, Index, Biblio., 2012
    — ISBN 978-1-926715-45-2

Four Eternal Women: Toni Wolff Revisited—A Study In Opposites
by Mary Dian Molton & Lucy Anne Sikes, 1st Ed., 320pp, Index, Biblio., 2011
— ISBN 978-1-926715-31-5

Becoming: An Introduction to Jung's Concept of Individuation
by Deldon Anne McNeely, 1st Ed., Trade Paperback, 230pp, Index, Biblio., 2010
— ISBN 978-1-926715-12-4

Animus Aeternus: Exploring the Inner Masculine
by Deldon Anne McNeely, Reprint, Trade Paperback, 196pp, Index, Biblio., 2011
— ISBN 978-1-926715-37-7

Mercury Rising: Women, Evil, and the Trickster Gods
by Deldon Anne McNeely, Rev. Ed., Trade Paperback, 200pp, Index, Biblio., 2011
— ISBN 978-1-926715-54-4

Gathering the Light: A Jungian View of Meditation
by V. Walter Odajnyk, Revised Ed., Trade Paperback, 264pp, Index, Biblio., 2011
— ISBN 978-1-926715-55-1

Celibacy and Soul: Exploring the Depths of Chastity,
by Susan J. Pollard, 1ˢᵗ Ed., Trade Paperback, 250pp, Index, Biblio., 2015
— ISBN 978-1-77169-013-3

The Orphan: On the Journey to Wholeness
by Audrey Punnett, 1ˢᵗ Ed., Trade Paperback, 150pp, Index, Biblio., 2014
— ISBN 978-1-77169-016-4

The Promiscuity Papers
by Matjaz Regovec, 1ˢᵗ Ed., Trade Paperback, 86pp, Index, Biblio., 2011
— ISBN 978-1-926715-38-4

Enemy, Cripple, Beggar: Shadows in the Hero's Path
by Erel Shalit, 1ˢᵗ Ed., Trade Paperback, 248pp, Index, Biblio., 2008
— ISBN 978-0-9776076-7-9

The Cycle of Life: Themes and Tales of the Journey
by Erel Shalit, 1ˢᵗ Ed., Trade Paperback, 210pp, Index, Biblio., 2011
— ISBN 978-1-926715-50-6

The Hero and His Shadow
by Erel Shalit, Revised Ed., Trade Paperback, 208pp, Index, Biblio., 2012
— ISBN 978-1-926715-69-8

Riting Myth, Mythic Writing: Plotting Your Personal Story
by Dennis Patrick Slattery, 1ˢᵗ Ed.,Trade Paperback, 220 pp. Biblio., 2012
— ISBN 978-1-926715-77-3

Creases in Culture: Essays Toward a Poetics of Depth
by Dennis Patrick Slattery, 1ˢᵗ Ed.,Trade Paperback, 228pp, 2014
— ISBN 978-1-77169-006-5

The Guilt Cure by Nancy Carter Pennington & Lawrence H. Staples,
1ˢᵗ Ed., Trade Paperback, 200pp, Index, Biblio., 2011
— ISBN 978-1-926715-53-7

Guilt with a Twist: The Promethean Way
by Lawrence Staples,1ˢᵗ Ed., Trade Paperback, 256pp, Index, Biblio., 2008
— ISBN 978-0-9776076-4-8

The Creative Soul: Art and the Quest for Wholeness
by Lawrence Staples, 1ˢᵗ Ed., Trade Paperback, 100pp, Index, Biblio., 2009
— ISBN 978-0-9810344-4-7

Deep Blues: Human Soundscapes for the Archetypal Journey
by Mark Winborn, 1ˢᵗ Ed., Trade Paperback, 130pp, Index, Biblio., 2011
— ISBN 978-1-926715-52-0

The Fisher King Review Series

Marked By Fire: Stories of the Jungian Way edited by Patricia Damery & Naomi Ruth Lowinsky, 1st Ed., Trade Paperback, 180pp, Biblio., 2012
— ISBN 978-1-926715-68-1

The Dream and Its Amplification edited by Erel Shalit & Nancy Swift Furlotti, 1st Ed., Trade Paperback, 180pp, Biblio., 2013
— ISBN 978-1-926715-89-6

Shared Realities: Participation Mystique and Beyond edited by Mark Windborn, 1st Ed., Trade Paperback, 270pp, Index, Biblio., 2014
— ISBN 978-1-77169-009-6

Pierre Teilhard de Chardin and C.G. Jung: Side by Side edited by Fred Gustafson, 1st Ed., Trade Paperback, 220pp, Biblio., 2015
— ISBN ISBN 978-1-77169-014-0

Phone Orders Welcomed
Credit Cards Accepted
In Canada & the U.S. call 1-800-228-9316
International call +1-831-238-7799
www.fisherkingpress.com

Made in the USA
Columbia, SC
30 May 2019